1988

Elementary Teacher's
Classroom Management Handbook

Elementary Teacher's Classroom Management Handbook

by Hal Malehorn

Parker Publishing Company, Inc.

West Nyack, New York

© 1984 by

Parker Publishing Company, Inc.

West Nyack, NY

Fifth Printing . . . . . April 1988

Library of Congress Cataloging in Publication Data

Malehorn, Hal
    Elementary teacher's classroom management handbook.

    Includes index.
    1. Classroom management—Handbooks, manuals, etc.
2. Education, Elementary—Handbooks, manuals, etc.
3. Teaching—Handbooks, manuals, etc. I. Title
LB3013.M32 1984   372.11′02   84-1925
ISBN 0-13-260605-4

Printed in the United States of America

ABOUT THE AUTHOR

HAL MALEHORN, Ph.D., Associate Professor of
Early Childhood Education at Eastern Illinois University, has taught five years at the preschool and
primary levels, and fourteen years at the university
level. He has also conducted workshop sessions on
materials and techniques for early childhood education. He has written several other books, including
Illustrated Treasury of K-3 Teaching Ideas.

USING THIS BOOK
TO HELP YOU TEACH

The demands on teachers' time, talents, and energies are considerable. Teachers have so many pupils to shepherd, such bookwork to complete, and so many routine tasks to tend to that it's miraculous any teaching occurs at all.

It is in this hurried and harried classroom setting that the *Elementary Teacher's Classroom Management Handbook* fits so beautifully. This book provides the professional with nearly 1,000 suggestions to simplify his or her responsibilities. Hundreds of time-tested ideas, handed along by generations of teachers, are collected here in this one spot, along with hundreds of other suggestions originated by the author.

Any single chapter proves the value of the entire volume. The book is packed with handy, brief entries that come to grips with the countless responsibilities teachers must face daily. Here is an incredible variety of ideas for 21 different sub-topics. From the very beginning of the school year to the testing and other assessments that conclude it, the author has included scores of ways to make the daily interactions more manageable.

It is not enough to keep ahead of the daily demands of teaching. The essential quality that differentiates the ordinary teacher from the extraordinary one is the extent to which he or she is able to introduce creativity, enthusiasm, and insight into the different tasks that constitute the teaching role. This extra effort converts what might be a humdrum, ho-hum experience into something that is unpredictable and delightful for both pupils and their teachers. Sample suggestions include the following:

- different ways to make name tags for your boys and girls the first day of school
- ideas to convert the regular clean-up chores into enjoyable and instructional experiences
- kinds of badges, certificates, and pins to reward pupils for outstanding achievement and appropriate behavior
- places in the community to seek free resources, along with what to ask for once you're there

If you're interested in specific things to start with right away, you might try one of these:

- make an all-purpose calendar that can be used month after month
- set up a permanent job chart that never needs to be changed
- use plastic jugs to prepare headbands for identifying your class members on field trips
- incorporate Disney characters and other cartoons to label buses for new riders
- invent original holiday celebrations to brighten the "blah" months

In addition to incorporating inventiveness and practicality, this book shows you how to accomplish hundreds of new ideas at virtually no cost. Many of the ideas illustrated with simple line drawings can be made from materials salvaged from community sources and from your children's own families. These devices not only recycle resources that would otherwise be thrown away, they also engage boys and girls in converting ordinary things into items of beauty and utility.

Take a few moments to jot down some of the problems that interfere with the smooth operation of your own classroom throughout the year. Then examine these pages carefully to discover those ideas that best solve your own situations. The chances are great that you will be glad you did. Through their more enthusiastic responses your students will thank you for your efforts on their behalf.

Hal Malehorn

ACKNOWLEDGMENT

I would like to thank Gaye Harrison, who drew the illustrations for this book.

TABLE OF CONTENTS

Using This Book to Help You Teach.........................vi

Chapter 1: Preparing the Classroom for the First Day 1

Getting a Head Start on Planning.....2

Bus Procedures • Color-Coding • Communications •
Community Data • Exchange Teaching • Idea File • Library
Books • Planning Cards • Planning Notebook • Plus
Planning • Professional Materials • Room Arrangement •
School Helpers • Summer Planning • Syllabus System •
Teacher Orientation • Teaching Pictures

Easing Pupils into the Year.....11

Alternate Sections • Bibliotherapy • Bus Procedures • Circus
Theme • Coloring Books • Convincers • Early Open House •
First Learnings • Helpers • Home Helps • Map Study •
Mascot • Moral Support • Name Recognition • Name Tag
Spoons • Participatory Planning • Parties • Promotions •
Round-Up • Routines • School Helpers • School Tour •
Security Items • Self-Portrait • Special Attractions •
Summer Letter • Summer Preparations • Surprises •
Transfers • Tree Treats

Icebreakers.....27

Adapted Games • Booklets • Circle Games • Circle Pass •
Guess Who? • Letter and Word Games • Mail Call •
Mixed-Up Names • Pair Presentations • Personalized Tags •
Photo Tags • Pictures and Portraits • Plastic Tags • Puzzle
Names • Puzzle Pictures • Reversed Names • Review Tags •
Shape Tags • Song Responses • Special Sharing • Tag Lines

Chapter 2: The Classroom Environment 38

Creating a Climate for Learning.....39

Absentees • Assignment Excitement • Bad Weather • Blah
Month • Breaks in the Action • Calendar Fun • Ceiling
Suspensions • Clock Treatment • Favorite Things •
Garments Glorified • Gracious Grading • Graffiti Spot •
Grand Entrance • Humor in Action • Inspiration at Work •
Interest Clubs • Keeping in Touch • Loyalty • Mascot •

Music and Moods • Names Are Neat • Old Hats • Outside
the Room • Personal Touch • Popular Choice • Questions,
Questions • Ratings Race • Scrapbook • Sharing •
Spontaneous Events • Spots of Color • Teacher Challenge •
Wall Treatments • Windows Well

Diagnosing Daily Discipline 57

Aggression and Acting-Out Alternatives • Anger
Alternatives • Appropriate Punishments • Attention Span •
Being Fair • Changing Positions • Confidential Criticism •
Consistent Treatment • Contracted Changes • Cooperative
Involvements • Corporal Punishment • Correcting Mistakes
• Expressing Feelings • Furniture Arrangements • Giving
Compliments • Giving Help • Handling Aggression •
Helpful Humor • Making Allowances • Making
Comparisons • Managing Monitors • Managing Upsets •
Note-Writing Alternatives • Sincere Apologies •
Withholding Blame

**Chapter 3: Generating Student Interest in the
Curriculum 73**

How to Make Fitness Fun 74

Accounting for Equipment • Calisthenics to a Beat •
Choosing Partners • Coping with Competition • Cue Cards •
Instructional Helps • Motivating Fitness • No-Fault Fitness
• Playground Guidance • Safety Sense • Signal Systems •
Skill Centers • Skills Charts • Squad Setups • Taking Turns
• Team Selection

The ABCs of the First "R" 85

All-Purpose Advice • Book Clubs • Book Festival • Book
Report Alternatives • Books in Comfort • Clever Containers
• Compatible Pairs • Diversified Basals • Kits and Kids •
Libraries and Librarians • Reading Group Alternatives •
Reading Materials • Reducing the Race • Reluctant Readers
• Sign-Out Sensations • Story Hour • Taping the Action •
Title Ticklers • Workbook Woes

The Craft of Handling Art 100

Assessing Art • Brushes in Use • Chalk Hints • Clay Helps
• Clay Substitutes • Clean-Up Time • Crayon Melts •

Display Variations • Fairs and Festivals • Fingerpainting
Surfaces • Giving Assistance • Handling Clay • Mess Made
Less • Mini-Gallery • Mixing Made Easier • Paint Additives
• Paint Alternatives • Paint Instruments • Paint Palettes •
Paint Principles • Paint Storage • Paper Cutting • Paper
Storage • Paper Uses • Paste Mess • Paste Pointers •
Patterns and Models • Personal Participation • Plaster
Possibilities • Project Keepers • Protecting Clothing •
Random Reminders • Recycled Art • Respect for the Artist •
Scheduling Art • Sculpture Armatures • Smocks • Time and
Space Considerations • Water Source • Ways with Paints

**Chapter 4: Organizing Classroom Equipment for Easy
Use** **121**

Organizing Spots and Spaces **122**

Ceiling Brighteners • Desk Arrangements • Display
Surfaces • Doing Doors • Dual-Purpose Items • Easel Ways •
Foldaways • Glare to Spare • Lightening and Brightening •
Mobility Management • Poles and Posts • Privacy Carrels •
Room Dividers • Space Conservation • Special Spots • Table
Flexibility • Table Ways • Work Space Markings

Less of a Mess with Storage **135**

Aprons • Bags and Baggies • Boxes and Cartons • Cans for
Keeping • Cardboard Carriers • Clotheshanger Reels •
Cubbies • Gym Shoes • Handy Hints • Homework Holders •
Interesting Containers • Irregular Materials • Labeling
Containers • Large Flat Items • Paper at the Ready • Paper
in Boxes • Pegboard Possibilities • Phonograph Records •
Plastic Drawers • Plastic Jugs • Puzzle Places • Safe and
Handy Scissors • Shelving to Shift • Small Hooks • String •
Study Papers • Tubes • Worksheet Extender

Learning Stuff and Stations **146**

Adjustability • Book Bus • Bulk Orders • Checking Out
Items • Color-Coding • Distributing Systems • Duplicating
Economies • Free-Fashioned Furnishings • Oilcloth
Covering • Panels and Partitions • Paper for Backgrounds •
Sending Notes Home • Stepped Effects • Stuff and Junk •
Substitute Materials • Tabletop Treatments • Worksheet
Ways

Chapter 5: Simplifying Routine Classroom Tasks............**156**

Techniques for Time and Tasks **157**

Activity Signals • Appointments • Before-School Privileges •
Dismissal • Movement • Quiet Signals • Scheduling Cycles •
Share and Tell • Signal System • Start/Stop Symbols •
Taking Turns • Time Cards • Timely Reminders • Timing
Turns • Traffic Lines • Transitions • Waiting for Responses •
Waiting in Lines

Maintaining Order in the Course **165**

Art Clean Up • Assigning Jobs • Bad Weather Tips • Clean
Up Campaign • Clean Up Concepts • Clean Up Roles •
Distraction Reduction • Emergency Items • Emergency Kit •
Emergency Response • End-of-Day Clean Up • Fabric Noise
Control • Faces and Figures Helpers • Give-a-Hand Helper •
Help-Wanted Helpers • Jobs as Occupations • Messy
Dressing • Nature's Helpers • Noise Abatement Ideas •
Noise Control Signals • Quiet Spots • Random Helper
Choice • Safety Inspection

Accounting for Kids **176**

Absentees • Attendance Clothespins • Bookkeeping •
Calendar Compartments • Calendar Lift-Ups • Choosing
Sides • Class Lists • Dial-a-Day • Diary Calendar • Food
Count • Head Count Hangers • House and School Counters
• Keeping Control • Lost and Found • Personalized
Attendance • Random Grouping • Wheel Calendar •
Sunshine Calendar

**Chapter 6: Using Resources Inside and Outside the
Classroom** **186**

Places to Go, People to See, Things to Use **187**

Alternatives Afield • Bag of Tricks • Catalog Sources •
Commercial Suppliers • Construction Sites • Counting
Noses • Emergency Trip Provisions • Evaluating Excursions
• Excursion Booklet • Factories and Agencies • Folders for
Subs • Fun for Subs • General End-of-Day Critique •
Helpers at a Distance • Introducing Substitutes •
Introducing Trip Concepts • Kids as Tutors • Lost on Trips •

Name Tags for Trips • Parents in Classrooms • Permission from Parents • Rest and Refreshments Afield • Rummages and Auctions • Seating for Subs • Secondary School Sources • Senior Citizen Aides • State Department Sources • Stores and Business • Textbooks to Salvage • Timing Your Trips • Trip Impressions • Walking Tours

Making Media Meaningful 205

Chalkboard Lines • Chalkboard Questions • Chalkboards in General • Chart Uses • Charts from Shades • Duplicator Masters • Films in Action • Filmstrips • Flannelboards • Frieze • General Handy Hints • Magazines • Maps • Murals • Overhead Projector Activities • Posters • Programmed Materials • Proper Patterns • Realia • Sand Table • Slides Suggestions • Tape Recorder Activities • Textbooks • Tracings • Typewriter

Telling Parents Tales Out of School 222

Communication Competencies • Conference Considerations • Educational Experiences Inventory • Enrollment Data • Facilitating Conference Attendance • Handbook Hints • Handbooks for Parents • Parent Assessment • Parent-Teacher Organizations • Pupil-Parent Conferences • Scheduling Conferences • Welcome Visitors

Chapter 7: Assessing Students' Progress .232

The Challenge of Child Study 233

"All About Me" Booklet • Autobiography • Fantasy Stories • Free Play • Inventories • Listing Rules and Rights • Parent Checklists • Picture Clues • Self-Reports • Sociograms • Story Situations • Unfinished Sentences • Values Scales

Activities to Enliven Reviews 239

Color-Coding • Computer Carton • Deliberate Mistake • Diary Details • End-of-Day Review • Expert Panel • Fact Mats • Fix-It Shop • Game Formats • Good Guesses • Peer Helpers • Puppet Tutors • Puzzle Papers • Quiz Slips • Shingles to Show • "Show Me" Cards • Signal System • Teacher for a Day • Trouble Spots • Wizard Cap • Wrong Answers

Measuring the Results 247

Anecdotal Records • Averages • Bowling Scores • Can-Do Can • Card Log • Checklist • Cumulative Folders • Cumulative Grading • Diagnostics • HappyGrams • Marking Papers • Measurement Message • Measuring Line • Open Report Cards • Original Report Cards • Parent Report Cards • Parent Visits • Passports • Peer Assessment • Physical Measurement • Pupil-Made Tests • Pupil Products • Questionnaires on Growth • Reinforcement Techniques • Self-Checking • Summer Carryover • Tape Recordings

Rewards for Winners 260

Achievement Tree • Animal Piecework • Badges of Honor • Bank Deposits • Certificates of Honor • Chest Decorations • Currency • Eatable Items • Fancy Phrases • Group Goals • Hall of Fame • Hats and Headbands • Military Markings • Quick Games • Real Objects Motivators • Secret Messages • Stamper Use • Stickers and Seals • Treasure Box

Index 269

1

Preparing
the Classroom
for the First Day

There is much truth in the adage, "Well begun is half done." To a pupil entering school for the very first time, or one who is new each fall to a certain classroom setting, having activities planned that are informal, friendly, and interesting can make the difference between a happy school year and an unhappy one.

Sad to relate, children are often thrust into new classrooms the first day of school in September without knowing even the names of their teachers. To further compound their confusion, the teachers frequently begin right away distributing books, handing out homework, laying down the law, assigning seating, and otherwise depriving children of a chance to get acquainted or to help determine their own destinies.

Wise teachers make a special point to prepare their classrooms for the influx of their learners. Their consideration for the anxieties and the curiosities of youngsters pays off in several ways—the boys and girls quickly discover that their teacher cares about them, and such thoughtfulness reduces the confusion and the disruption that are otherwise a part of school beginnings. Where extra measures of effort are given by the teacher, fewer youngsters arrive in tears or leave in frustration; older pupils are more comfortable in arriving when they know in advance which bus they are to ride, which crossings to use, what doors to enter, and where the bathrooms are located. No teacher ever lost anything by showing concern for the pupils' basic human needs.

In addition to preparing the children and the classrooms, effective teachers prepare themselves. There are many important tasks that can be completed well before the opening of school in the autumn. Teachers who use their summers to get ready for their assignments find that they have daily routines under better control once school is under way.

In view of the fact that first impressions tend to be lasting ones, it is also to the advantage of teachers to convince the parents of their humanness from the very first contacts. Fathers and mothers are much more likely to both support and respect a teacher who quickly captures children's attention, interests, and energies, and who is demonstrably ready to embark on a worthwhile and exciting school adventure.

In spite of their public disclaimers, most children really do look forward to the first days of school. There is an electricity in the air and a level of expectation that are ordinarily not found anywhere else in childhood. What a remarkable bonus it is to maintain this level of enthusiasm throughout the school term, just by providing each day a few highly interesting activities, beginning with the first get-acquainted times.

GETTING A HEAD START ON PLANNING

Bus Procedures

Find out before the beginning of the school year the names of your children who will be riding the school bus or who will be accommodated in car pools. Make a map of your attendance region adjacent to the school and use colored pins to indicate on this map which riders use what means of conveyance. As the year begins, label each vehicle with a different colored sign. For riders who are so young as not to be able to read, include a symbol or cartoon character. Provide each of your students with a different label that matches the color or the figure on the poster labeling the appropriate conveyance. Have aides and bus drivers who supervise the loading and the transportation similarly identified.

During the first few weeks of school, ride the bus a few times to check on the appropriate behavior of your children and the procedures that are used to ensure the safety of the riders. Reinforce these principles in your early lessons on safety. Ask some of your more responsible students to take turns reporting to you those riders who are especially considerate of others and supportive of good safety measures as they ride.

Involve the students early in the year in preparing colorful posters on rider safety. Get permission to post these reminders in each bus or other vehicle that is used regularly to transport pupils to your school.

Color-Coding

When you teach several subjects in the same room, prepare folders, one for each subject, using folders of different colors for the various subject areas. Use such folders to hold the lesson plans in one pocket and the papers and other appropriate materials in the other pocket. Further differentiate among these folders by decorating them thematically with pictures or symbols. Use colors as well in collecting anecdotal record cards as you make note of particular pupil behaviors in your various classes; a different color index card might be used for each subject you teach, for one type of behavior, or for a given unit of study.

Communications

Maintain a permanent file of all your communications, separating them by type as necessary. For example, keep one folder with all the administrative bulletins, important memoes, and calendar information that are distributed during the typical school year. Have a second folder handy for containing parent letters and notes. A third folder might include copies of occasional newsletters you and your children share with the parents. A fourth set of data might include the anecdotal records you compile on the achievements and the needs of your boys and girls, particularly as you send carbon copies of these evaluative items home to the parents. To help you file more quickly the information you are thus accumulating, color-tip the tabs of each folder.

Community Data

When you are new to a neighborhood, find out as much as possible before school begins about the community served by your school. This information will help you understand the backgrounds and the needs of your students, and will help you deal with the logistical aspects of the teaching tasks. Inquire of your school administrator, or discover through your own field inquiry, elements such as: the language that is predominantly spoken, the main occupations, and the general community attitude about and support of the school program. Discover as much as you can about the persons who influence the local decisions that affect schools, such as the members of the P.T.A. and the school board of directors.

Exchange Teaching

Enhance your own teaching skills and motivate your students by arranging exchanges of several types. One possibility is to arrange with a colleague in your same building or in a nearby school an agreement for exchanging products your children make as a result of their learning. Also explore the possibility of swapping tape recordings as well as pictures, stories, and other related materials. With more mature and more ambitious students, arrange a similar exchange with same-age pupils in foreign countries or distant states, using as your contacts names supplied by professional teacher magazines, members of the armed services, missionaries, Peace Corps workers, foreign exchange students, and members of diverse cultures represented in your neighborhood.

You can also gain a helpful perspective on your own teaching by visiting another teacher or a comparable grade level or subject area. Where you are not granted professional leave for such a purpose, take the initiative in setting up a correlated exchange with another teacher who would be willing to swap two or three days of instruction. In addition, consider spending some of the free time for planning during your daily schedule in observing some of your colleagues, particularly those professionals who are demonstrably successful in their classroom instruction. (Be sure those teachers you visit feel at ease with your presence.) Make a point to visit on occasion a teacher of the grade just ahead of or just behind your own, in order to acquire some further insight into what the students at these various levels are involved in.

Idea File

Maintain an ongoing collection of teaching ideas that come to your attention during the year. Such new notions add an element of change and surprise to your daily instruction. Explore your colleagues' classrooms for their best techniques, and share your own suggestions with them in turn. Examine the teacher magazines for further hints for making teaching more effective. Record all ideas on cards, one per card, and assemble them in a file box that is organized by topics. Or, prepare looseleaf notebooks with separate pages that can be added or removed from time to time during the school year. At least once a week examine your idea file for new ways to approach a given subject. Also, let the boys and girls in your classroom have a ready access to your file for the purpose of choosing unique ways of expressing their interests and their skills. Encourage these same students to invent their own original ways of managing the daily routines, their own behavior, and their learning responsibilities. Award extra credit for the more insightful and original ideas they contribute.

Library Books

During the summer months and at spare moments during the year make a point to read as many books in your library collection as you can, selecting especially those books that are particularly interesting to or useful for your students. If appropriate, add to each book spine a piece of fabric tape color-coded to indicate books that are of a particular subject or a given level of difficulty. On a card selected to fit inside the card pocket in the book, write a brief summary of the story. Whenever a child borrows one of the books, remove the card and use it to remind yourself of the content of that particular volume. Then place that card in the appropriate spot on the shelf to mark the placement of that book. As you read each book, too, make a point to write simple questions that will guide your pupils' reading in the event you plan to have conferences with them after they have finished reading.

Planning Cards

Instead of using the traditional plan book which contains only a limited space for writing, do your planning on index cards, one for each subject area or for each area of responsibility you have assumed. In this way, your plans are made permanent for use during subsequent years. You can write on the back of each card comments that might help you handle the lesson more effectively next time. In addition, the use of cards enables you to change your order of business as needed, simply by relocating the cards in appropriate sequence in the daily activities file kept on your desk. Make a point to use colored cards for your plans, one color for a different subject area.

Planning Notebook

As an alternate to the usual spiral-bound plan book, organize a looseleaf notebook for which you prepare a set of duplicated sheets, each sheet for a different day of the year. On the lefthand edge of this master sheet have a column of squares, one square beside each activity that might well be required at some time during a typical instructional week, whether or not it occurs every day. As you plan each day's activities, make a single mark through each appropriate box using a green pencil or pen; then write out briefly beside each marked box the specific thing you plan to do that day. At the conclusion of the day, review what you have accomplished, and mark out with a cross-mark of red ink the items that were satisfactorily completed. If for any reason you have not accomplished everything you had planned, transfer those incomplete items onto the appropriate spot on the next day's master list. On the reverse side of each sheet write your reflections on the general success of the day, anecdotal details of your children's progress, or suggestions for improving your subsequent instruction.

Plus Planning

Whenever you plan for a day's activities, make a point to have on hand far more activities to be achieved than you are likely to complete. In the event something does not go well, or if the pupils progress more quickly through the concept or skill than you had anticipated, you will have something else to suggest. Such overplanning will also lend a sense of urgency to your teaching, as the students will perceive not only that there is much to do but also that such efforts are important to you and to them.

In like manner, try to end any class on a high note when the children are at a high level of enthusiasm. Do not pursue any activity until fatigue or boredom or frustration sets in. Have a collection of surprises to use in concluding an instructional period: a game, a stunt, a story, a riddle, a joke, or a song are all appropriate ways to conclude a time of concentrated mental or physical effort.

Professional Materials

Set up an instructional file that can be used by you and other professionals in your school, as well as the more mature pupils enrolled. For example, include a folder for each topic of study, and in each of these folders place articles you or the children have clipped from magazines and newspapers that relate to the topics at hand. Make similar collections of recipes, art suggestions, holiday and seasonal suggestions, and ways to improve parenting and parent support of schools. In addition, assume the responsibility for consolidating the professional subscriptions that are personally undertaken by various teachers in your school. By combining these magazines, the diversity of teaching ideas can be increased dramatically without any further expenditure of money. Institute in some central location, such as a teacher center, a master file of clippings that have been cut from these professional sources.

Room Arrangement

When you plan the periodic rearrangement of the furniture in your classroom, make a scale drawing on graph paper and prepare on appropriate pieces of colored construction paper scaled items to represent the major pieces of equipment that are to be considered in the placement. Miniatures are much easier to manipulate than moving the actual furniture. In planning the classroom, consider the traffic patterns, the light sources, and the acoustics. Make a special effort to tie in the children's desks or table space with the purpose of your instruction. For example, a circular or U-shaped furniture arrangement gives everyone a good view of the proceedings and an equal chance at classroom interactions. Clusters of desks are especially appropriate, on the other hand, when you schedule small group projects. Ranks and rows and columns are best suited to traditional lectures. A theater-style shallow curve facilitates viewing during television programs, movies, and other visual presentations.

School Helpers

Make a point to keep in close contact with the support persons who work in your school. Help your children to understand and appreciate the services provided by auxiliary people. Keep track of the birthdates and other special events represented among the staff members in your school. Suggest to your boys and girls that they prepare homemade greeting cards as appropriate. Some of your pupils might also make helper coupons, consisting of booklets of service slips, on each of which the children write small services they are willing to provide the principal, the secretary, the nurse, and other help-ers. You would also do well to call on these helper persons to explain their work to your students, particularly as a part of a unit of instruction on community helpers or career choices. Or, incorporate their special skills in particular subjects of study: the engineer, custodian, or maintenance person, for ex-ample, can contribute to your pupils' understanding of some of the basic systems in the building as you undertake certain topics in science; the cook or the dietician can assist with nu-trition; and the school nurse can share information on various aspects of hygiene. Make a point to send thank-you notes after such assistance as a way to express communal appreciation of their help during the year. An occasional tea party or small tokens or gifts are also thoughtful ways to express your thanks.

Summer Planning

Whenever you are on summer vacation, you can do a lot to improve your instruction for the following school year. If you travel, for example, make a collection of descriptive liter-ature that pertains to the places you visit. Compile sets of fos-sils, rocks, vegetation, and soil characteristics of the places you visit. Invest small amounts of money in souvenirs that re-flect the various points of interest. Maps are also an appropri-ate aid to social studies activities.

During the time you are not traveling, spend your spare time reading the records of the pupils you will be teaching the following term, make learning aids and games to enhance your instruction, develop duplicated worksheets, examine alternative materials for subsequent use, send away for free and inexpensive and sample items, revise the use of your classroom space, and plan bulletin boards and classroom decorations.

At the conclusion of each school year, send home to the parents of your incoming students a note requesting similar contribution of free time and items collected during summer travels.

Syllabus System

Before the school year begins, prepare a simple syllabus set, one for each course you teach, in which you outline in general what you plan to be working on during the year, as well as an explanation of your evaluation methods and an overview of the sequence of your units of instruction. Give original names to these units. Pose questions to pique the curiosity of your pupils. As the year begins, send these syllabi home with the children to share with their parents. Encourage the parents to help assess their offspring as the boys and girls progress through each syllabus.

Teacher Orientation

If you are new to a particular school, make a point that as the year begins you are informed about matters of policy in areas such as these:

discipline methods

birthday celebrations

reporting procedures

testing program instruments

textbooks and manuals

parent organizations

school calendar

attendance procedures

curriculum guides

substitute teachers

cumulative folders

grading guidelines

professional organizations

budgeted funds

homework policies

school board meetings

committee structures

special resources

rules of pupils' behavior

hours of work

consumable supplies

disaster and emergency procedures
lesson planning
promotions and retentions
teaching schedules
professional materials
aides and volunteers
pupil fees
insurance coverage
parent conferences
inventories
requisition procedures
bus routes and policies
teacher responsibilities
sample forms
salary and benefits

Teaching Pictures

Use magazines and other publications as sources of teaching pictures. Photography magazines, such as those on travel, flying, sailing, hot rods, racing, and athletics, as well as other specialty publications are particularly useful. Old textbooks provide handy pictures and supplementary reading material at the same time. Discarded catalogs and homemaking magazines enhance vocabulary and develop creative writing. Story magazines are also good for these purposes. Mount and laminate each item on sturdy paper to preserve its usefulness.

EASING PUPILS INTO THE YEAR

Alternate Sessions

For kindergarten or other children who are attending school for the first time, arrange to stagger the days they attend during the first week. This will reduce the number of pupils present; half will come one day, and the other half of the class will come the next day. Or, you might reduce the time these few days the children attend, thereby making sure that the students are not overtired or confused by too many activities.

Bibliotherapy

Sometimes young children become anxious when confronting new situations such as attending a different grade, meeting new classmates, riding a bus, and crossing busy streets. Children's books on these special topics can be very helpful in allaying your pupils' uncertainties. During the first days of class, share some of these library books and encourage the students to discuss openly their feelings about new experiences. Encourage them, too, to take some of these books home to read at their leisure. Further suggest to the class members that they prepare original compositions that tell about their uncertainties, illustrating each one with their own artwork.

Bus Procedures

Since many children who are new to the area are uncertain about bus procedures, ask parent volunteers to ride the bus during the early weeks of school. Enlist these volunteers from members of the communities who are familiar with particular neighborhoods and who are well known to the student body. Ask the aides to remind the children about proper rider safety, as well as appropriate ways to mount and dismount the vehicle. To identify the riders who belong with each bus, prepare colorful headbands that match in motif a symbol that is placed in the window nearest the door on the bus. In addition, set up a buddy system of children who live in the same neighborhood as a further way of looking after their safety.

Circus Theme

To welcome your students the first day, decorate your classroom like a circus, complete with flags and balloons and animal cutouts. Dress up like a clown, but leave off facial make-up to assist the boys and girls in recognizing you readily. Provide a snack of fresh popcorn and juice. Have on hand a collection of animal masks salvaged from previous Halloween

parties. Issue these masks or have the children make their own as one of their first in-school experiences. As each child is introduced by name, have the child act the role of the animal whose mask he or she is wearing. Introduce some sprightly band music and have a circus parade around the school building after you have marched around your classroom.

Coloring Books

To help the children who are entering your classroom in the fall, have the prior group of children in the spring make a simple set of coloring books by duplicating their original drawings that accompany your own explanations or diagrams of the new classroom the incoming pupils will encounter in the fall. For example, the pupils might draw a school bus; a portrait of you, the teacher; the school itself; or the foods typically served in the cafeteria. As your new students arrive after summer vacation, give each person a booklet to color in during their spare moments, to accompany the written material you have also included.

Convincers

Some young children may find it unsettling to come back to school the second day in the fall. If this is likely to be a problem for your students, make a point at the close of your first session to read just the first half of a particularly exciting or interesting story. Then tell the students as they are about to leave that you will finish reading that particular story the very first thing the next time they come to class. Or, you might similarly ask them to decide on an activity to begin the following day's session. Another successful approach is to let each boy and girl take home the first day something special—a book borrowed from your library, a puppet, a toy, or a game. As the students sign out their items, remind them that they will be returning these items the first thing the following session.

Early Open House

If it's permitted by your school district, send a notice in the summer to all your new students. Explain to these youngsters that you plan to be in your classroom a certain stipulated portion of the day for a week or two at the end of the summer. Further inform them that your classroom is to be open for inspection by them and by their parents and other family members. Tell them where your classroom is located in the building. As the people arrive at your classroom, have available some of your best materials for the new children to explore. Use this time for getting acquainted, and engage in informal diagnostic procedures as you ask the boys and girls, for example, to read from one of the readers, to demonstrate their math skills through a game you have put out for that purpose, to put together a typical puzzle, or to play other educational games that will give you some clues as to their cognitive and physical skills.

First Learnings

Children are always anxious to learn something new and important the very first day in school. Instead of introducing the usual items they may be familiar with, teach them something that is likely beyond the experience of the entire group. For example, teach them some simple phrases of greeting in a foreign language. Share with the class some of your graphic materials collected during summer travels. Or, discuss with them your own special hobbies, illustrated with materials you use or construct. In the case of young children, be sure they can tell their name and address and telephone number the first day, as well as their bus number. Introduce them to one or more important words having to do with safety. With older children, help them read several large and unusual words they might want to "spring" on their friends and family members. Present to young children a simple homemade certificate that indicates some of the things they accomplish the very first day of school.

Helpers

Since the first few days of school are usually rather hectic, ask some of the parents to help take care of the routine tasks that so often encumber teachers at this time. Parent volunteers could do things such as collect money, check enrollment registration, organize name tags, distribute books and supplies, and supervise bus loading/unloading and riding. Suggest as well that older students in the school, particularly those who have brothers and sisters or neighbors in your classroom, help shepherd the youngsters in the early weeks of school.

Home Helps

Send home to the families of your children during the spring or the summer a booklet in which you outline some of the procedures and expectations of the boys and girls who will be entering your classroom in the fall. Items to include in this simple handbook might be:

- explanations of how to send various items to school, such as lunch money and responses to notes
- ways to mark all clothing and supplies to identify the owner
- suggestions for providing a place that is conducive to quiet study at home
- instructions for what to do in cases of emergencies
- a description of the safest route to use when walking to school

- times when you can be reached for consultation either at school or at home
- telephone numbers of the school and your own home
- emergency slips for the telephone numbers, names, and addresses of medical facilities and personnel to contact

Map Study

During the first few days of school, introduce the children to a large map of the local area and have each child make a small replica of a house. Lay this map flat on the floor oriented to north. Help the boys and girls place their small homes on the map in approximate sites corresponding to actuality. Use yarn to represent streets. Find out which children live in the same neighborhoods. Examine the map to identify the safest ways to walk and ride to and from school. See which class member lives the closest to the school and who lives the farthest. Identify with cardboard stand-up figures the relative positions of police personnel or safety patrol monitors. Note with other stand-ups the location of stop signs and stoplights. Consider, too, the bus routes that are to be used during the year.

Mascot

In the event you have children who are likely to be insecure in new situations, provide a stuffed animal for them to hold onto or sit with. Sometimes simply having an old fur coat, a shag rug, or a piece of satin or velvet to feel is sufficient comfort. Another good idea is to have a puppet that you can use in talking to the children. As the children respond to your own use of the puppet, offer the item to them to use for a time.

Moral Support

Sometimes young children find it difficult to stay in school without the comforting presence of a parent or some other friend or family member. Where this is a problem, encourage the parents to provide prior to the opening of school experiences for the child in being away from home. These experiences include attending church school or sabbath school, enrolling in nursery school for a short time each day, or arranging for a baby sitter to occasionally be in the home. Allow parents to remain with their children the first few days if that is likely to help those few pupils still unsettled at the experience. However, encourage these parents not just to sit and watch or comfort their offspring. Rather, ask them to assist you in the routine tasks in the classroom, or even have them leave your classroom for a few minutes at a time. Gradually increase this time of separation until the child in question is capable of working into the regular group activities.

Name Recognition

During their first schooling experiences, boys and girls want and need to learn to read their own names. To stimulate this curiosity, have available a set of name cards on which you have printed the first names of all the boys and girls in the class. On the back of each card print each person's last name in turn. As soon as any child can recognize his or her first name, the tag may be reversed with the last name showing. If any child can recognize both the first and last names, he or she may then wear that tag for the rest of the week.

A second suggestion is to make the cognitive task more interesting with bits of food. If a child has any letter with a round part in it, make a name card with a round candy glued to the surface of a card. As soon as the child involved can consistently recognize his or her name, give him or her another round candy as a reward. For persons with straight letters in their name, use a straight pretzel as a reward.

If your children are beyond the point of merely recognizing their names, include more challenging situations, such as spelling their names correctly; recognizing the spelling of middle and last names; and reading and spelling names of siblings, other members of the class, and names of roads and cities.

Name Tag Spoons

Collect and wash sets of wooden spoons or tongue depressors. Bring to school macaroni alphabet letters or letters from an alphabet cereal. As soon as any child has learned to recognize his or her name from a card stimulus you have prepared, let the child compose the name by gluing the letters in place on the wooden item. These spoons may also be used with older boys and girls as they draw on them in miniature any learning activity, past experience, or present interest they would like to talk about with their classmates. Ask each person to write his or her name on the back of the spoon. During a get-acquainted period, suggest that the children talk in pairs, one person trying to guess the other person's activity. If the guess is correct, that child may keep the spoon. The child with the most spoons at the end wins. Or, simply have the children swap their spoons to get acquainted, making sure that no one ends up with his or her own spoon at the end of a designated time.

Participatory Planning

Children are always flattered when they are consulted regarding the elements of classroom procedure they will be working under during the school year. For example, suggestions regarding the arrangement of the furniture, the ways in which groups of pupils might be organized for instruction, and the reasonable rules to govern their behavior can all be asked. You might solicit suggestions for consumable materials to order or titles of books to request from the librarian. The class members might also offer input regarding the decoration of the classroom.

Parties

Surprise the children just enrolling in your classroom by scheduling a party for the first or second day of school, complete with games, songs, and simple refreshments. Decorate balloons with smiling faces, and label each one with the name of a child in your class. Provide simple party favors, masks, and decorations. These festivities might be accompanied by a "Grand Opening" display, complete with flags and banners such as those used by supermarkets and other commercial agencies. Or, you might call this celebration a "Happy New

Year" party, complete with hats, streamers, and noisemakers, thereby observing the beginning of a brand-new year.

Promotions

In the spring when your children are on the verge of being promoted to the next year's grade, make a point to introduce them not only to the new room but also to the next year's teacher. Return this same favor to the children in the next lower grade to your own, arranging for a time for these incoming children to visit your classroom. This will give an opportunity to write personal letters of introduction, one letter to a new child written by each member of your present group. Ask your own students in turn to write letters introducing themselves to their receiving teachers. These personal missives will provide teachers with a sample of handwriting that may reveal something special about each pupil. Also ask your students to write letters to the incoming students; these will help the younger students feel more at home in their new environment. Another idea is to have each student prepare original art work to share with these same two sets of people.

Round-Up

If you are a kindergarten teacher, sometime in the late spring schedule a registration of all the children who will be attending your class the coming year. Plan this event so that the boys and girls will come with their parents. Stagger the registration by letters of the last names so everyone will not arrive at school at once to register. If school is in session during the registration, encourage the boys and girls and their parents to spend at least a few minutes observing and participating in your classroom occupied by your present children. Make a point to introduce the boys and girls who are familiar to the newcomers. To add special interest to this "round-up," ask your parents or your present students to make cowboy and cowgirl cutouts for the children to wear as name tags as they register. Further add to the theme with decorations that feature western ideas.

Routines

When your pupils enter your classroom for the first time, spend some time helping them to adjust to the new setting and their new responsibilities. Explain where they may sit and allow them to choose their own locations as much as possible. Point out where each pupil is to hang his or her coat and make labels or picture or work clues to help them remember each spot. Be sure that everyone knows where the restrooms are located. Set up informal classroom groupings of children who live in the same neighborhood.

School Helpers

When children are involved in learning about the various school personnel early in the year, make a display of the people who provide support services in your building. Take instant photos of these staff members and provide both a label and a picture clue indicating where they work and the kind of work they do. Post this display prominently either in your classroom or in the entrance to the school.

A second suggestion is to take a singing tour of your facility. At each worker's station stop and parody the children's tune, "Do You Know the Muffin Man?" substituting the names of the school helpers at each site. Or, you might prefer to parody other songs for this activity, such as "Where is Thumbkin?" or "Mary Wore a Red Dress."

School Tour

In addition to introducing the children to the staff, let them locate the rooms where older brothers and sisters are enrolled. On behalf of young children make a different symbol for each classroom to enable your boys and girls to find their siblings when necessary.

If you teach young children, take them on a gingerbread tour. This involves your telling the children a simple story about a gingerbread boy who ran away. You must then take the children on a tour of the facility and, at each area you stop, there has been placed beforehand a clue you must read to tell the group where the gingerbread boy went to from that spot. Each site, of course, is one of the offices or other places where the staff members work. The final stop to which your class is directed is, of course, the school kitchen where you find a gingerbread boy baking in the oven. At that point the story ends and you all have a snack.

Security Items

Allay children's school anxiety by encouraging them to bring from home their favorite dolls, stuffed animals, toys, or other favorite items. Be sure to label each item with the owner's name. Also, when your pupils arrive at the school grounds for the first time, greet them outside the building. Later on indoors choose a nursery rhyme, poem, story, or finger play they might enjoy. Also suggest that they bring to school the special things they accumulated during the summer and spend the first class period discussing these items.

Self-Portrait

Before the school year begins, write a letter to each of your incoming students requesting that they draw and then mail to you at your home or school address a self-portrait they have made during the summer. Suggest that they add to their picture some special feature that will help you recognize them when you meet for the first time. As these pictures are sent, arrange a portrait gallery somewhere in the classroom.

A second idea is to duplicate a picture of a boy or a girl that you have prepared. Then cut these pictures apart to make a simple puzzle. Send a copy of this picture to each of your students. Include directions to the recipients to put the picture puzzle together, color it, and bring it back to school the very first day to make an attractive bulletin board display.

Special Attractions

To inform your new pupils of what they might reasonably be expected to accomplish during the coming school year, have available for their inspection a scrapbook of typical projects completed by pupils during the preceding term. Or, have a set of photographic slides you have taken of last year's activities. Invite your pupils' parents to view this slide show as a part of your first days of introduction to your classroom. Another surprise you can prepare is a set of small flags to distribute to the children before they arrive at school the first day. Lead them in a parade around the playground before you enter your classroom. You can also use flags and balloons to identify your classroom. Expand upon this theme by scheduling a special surprise for the first several days of school. (See "Surprises.")

Summer Letter

During the weeks just prior to the beginning of the fall term, duplicate copies of a letter you have handwritten on a ditto master. Include in this letter material that introduces you to your children. Include interesting information about yourself, your family, your hobbies and interests, your pets, and a general description of the main activities you have planned for the school year. Include an inexpensive copy of a picture of yourself. At the bottom of each letter add some personal comments on any aspect of that particular child's background that has come to your attention as you have reviewed his or her records from preceding years. Address and mail these letters to your children personally, even if they are still too young to read.

Summer Preparations

Just prior to the beginning of school in the fall capitalize on your children's enthusiasm for coming to school by sending home to them a copy of the schedule of daily activities you have planned for the year. Suggest that they and their parents practice some of these daily activities, such as, a sharing time at 9:00, reading a book and talking about it at 10:00, singing a song at 10:30, and painting a picture at 11:30. If you have the time, you might also provide your pupils a summer contact by calling them on the telephone, or visiting them at home, carrying with you a suitcase filled with some of the special learning materials you plan to use during the coming school year.

Surprises

The first day of school surprise your children by inviting them to join you in a playday on your playground or a local park for at least the first hour of the day. You might combine this event with a picnic lunch provided by parent volunteers. You might otherwise suggest a nature walk or take a hike around the neighborhood. Or, simply have the children join you in some games played in the classroom or in the gymnasium. It is also interesting to schedule for the first week of school a tea for the children and for their parents. Parent volunteers might help you produce such a surprise, and you might want to invite the school principal and other resource persons to share in the event to help the children become better acquainted with the school staff.

Transfers

Whenever children are added to your class roster during the school year, assign one particularly responsible child to help acquaint the newcomer with your classroom procedure. Collect from these new pupils personal information and share this with the other members of your class. Invite the new child's parents to come to school to be introduced to the other boys and girls. Set up a convenient coaster wagon as a "welcome wagon" for the new pupils, filling it with products your children have made in the meantime: booklets, paintings, and small gifts. The other class members might also provide a card on which they too have written personal information to introduce themselves to their new classmate. Similarly, at any time during the year when a child moves away from your school, ask your pupils to prepare mementoes for the person to take along. Mail to the receiving teacher a set of sample items prepared by the transferring child and include your own personal observations as well.

Tree Treats

On the first day of school, have in your classroom a sturdy tree branch set in a bucket of hardened plaster, pea gravel, or sand. To each twig on this branch tie a shiny red apple. Or, prepare a mystery box to place at the foot of this tree. Inside the box put small dried fruit, nuts or raisins. Encourage the children to guess what is hidden inside this mystery box, responding to the clues you provide them. Or, have a special set of name tags that you tie to the branches of the tree. As each child is introduced to the group, the child removes the appropriate label and wears it the rest of the day. Or, prepare personalized sacks or cartons that the boys and girls can decorate during the first day and then use as carriers to transport to and from school their materials and papers. These carriers can also be tied to the tree. This tree might also become a part of a nature center in which you have temporarily placed an unusual insect, a bird, or a small animal.

ICEBREAKERS

Adapted Games

Use ordinary children's games that involve calling out the names of the boys and girls in your class. For example, "Spin the Platter" requires a child when called to dash out to the center of a circle of children and catch the platter or pie tin before it stops spinning. "Spud" involves tossing a playground ball straight up into the air while the child who is "It" calls the name of a classmate in the circle of boys and girls. This second child whose name is called must catch it before the first bounce, and then either toss or roll the ball toward any other member of the circle, all of whom run outward from the circle until the ball is caught by the child whose name has been called. The child who tosses the ball must say the name of any classmate who has been hit.

Booklets

For the first day of class, make a set of autograph booklets. Or suggest in a summer letter to the children that they bring their own construction paper autograph books to class the first day. During the first week of school in the fall, give the boys and girls time to circulate among their peers collecting autographs. This might be a timed exercise to see how many different signatures each class member can get within the time stipulated. If the children are too young to write their own names yet, distribute stickers for them to use, or suggest that each person draw a face in each booklet, representing a unique self-portrait. Later during the year let the children continue to collect personal messages in these booklets that they will use as mementoes in later years.

Another possibility is to make a large booklet on behalf of the entire class, using a different page for each pupil enrolled. Give the students ditto masters and ask them to write such personal information as names, addresses, telephone numbers, family data, hobbies, interests, favorites, and the like. Duplicate these pages and combine them into booklets to send home with each pupil. Encourage the students and their parents to use these sources of information in distributing greeting cards and in organizing the room for special projects.

Circle Games

Arrange the children in any familiar circle game that requires them to run in opposite directions around the outside of the circle as one or more players are tagged. When the runners who have been tagged get to the opposite side of the circle, however, ask them each time to stop and shake hands and say their names aloud to the other class member before continuing to race on around the circle.

A second activity is to get a large playground ball and have one child stand in the center of a circle. This child must catch the ball as a member in the circle bounces it to him or her, and then bounce the ball to anyone else in the ring, first saying the name of that particular child before bouncing the ball in that direction.

Circle Pass

Arrange the children in circles, with six or eight members in each ring. Hand to each group a toy or some other small object. Require the children to pass this item around the group, with each person who passes it along using his or her own name and the names of all the classmates in turn who have preceded in the passing of the item. If the students are already well acquainted, challenge the persons in the circle to remember the names in proper sequence, without looking at them as they stand in the ring. Similarly, ask each member of the class to bring some small personal object to class. Seat the boys and girls in a circle, and have each person describe the object.

A second circle-passing activity involves the students in handing along a large ball of twine. As each child in turn handles the ball of twine, he or she must mention his or her name and tell some interesting fact of a personal nature. Then that particular player tosses the string to any other member in the circle, while holding onto the end of it. As each person in turn tosses the ball of twine elsewhere, the string will unwind and will crisscross the group, symbolically tying the entire group together for the school year.

Guess Who?

Have each student write a story about himself or herself but without signing his or her name. Mix up these stories and randomly distribute them to the children. Allow a few minutes for the boys and girls to read each tale silently, and then challenge the students to match each tale with its author. With younger children prepare a list of characteristics and see how quickly the boys and girls can name the appropriate class member, who, for example, has freckles, wears braids, and is missing one front tooth. A third possibility to test powers of observation involves standing the boys and girls several at a time behind a cardboard panel or an old piece of fabric. One at a time the pupils can put a hand, a foot, or an ear through a hole in this panel. The boys and girls in front of this partition must try to guess the person to whom the particular body member belongs.

Letter and Word Games

Let the children have some fun with their names as an introductory activity. For example, ask them to say their names and then tell one thing they like that begins with the same first letter. Or, ask them to write their names vertically and think of an interest or a characteristic that begins with each successive letter. Similarly, see if anyone can make a simple crossword puzzle, writing first, middle and last names at right angles to each other, and including other words, such as names of streets, siblings, and pets. Or, see if the boys and girls can make a rebus card of their names, using either the sounded syllables or spelled items in their names.

Make a name tag by cutting out of cardboard one or more of each child's initials. For each initial let that child make a list of self-descriptive words that begin with that particular letter. These initials can then be combined into a necklace for wearing about the classroom the first few days of school. Each child might also cut out cardboard replicas of letters included in his or her name, punch holes in each one, and then thread them on a long piece of yarn.

Mail Call

On the first day of school give each child a salvaged envelope and ask each student to put his or her name on one. During the day these envelopes are randomly placed in a box. From time to time ask individual children to take out the envelopes and deliver them to the appropriate classmates. See how quickly each pupil can learn the names of all the other members of the class. A second approach is to include family relationships in the activity by having the pupils bring to school various letters delivered to their homes. Convert these letters into name tags, complete with home addresses.

Mixed-Up Names

When the children first arrive in your classroom, prepare a list of the names of all the class members, but have each name mixed up in its spelling. Also prepare a second list of the actual names. Challenge the pupils to see how quickly they can unscramble all names in one column, drawing lines between the correct and the incorrect spellings. After the corrections have been made, let students check off the names of the persons they already know.

A second suggestion is to prepare a name tag for each pupil. As the children arrive on the first day of class, give each pupil a tag drawn randomly from a box. Let the boys and girls circulate around the classroom during the first few minutes to find the right name tag. Or, you might make a slight deliberate letter reversal or spelling error in each name. Hand out a list of correctly spelled names and let the children find the persons indicated on the list as they all get acquainted.

A third idea is to provide for each student a name tag made in an interesting shape and cut apart in two pieces in such a way that only one set of halves will fit together. Then ask the children to place one half of their name tags randomly inside a box. While holding the other half of the tag, they withdraw any second piece from the box. The pupils finally move randomly around the room to see if they can find the person who belongs to the second part of the name tag. Or, you might prefer to have the children hide the other halves around the classroom for a brief scavenger hunt as a get-acquainted activity.

Pair Presentations

Suggest that the boys and girls pair off randomly by drawing names or numbers from a box. Then ask these persons to interview each other, asking about siblings, birthdates, addresses, pets, hobbies, and interests. At the conclusion of a stipulated period of this informal conversation, ask each class member to introduce his or her partner. Suggest that the boys and girls try to find out something truly unpredictable or unusual. You might vary this activity with other children by having them record in writing some of the most interesting details, and then place these cards in a box for drawing out and guessing the identity of the person described on each card.

Personalized Tags

Early in the school year involve the class members in making unique name tags to wear. Suggest that each tag be decorated with original art work, including elements of special design that might tell something special about the artist.

After all the pupils have been acquainted, set these tags aside to be used when substitute teachers or visitors come to the classroom. Encourage the children to consider different media (print, glued sequins, etc.), various textures, combinations of colors, and unique shapes to make sure that no two tags are the same.

Photo Tags

Make special name tags for your children by taking instant photos. Arrange the children in small groups and then take the picture of several persons standing or seated not too closely together. This will allow enough room for you to cut out the individual figures and paste each one on a name tag. Enhance each item further with original designs drawn by the individual pupils, and add fingerprints and other personal information. After these tags have introduced the students to each other, set them aside to use as reminders when the boys and girls need to be out of the classroom during the instructional day.

Pictures and Portraits

Distribute to the boys and girls cardboard ovals, along with crayons or colored pencils. Ask each member of the group to draw a self-portrait, adding particular features that would help the other class members to recognize the owner and to associate the name with the face. At the bottom of the tag, each child may write his or her name. Such tags may be used in a card game in which they are shuffled and drawn from a face-down stack of ovals. They then try to match the name on any card drawn with a member of the small group with whom they are playing the game. If any child draws the name of a member of the group and can match the name with the proper face at the table, he or she may keep that particular card; or, any card that can be matched correctly with any other member of the entire class may similarly be kept.

A similar activity for the first day or two of school is to let the youngsters trace and cut out of kraft paper a full-figure portrait, with clothing and features added to identify each artist. These drawings can be posted on the windows or the walls to show passersby the names and portraits of the students in your classroom.

Plastic Tags

Before school begins ask the families of your children to bring to class plastic jugs that have been thoroughly cleaned out. Show the boys and girls how to cut out curved pieces for making small name tags to wear or to place at their work sites in the classroom. You might suggest that the pupils experiment with drawing their pictures first, and then cutting out the shapes they are interested in producing for their tags. Young boys and girls might prefer to convert a portion of their plastic jugs into a headband with or without feathers or other decorative elements; thus, each person's name can be displayed by wearing it on the head during the day. Older boys and girls might want to cut off the handle and the spout

portion and wear that section as a beanie, appropriately labeled with their names and decorated according to their interests. Show students how to make interesting yarn balls, flowers, or feathers that project from the spout opening at the top of each beanie.

Puzzle Names

As the children enter your classroom the first day of school, ask them to sign in on a large piece of cardboard. After all class members have registered with their signatures, cut this puzzle apart. Later in the day ask the group as a play activity to reconstruct the sign-up board. When all the pupils have had sufficient experience with this puzzle, reassemble it one final time and glue it permanently to a cardboard backing.

A second approach is to prepare a large graph paper matrix. On this matrix print the names of your children, one letter per square, either left to right, right to left, top to bottom, bottom to top, or diagonally. Duplicate this puzzle and challenge the children to see if they can find all the names of their classmates, circling each name as it is found. Provide the pupils a duplicated list of names to help them know what they are looking for.

Use graph paper to make strips. Then give each strip to a particular child containing only as many squares as there are letters in his or her name. Ask each child to print that name on the strip. When the names are on the strips, ask the boys and girls to move about the classroom trying to arrange their names in a stack in such a way that the letters vertically spell "Hello," "Welcome," "Greetings," or any other word of particular interest, including the name of the school itself.

Puzzle Pictures

Ask each child to draw a self-portrait on a large piece of paper or cardboard and then print his or her name underneath this picture. Have the pupils cut these pictures into several pieces and put these pieces inside an envelope. During the first few days of school, the children may select an envelope at random and remove the pieces to reassemble the puzzle, passing it along to its owner after the puzzle has been put back together again.

Reversed Names

Add variety to your getting acquainted activities by asking each student to write his or her name on a separate piece of paper, under which a sheet of carbon paper has been placed. When each name is written, cut out the name with the name reversed on the carboned side, so the letters appear backwards. Each name may then be used as a name tag. The boys and girls must circulate among their classmates attempting to decipher each name. If the group members are already familiar with each other, use some other item, such as a street address or telephone number. Have handy a mirror that can be used to confirm the children's guesses.

Review Tags

Use name tags to challenge your students to review certain concepts and skills. For example, check on young children's ability to recognize certain letters, associate first names with last names, identify shapes and colors on the tags, spell the first and last names, and name objects that are pictured on the tags, particularly if a given object pictured begins with the same sound used in that person's name. Older boys and girls can use their name tags to explore more complicated phonetic elements, alphabetize their names by first or last name, perform mathematical operations, graph the numbers of letters in the names, and appropriately place the name tags on a map of the immediate neighborhood.

Use these review activities in a game where a student who can answer any question posed by another student gets to keep that student's name tag. The questioning continues until all name tags have been exchanged.

Shape Tags

Make unique name tags by asking the children to cut out paper dolls on the double fold and decorate each one according to their interests and appearance. Young children might want to cut out name tags in the shape of a butterfly, a feather, a police badge, or a sheriff's star. Or, you could consider making a bracelet, a headband, a crown, or a hat. A stand-up desk label or one that hangs down from each individual's work space is another possibility.

Song Responses

If you teach young children, use a melody such as "Are You Sleeping?" to call the names of the children in turn. For example, sing, "Where is Tommy?" Tommy must then reply with the phrase, "Here I am, Here I am." The song continues with "How are you today, sir?" "Very well, I thank you." "Have a good day, have a good day." Let the children take turns leading this song, too. Use other familiar folk songs to substitute the names of your pupils in the appropriate spots. "Mary Wore a Red Dress" is one example. Or convert familiar nursery tunes to your own get-acquainted purposes.

Special Sharing

Children in the early grades feel more comfortable in a new grade or a new classroom if they are given an opportunity to share some of their experiences with classmates. In a summer letter to your new pupils ask each one to bring to school a special item to describe, such as a favorite toy or some souvenir from summer travels. With older pupils suggest they bring to class a baby picture. Have the classmates try to match the pictures as they are posted on the bulletin board. (NOTE: Be sure to warn parents against sending an heirloom or an irreplaceable photo!)

Tag Lines

Combine names with addresses by obtaining sturdy tag-type shipping labels. Ask the children to write their names on one side and their home address on the reverse side. Another suggestion is to attach original name tags to spring-type clothespins and wear these clipped to various parts of clothing during the day. When it is necessary to remove these tags for a part of the day, set up your own clothesline and clip the pins to that. You might also set up several different lines of twine and color code the name tags by areas of the school district, or by the mode of transportation to and from school. This will help you take attendance each day and will also enable you to become acquainted with other ways of managing your classroom.

2

The Classroom Environment

The success of any instructional program depends on the classroom atmosphere in which pupils spend as many as 1,000 hours every academic year. It is important, therefore, that you plan surroundings that will be as homelike as possible and allow students to be at ease as they undertake their daily tasks.

This means that the physical appearance of the classroom must be conducive to study and informal interactions: adequate space, occasional privacy, colors and textures that are appropriate to children's visual and psychological needs, furniture that fits, and materials that supply a variety of learning opportunities.

Equally important is the environment of the intangibles. Learners respond much more quickly in a setting where they perceive they are respected, trusted, and challenged. Sensitive teachers can do many things to put the children at ease and to convince them that they are important and worthwhile. Teachers can also demonstrate a sense of wonder, a sense of humor, and a certain enthusiasm for living, elements students are quick to perceive and ready to imitate. Special events that occur in the classroom with and without advanced notice are also bound to intrigue pupils and attract them to the school building day after day. Such consideration on your part also shows that adults do care about the happiness of students. Therefore, it is almost inevitable that greater learning will occur under such optimal conditions.

Similarly, you need to anticipate and prevent the behavior problems that so often erupt as a result of inattention to student discipline. In all too many cases, disruptions and conflicts interfere with the flow of instruction, thus robbing both the misbehaving students and their innocent classmates of the educational tasks at hand. In addition, recurrent discipline difficulties create stress that steals from your energy, which can be better used for planning and supervising instruction. Tensions created by conflicts and confrontations spill over onto unwitting bystanders too, and affect almost everyone.

The sensitive and sensible teacher prepares for such situations long before they occur. This awareness both prevents many interruptions and enables the teacher to deal more adequately with those occasional intrusions that cannot be foreseen or planned for. It has long been said in the teaching profession that most difficulties in discipline are as much teachers' problems as they are pupils' problems. Professionals who invest their time daily in examining the best principles that motivate pedagogical behaviors are most likely to elicit effective interpersonal practices for classroom application. The results will be more satisfied students, better pupil achievement, happier models of pupil behavior, and a considerable saving of time.

CREATING A CLIMATE FOR LEARNING

Absentees

When students are absent for long periods of time, maintain contact with them, ameliorate feelings of isolation, and continue their learning. One suggestion is to have your children who are present in the classroom compile a booklet containing original stories, jokes, cartoons, riddles, art projects, and a resumé of class notes. When your daily worksheets and other materials are routinely distributed during the day, make a point to set aside one copy of each item for the absent child. Fill a small suitcase with books, toys, games, and other objects of high interest and send it to the absentee's home. Engage the other pupils in writing occasional cards of remembrance appropriate to the reason why the student is absent.

Assignment Excitement

Add special interest to your routine homework tasks by varying the ways you make these assignments. For example, occasionally roll up duplicated papers and insert them into colorful bottles, boxes, or other interesting containers. Or, wrap them up like Christmas presents for the children to open. In general, you might substitute for the word "work" terms such as "games," "puzzles," "mysteries," and "inquiries" which indicate some element of challenge.

When it becomes necessary for the children to bring their papers home, let them carry these in colorful folders or envelopes that are not so easily mislaid once the children get home. Or, you might suggest the boys and girls wear a simple fabric jacket or vest to which various pockets have been attached. You might make a similar garment for your own use during the day; then, as various subjects of study are introduced, pull a card from each pocket and share that task with the boys and girls. Or, let the children take turns in withdrawing a surprise assignment from a pocket. From time to time have in one pocket a card on which you have written something like, "For the next ten minutes everyone may read a book," or, "Beginning immediately we will have a 15-minute recess."

Bad Weather

Sometimes changes in weather make it necessary for the children to stay indoors when they would rather be outside. At such times, have special activities—games, stories, and puzzles stored in a secret spot—for "rainy day" use only. Another possibility is to take advantage of the bad weather. For example, you could make a point to help the children view and appreciate the beauty of a rainy day: the rainbows present in oil slicks in the pavement, the way a leaf sails down the gutter, or the rainbow after the clouds dissipate. A rainy day is also a good time for playing in puddles and in rivulets, just as a snowfall invites "Fox and Geese" or building a snow fort.

Blah Month

Sometimes children's interest begins to wane simply because of prolonged bad weather or the number of weeks that elapse between holidays or vacation time. Perk up your classroom by transforming your windows into rays of sunshine by covering them with strips of yellow cellophane that catch and color the lightfall. Each child might make a window hanging by stapling cellophane or tissue paper between circles of construction paper.

You might also have in your classroom a box in which you have stored especially interesting things. Label this container, "Do Not Open Until You Need a Pick-Me-Up." Each day one child could select a surprise object or activity from this box.

Breaks in the Action

Good timing is an important element of teaching, so occasional breaks in the daily routine are just the thing to relax tensions and restore enthusiasm for the tasks at hand. One suggestion is to set a kitchen timer randomly and hide it in the classroom, with the understanding that whenever it rings, the class will be interrupted for some fun, such as a treasure chest of books, pictures, games, filmstrips, or puzzles. Or, you might provide a grab bag for one child to reach into, removing a slip with a special group privilege written on it. A "Joke in the Box" is a collection of jokes cut from children's magazines and other joke books. Pantomiming with old hats and puppets is yet another possibility.

Calendar Fun

Interject a note of special interest into your study and use of the daily calendar. For instance, introduce the study of Roman numerals from 1 to 31, and let your boys and girls use these symbols to date their papers from time to time. Find similar variations of numerals, such as hieroglyphics, cuneiform, and early Arabic symbols. When celebrating the birth dates of famous people, challenge your boys and girls to find out if that historical person would be older than 100 years or 200 years. Then make and count out the number of paper candles required for a cake to celebrate that occasion. Make a point to sing "Happy Birthday" to the person being honored, and let the boys and girls make temporary paper decals to wear about on their clothing to draw attention to the special person. Try to discover some figures from the past who would not be readily recognized by other children in the school. This could develop into interesting cafeteria and playground conversation and might stimulate personal research into the background of the person being remembered on that particular date.

Ceiling Suspensions

Show your children how to make mobiles and then suspend these from the ceiling. Let the boys and girls use these for permanent display purposes; the items they choose to post on these mobiles will gather much attention as they slowly turn in the air currents. Another suggestion for a mobile is to suspend several commonplace objects that are used in classroom activities. If you want to perk up the environment with color, bring to school some inexpensive balloons and ask the children to help inflate these. Suspend them from strings attached to the ceiling, along with flags, streamers and other readily accessible but inexpensive decorations. Do not feel you must wait for a festive occasion for such a display; you might ask the children themselves to think up a reason to celebrate with these suspensions.

Clock Treatment

If you have in your classroom a circular wall clock, convert it into a large colorful flower by cutting out large bright petals, a stem, and leaves, and attach these pieces to the clock. Or, you might incorporate the clock into a large cluster of paper balloon shapes, with pieces of yarn running down to a common point beneath the clock. A clock can also change into a bright glowing sun with the addition of fluorescent yellow rays and a piece of yellow cellophane placed directly over the clock face. If you have a rectangular clock, it can become the head of a robot, a window in a building, or the top of a rocket ship. Ask the boys and girls for still other suggestions for clock decorations.

Favorite Things

Combine an appreciation for pretty things with your children's natural interests by having a personal box for every member of the class, including yourself. Inside each container have a set of favorite things: photographs, examples of hobbies and crafts, and interesting stones or marbles. You might set up one special box with a velvet or satin lining with costume jewelry. Still another suggestion is to make a display of flowers in season, and encourage the children to bring some cut flowers to share with their classmates. Make a point to wear on your own person selected blossoms that are brought you by the students. Take time, too, to press-dry some of these contributions to keep in a personal scrapbook you maintain during the year. Also, if you grow flowers yourself, occasionally bring enough blooms to share with your students.

Garments Glorified

Have available for your children lengths of muslin or other plain fabric. Distribute to the group liquid embroidery or permanent felt-tip markers. Let your boys and girls each set aside a portion of this fabric and decorate it in keeping with their interests, their names, the date, and anything else that would remind you of their achievements and their presence in the room during the year. When the fabric has been completely decorated and dried, convert it into a simple sacklike garment just by running a few seams and cutting holes for head and arms. The scraps, if any, can be used to make an apron. A similar idea is to obtain a plain T-shirt, large enough to fit the biggest member of your class. Let the children not only help decorate it, but also take turns wearing it during the day.

Gracious Grading

One of the least satisfying elements of schooling for many students is grading. To help them overcome this difficulty, make a point to look for new ways to assess. For example, you can begin simply by marking at the top of papers only the number of right answers instead of the number of wrong ones. This will help the children begin to think positively about themselves and to upgrade their self-confidence and raise their goals. Make a great fuss about the number of correct answers and the extent of their improvement. Use smiling faces, "Gee" for Good, "X" for Excellent, and other unconventional marks. Suggest that the boys and girls record on a graph their math papers and spelling marks to give themselves a personal record of growth from time to time. Make a point not to compare pupils with each other, and encourage boys and girls to select, if they want, their own best work for display or distribution among their classmates. Let the boys and girls check and correct their own work. Encourage them also to think of new and wild words to put at the top of their outstanding papers, such as "groovy" or "splendiferous." Contact speakers of foreign languages to suggest yet other words you can write at the top of papers that show major improvement or achievement.

Graffiti Spot

Set aside a place in the classroom where your children can register freely what is on their minds, anonymously or otherwise. This might be a part of the bulletin board or a large piece of kraft paper spread over a table, renewable from time to time. Suggest that the children leave their names or their initials, as well as comments, poems, greetings, wise sayings, or quotations. Or, as a therapeutic device, suggest that the children write some of their personal problems anonymously, and challenge the other members of the class to help find solutions to these difficulties. Original pictures can also be welcome at such a site.

Grand Entrance

Make the prospect of coming to school a pleasurable adventure as you add decorations to your doorway. One good idea is to convert a large cardboard carton into an archway that the boys and girls must climb through or crawl under. This item can be made collapsible so it is not in the doorway to impede traffic once the day has begun. Or, festoon the doorway with crepe paper streamers that will gently blow in the breeze. Strings of gaily colored beads made by the pupils, or cellophane or tissue decorations are good ideas, too. Make a label for your classroom that identifies it as a castle, a fort, a space ship, or any other spot in fantasy. Then enlist the children in decorating both the inside and the outside of your doorway appropriate to the theme you have jointly decided upon.

Humor in Action

A sense of humor is a priceless pedagogical ingredient. Display and sharpen your wits by bringing in jokes you hear from time to time, or cut out some from comic pages and joke books. Encourage the children to set up a center for humor with an appropriate label such as "The Laugh Line" or "After Laughter." Embellish such a center with a communal clown shape made by tracing each child's hands and feet and cutting out these tracings to assemble them in a large area on the wall or the bulletin board. Or, let the children either bring to class or make original masks and hats that honor their favorite funny television or storybook characters. These items might be worn during the day at recess or story hour.

Inspiration at Work

Lift your children's spirits from time to time with just a dash of thoughtfulness. Ask the boys and girls to invent an original cheer for your classroom or adapt one from your own school's collection. Use these cheers for recognizing the accomplishments of the members of your class. At the end of the day, ask the pupils to join in on a song of fellowship before dismissal. Suggest that the boys and girls make up their own words and tune. In addition, ask the children to think of original mottoes that would help them focus on their tasks or to cope more effectively with their daily interpersonal relationships. Such mottoes can be made in the form of cardboard stand-up items to place on desks or wooden ones to hang from the walls.

Interest Clubs

Set aside a certain time, such as Friday afternoons, when the children have at least a brief time to work together in groups according to special interests. Set up a separate table for each club, and designate materials for them to use. Encourage the boys and girls to bring in their hobbies and to work on these together. Each interest group can be identified with its own banner, flag, or sign. Also maintain a notebook or a box to which each class member can contribute pictures, stories, or real objects that relate to these interest groups. Encourage the pupils to share their products and discoveries with other classes that might have similar interests. They might also want to convert some of their items into aids to assist in the instruction of their classmates or students in other classes.

Keeping in Touch

You can help your children and also build parent support by going out of your way to maintain contact with your pupils. One handy technique is to send them post cards and personal messages whenever you might be away from your community at any distance. Make a note to send birthday cards when these important dates come due. As the boys and girls move out of your room into higher grades, send along with them sample materials they have produced in your class as a way to inform the new teacher of progress and potential. Occasional follow-up notes and cards the following year are also in order.

Loyalty

Develop a sense of loyalty to the nation as well as to your classroom group using several interesting techniques. For example, enlist your children in designing and producing a banner that represents a theme selected by the class members. This can be fashioned like a pennant, a flag, or a streamer, and can be constructed of muslin, felt, burlap, or any other appropriate fabric. Such a room banner may be taken along on a simple pole-and-floorboard arrangement to all-school assemblies to not only identify where your pupils are to sit, but also help them sense they are unique. This may encourage them to be well behaved!

You can also make your own stars-and-stripes banner by placing miniature photos of your children in place of the stars that are ordinarily found on the flag, using more than the stipulated number of red and white stripes so as not to appear to be desecrating a real flag. These stripes could well include the children's own patriotic statements, written right on the stripes by them. Yet another approach is to have the boys and girls each make their own personal replicas of the American flag, using paper, sticks, and a lump of clay as a desk holder. These then could be used in the special observances of George Washington's or Abraham Lincoln's birthdays.

Mascot

Contact a department store or a men's clothing shop for a manikin that is to be discarded. Using just the torso portion as a silent member of the class, let the children decorate or dress it according to a name they have invented for it. Use this manikin as a silent messenger for the class as you place in its upraised hands the notices that the children are to become aware of during the day. Let this mascot also serve as a silent partner in oral reading activities.

A second possibility is to obtain a small animal as a mascot for the classroom. Children often relate well to a warm and furry animal when they are feeling sad or otherwise in need of an undemanding friend. If it is not possible to have a real creature, a stuffed version can be an acceptable substitute. Make a point to cover any fabric mascot with a washable sturdy garment to make it easier to keep clean. A similar version of a mascot is to obtain a set of discarded clothing and engage the children in stuffing a life-size "person" with clothing scraps. A scarecrow, a clown, or a spaceperson are just three of many possibilities the children could create.

Music and Moods

Sometimes music has its own particular charm in stimulating children's efforts. For example, when the weather is inclement or when the children otherwise seem not quite as sprightly as they usually are, a cheerful march might be just the thing. On the other hand, when they are fatigued from recess or study, a quiet orchestral selection might be in order. Since listening to music is often viewed by the children as a special privilege, use it sparingly and under the stipulation that it is done only under special circumstances. Whenever the tensions are running high, use some silly song to relieve the stress. Or, begin your instructional day by singing the children's names and asking them to answer your call.

Names Are Neat

Encourage your boys and girls to invent bird-like names for themselves that will reflect their individual interests and abilities. For example: "freckly-faced rope-jumper" or "red-headed car-racer." Encourage them to make drawings of themselves in their bird-like roles, complete with appropriate feathers and other avian features.

Children also enjoy having titles along with their names, particularly as these identify different roles and relationships in the classroom. Whenever boys and girls are designated to be a tutor or any other specialist with a particular responsibility in your room, encourage them to make labels to identify these tasks. These labels may be worn during the day as badges of distinction, or the pupils may devise stand-up desk markers that similarly identify areas of expertise.

A third suggestion is to prepare replicas of the old-fashioned "wanted" posters and place these prominently about the classroom. From time to time, place on these posters the names of children who have done a particularly outstanding job, such as "Wanted: applause for Suzy who has learned her times table." Or, you might choose to indicate needs that the children have expressed, such as "Wanted: someone to help me review my spelling words." The boys and girls can use their own name cards interchangeably on these posters, appropriate to the legend or caption expressed on each one.

Old Hats

Engage the children in assembling a collection of old hats for your classroom. These can be used for impromptu dramatic activities when appropriate. Or, the boys and girls may be permitted to wear them informally during the instructional day. Furthermore, let the children decorate these hats as a part of their crafts experiences. If there is sufficient interest, let the students each purchase or make identical hats that display not only their own names, but also the identity of their classroom, grade, or school. Old hats are useful to pass around the classroom when items are either to be collected from or distributed to the pupils. A hat can also be converted into a grab bag for the children to reach into and pull out some surprise or announcement of the next activity you have planned for them.

Outside the Room

Bring the outdoors inside your classroom by having small tubs and large flowerpots into which you have planted small trees. Place these containers on a caster platform for ease of moving about the room. When school is over in June place these outdoors in the natural elements.

A second suggestion is to give the students long strips of crepe paper and let them interweave these through the openings in a chain-link fence that encloses your playground. They can each make their own unique designs in this way. After the paper has faded, be sure the students remove the unsightly material, which can then be saved and used for a future papier-mâché project.

A garden spot is always a good way to beautify the outdoors and to help the boys and girls learn about science while gardening. Ask the children's parents to send to school packages of seeds and extra bulbs dug up in the fall. Encourage the children to make small but permanent markers for each kind of growing thing, as a service to the younger children in your school.

Personal Touch

A little extra personal effort will endear you to your students and will enlist their support and cooperation during the entire year. One suggestion is to use an instant camera to take occasional pictures of your children in outstanding or interesting performances or poses. Have the students write a brief paragraph about their photos and send these home to be shared with their families.

Make a point to write a personal note to each child at least once a year. Also send away for free materials that will be sent directly to the children at their homes, thereby giving them extra occasional mail deliveries. Mark the pupils' birthdates and other special holidays and seasons to send them personal greeting cards.

Since young children are especially proud of losing their baby teeth, keep on hand a *Tooth Is "Looth"* book in which you record each event as it occurs. Make a large replica of a tooth and let children wear it around their necks any day they lose a tooth.

Challenge the children to think of a special name for your class. This may relate to a particular interest most of them have or it may be a play on your own name or on the grade level you teach. Encourage the pupils to make their own inexpensive T-shirts with the name of your group on them.

Occasionally, as the boys and girls come into your classroom the first time that day, shake their hands, bow, and address them as "Mister" or "Miss."

Give the children turns in performing as the teacher of your class, particularly during review experiences or other low-level types of activity. During these times you must pretend to be a child, occupying the desk of the person now in charge, and participating in the activity at hand.

Assign each child to be in charge of one day each month. Challenge each person to find out some special event associated with that date, and then share that event with the class members. Schedule birthday parties for obscure figures of history, or have special celebrations for obscure events or for days or weeks of national interest, such as "National Dill Pickle Week."

Popular Choice

From time to time during the year let the boys and girls in your classroom help make some of the decisions that determine what will be done by the group during the day. For example, ask for a show of hands regarding which subject to begin the day with, especially if you have gotten into a routine of having the same subjects at the same time every day. You might ask the students to decide the sequence of events during the remainder of the session. They might also want to determine when free time might be granted. Let them participate in other areas, too, such as giving directions for assignments, calling the class together as a group, and engaging in some of the other privileges and responsibilities usually reserved for teachers.

Questions, Questions

Whenever you introduce a major unit of study, especially history or geography, and before the children have had a chance to learn about the topic at hand, challenge them each to write one important question they would like to have answered or would like someone to explore. Then, during the course of your instruction, identify these queries along with their authors. Have these written on paper prominently posted on a bulletin board, and be sure that each child's name is included on each one. In a sense, then, that particular pupil will take charge of a given aspect of the group study. When that question has been answered satisfactorily, the answer can be written on the reverse side of the question card, and removed and used later during review activities. As a culminating experience, you might compare the answers obtained with some of the guesses made by the children at the initial contact with the content of that particular unit. These guesses can be written on cards and later on compared with the legitimate answers the boys and girls have discovered as a result of their study.

Ratings Race

Whenever you would ordinarily make a chart to keep track of how many times children respond correctly, reconsider the customary use of competition to stimulate students' responses. Whatever you are sampling—whether it be how many books each student has read or how often he or she has brushed hair or teeth—you would do well to turn the process inside out, thereby stressing individual responsibility rather than success as compared with each other. For example, in stimulating reading, make a list of 10 or 20 books appropriate to your children and ask the boys and girls to sign their names after each one when they have completed reading it. This will give the students a chance to see which books are the most popular in your collection, and will be motivated by their peers to read them. Thus, the reading will not deteriorate into a race to see which child can read the most books. Similarly, if you have a chart showing good habits of health, let the children make their own checkmarks early in the day. In this way individuals will be in charge of their own responses, and the chart will show cumulatively which habits seem to be either the easiest to tend to or the most important to the children enrolled.

Scrapbook

Encourage your children to keep scrapbooks—individual ones as well as cumulative ones—for the classroom. Such a collection might include representative work completed during the year, and the colors, motto, mascot, or emblems that identify your classroom. Outstanding events during the same time period are also appropriate, along with special honors. One particularly effective approach is to salvage wallpaper sample books from local businesses and convert these into class diaries, one page written on by a different child, in turn, each day. Classmates can cut or decorate each page with different original drawings or embellishments of the samples on which the writing is placed.

Sharing

There are many occasions for sharing during the usual school year. Much of this occurs as you share your own hobbies and activities that take place outside of school. Bring to class the pictures of your family, souvenirs from your travels, and examples of your handcraft. Another possibility is to have your students share their songs, poems, stories, and art efforts with elderly residents of your community, or with other children in the district or region. Encourage the members of your group to contact by telephone those familiar persons who would appreciate hearing from someone like them. You might also share your own home with the children. Having first obtained parental and administration permission, invite several children at a time to visit your home, to share in a simple meal, or to participate in some activity, such as shopping in the neighborhood. You might ask for parent volunteers to help with these activities.

Spontaneous Events

Make or salvage an apron and add several pockets to it. Fill these pockets with cards on each of which you have written some unexpected surprises. Let one child wear this apron around the classroom. From time to time the other class members may randomly choose one card from a pocket and announce the special treat. A similar idea is to have a wildly decorated hat for a child to wear about the classroom. Attach to the surface of the hat various jokes, riddles, cartoons, and other interesting items contributed by the boys and girls themselves. When you feel the need for a break or when one child is in need of a laugh, let that pupil pick one of the items off the hat and share it with the classmates.

Spots of Color

Just a bit of paint can do wonders for dressing up your learning environment. For instance, if you have venetian blinds, get permission to create a temporary mural on one or more section. Clean the slats thoroughly beforehand, and let the children use tempera paints to make an interesting picture or design. If necessary, add soap flakes to the paint to help it adhere to the slippery surface of the blinds. Paint can also be used in designating certain areas of activity in your classroom. For example, use red, orange and yellow to decorate those areas of greatest physical involvement, while blue and green can designate areas for subdued activities. A further idea is to have the children cut from discarded cardboard large random shapes to be hung from the walls or ceiling. Paint these items with bright colors and discard them when the children seem to tire of them or when they get dirty.

Teacher Challenge

"I'll eat my hat" is a traditional challenge that children find hard to resist. When you introduce a particularly difficult concept or unit to your class, make a statement beforehand that if they manage to attain a stipulated level of performance, you will eat your hat. Propose that the competency be one that shows major progress rather than perfection, so as not to make it impossible for the children to attain it. If the class members reach the level of proficiency you have agreed to, carry out your part of the bargain by bringing to the classroom a sheet cake arranged and frosted like a top hat. Or, bake and bring to school a set of cookies that are cut and decorated to resemble a hat.

Wall Treatments

One way to brighten a classroom is to make huge sunflowers to cover part of a wall. On each petal of a sunflower blossom write the name of one of your students. On the inner portion of the flower write a legend such as, "You brighten our day." You can also convert a corner into a replica of the American flag, with half the flag on one wall and the other half on the other wall, bending around the corner. A gigantic beanstalk is yet another possibility, with a cutout of Jack climbing the ladder of major achievements characteristic of your grade

level, each leaf representing one major accomplishment. Add still other interest by cutting out pictures of high adventure, such as explorers, athletes, and dancers. Project these against large colorful pieces of paper and let the children trace them and cut them out for posting.

Favorite pictures from the children's story books or textbooks may similarly be projected on the wall using an overhead or an opaque projector. Save colorful Sunday comic sections and use these to embellish temporary partitions in your classroom.

Windows Well

If your classroom has a strong outdoor light source, hang interesting plants in your windows. Or, fill a fishbowl with water to which you have added food coloring. Add colored rocks and plastic foliage to make a pretty underwater scene. Be sure there are no fish in the tank since food coloring can be toxic to fish. Small prisms, foil, glass, mirrors, and other sparkling items such as jewelry are also good for decorating strong light sources. Colored clear bottles and jars are also suitable for adorning shelves that are in the sunlight.

You might set aside one window in your classroom as your "Window on the World." Keep this window decorated with the children's art work, especially those incorporating transparent cellophane tissue paper. From time to time add compelling legends to call attention to your children or to greet passersby.

DIAGNOSING DAILY DISCIPLINE

Aggression and Acting-Out Alternatives

There are many situations during the year when children who have energy to burn, who need an outlet for their frustrations, who have aggressive tendencies, or who simply seek attention turn to acting-out behaviors that are either nonproductive or outright destructive and disruptive to the regular routine. If you have children who have a legitimate need for this kind of activity, set aside a special place and materials for the purpose, with the understanding that the other members of the class are not to be disturbed. Depending on the individual child involved, you might also want to stipulate that he or she may remove him- or herself to this location without asking your permission. There are many activities that such a child can engage in during free play times, especially outdoors, to release strong emotions. Here are samples:

- Blow up and burst paper bags.
- Tear newspapers into strips or bits for papier-mâché experiences.
- Pound and knead clay to get the air out for later firing in a kiln.
- Throw a sponge ball at a target.
- Hammer roofing nails into a thick piece of wood.

- Tear apart a large cardboard carton.
- Saw holes in a large cardboard carton using a keyhole saw.
- Dig a garden outdoors to prepare soil for planting.
- Shovel snow off the playground.
- Sweep the sidewalks with a broom.
- Tear up strips of fabric for weaving experiences.
- Build a tower of cardboard cartons and then knock it down.
- Rake leaves off the playground, stuff them into a sack, and stomp the sack.
- Jump rope for five minutes.
- Scribble on a chalkboard.

Anger Alternatives

Whenever one of your pupils either loses control of his or her temper or is on the verge of doing so, encourage that person to get into the habit of cooling off and regaining composure. One way to do this is to count something. While some adults traditionally advise counting to ten, let the child count ten objects or find ten items of the same kind. By the time the counting is done, the emotions will likely have subsided. Another idea is to let the child talk to a puppet or a classroom mascot. Some children might prefer talking into a tape recorder that will enable them later to recall how they felt and sounded when the situation is discussed in private. A related suggestion is to ask someone with a foreign language background to teach a socially acceptable expletive which can be thundered out in a moment of anger. If you have a pupil who needs to shout his or her anger, provide a small storage closet; or sound proof a cardboard carton with cushions, pillows, and carpet scraps and let that person release pent-up emotions.

Appropriate Punishments

Use punishments for misbehavior sparingly; but when it is absolutely necessary, make sure that these acts are directly related to the misdeed. For example, a child who destroys someone else's property should reasonably be expected to help pay for its replacement, in keepng with that child's resources. The student who makes a mess should logically clean it up. Wherever possible, let the misbehaving students themselves participate in deciding what they think would be a reasonable penalty to serve as compensation for their misbehavior. In this way they will have to consider the consequences of their misdeeds the next time around. Another suggestion is to offer two or three possible consequences and allow the children to choose from among your list. Before any penalty is imposed, however, make sure the child understands its necessity by asking that pupil to explain to you in his or her own words the reason for your action.

It is equally important that you avoid punishments that are counter-productive. Traditionally, teachers have chosen certain kinds of penalties that not only fail to relate to the misdeed and its consequences, but turn the children away from respecting the teacher as a fair and humane person and turn them away from certain subjects of study. For example, the practice of assigning children to write "I will not chew gum" 500 times tends to make them more determined to chew gum. If a child places gum where it does not belong, on the other hand, there would seem to be some sense in asking him or her to spend some time removing the dried wads stuck under the tables in the cafeteria. Assigning longer "doses" of punishment homework similarly turns children away from writing essays, using reference works, or doing mathematics problems. They learn to hate their subjects of study when homework is used as punishment. Perhaps the best way to tell if a punishment is reasonable, other than asking your children, is to ask yourself how *you* would feel in a similar situation.

Attention Span

It is generally said that children have a short attention span. While this generalization is sometimes true, the intensity of their response to a learning situation is much more likely to be a function of their interest in it, rather than time itself. Therefore, it is appropriate to plan frequent changes and include a wide variety of learning experiences. When the students lose interest in your activity, change directions to perk them up. Select projects and materials that both relate to the pupils' interests and reflect their need to perform well at tasks in keeping with their abilities. If one individual's attention begins to wander during a session, subtly bring that person back to the group by casually interjecting his or her name into the narrative or the question or the discussion. Make a point to involve all pupils equally in the proceedings each day, instead of calling only on those pupils who are bright and responsive. Chart the flow of the conversation during the day to see how many boys and girls are involved in it. Try to have the discussions moving from pupil to pupil at least part of the time, rather than expecting the children to respond only to your questions and comments.

Being Fair

It is almost impossible to be absolutely fair with all your students all the time. Boys and girls in the elementary school are just developing a strong sense of social justice, however, and so their ideas of fairness may or may not coincide with your own. Make it apparent to the children in your room, though, that you will try your best to treat them equitably, even though treatments sometimes may vary depending on the differential needs of the pupils present in the room. Let them know that you will listen to their expressions of complaint concerning perceived unfairness. Make a concerted effort to avoid having children thought of as "teacher's pets" by randomly assigning tasks or dispensing privileges, except in situations where such duties or rewards are already assigned or earned outright. At intervals during the year distribute a questionnaire to be answered anonymously on which you ask, among other things, whether or not you have provided fair treatment.

Changing Positions

Sometimes children misbehave simply because the adult in charge is unmindful of physiological limitations. To sit still for any length of time is not natural for the human frame; and to remain in an uncomfortable position, such as sitting cross-legged on the floor, can actually turn into a subtle form of torture. Similarly, children should be allowed to move about the classroom, within reason, simply to change their site for studying. Learning can occur, surprisingly enough, underneath desks and tables, on rugs and carpets, and in rocking chairs. The novelty of such variations will, of course, wear off after a while, and your students will find the places and positions that are most conducive to learning in pursuit of each instructional task. Your only stipulation should be that wherever the children choose to study during a general activity time, they should not interfere with either the concentration or the physical safety and comfort of their classmates.

Confidential Criticism

Whenever it is necessary to comment negatively on a child's performance, behavior, or attitude, make a point to protect that person's feelings by conferring in private. No one appreciates a public audience when being reprimanded; and to do so is to humiliate a child. This humiliation tends to not only drive the inappropriate behavior underground, but also causes resentment that frequently lasts a lifetime, thus impairing the quality of one's attitudes about schooling and about a particular teacher. Also, you would do well to direct your criticism at the act itself, *not* at the child. You can demonstrate that there is a difference between disliking the act and liking the child with comments that reflect that important distinction. "You're a bad boy" can't help but reflect negatively on a child's character, while "You shouldn't have thrown that stone" comments on the deed.

It is equally important that you keep your comments confidential from other professionals in the school, unless the consequences of a particular child's behavior are such that sharing information is absolutely necessary. Unfortunately, much data that is passed from one teacher to another borders on gossip, and this accomplishes nothing constructive. Even when information is accurate and objective in nature, to pass it along without due cause tends to set one's mind to expect certain kinds of behaviors from that particular child. And since teaching is one profession where self-fulfilling prophecies are commonplace, it is advisable to protect the students from distorted expectations by keeping most information private, however factual it may be.

Consistent Treatment

One of the things that children most appreciate is consistency in approach. If you propose certain consequences for certain kinds of behavior, whether positive or negative, carry through on your plans without fanfare. This suggests that you should avoid making idle threats you either cannot carry out or would rather not carry out. Children like to know what to count on from day to day. Of course there are times when circumstances intervene; for example, you may be extra demanding because of fatigue, illness, anxiety, or any other factor that similarly conditions children's behaviors. In such an instance, a sincere apology and an explanation ought to be given your pupils. If you make a mistake in judgment, such an error should be readily admitted and an adjustment made, just as (presumably) you casually treat the children's misjudgments and misdeeds.

Contracted Changes

When a member of your class is coping with a particular difficulty, set up a simple contractual agreement with him or her to focus on the one behavior problem. Be sure that the child really does want to improve, then establish a baseline of behavior consisting of the number of times that negative behavior occurs each day or every week. Make a chart or a graph of this information and challenge the child to take charge of recording this information. Help the child to prepare a document that states the goal and carries a solemn signature as a part of the agreement. As your part of the arrangement, stipulate the kinds of support you will provide, as well as any reasonable reward you will offer if and when the goal is attained. At whatever time the student achieves an appropriate level of behavior or achievement, attach a seal to this contract and send it to the principal and later to the children's family for sharing.

Cooperative Involvements

Some teachers make the mistake of approaching their daily tasks as a series of confrontations that call for their exerting their legal power over children. They establish long lists of rules that their pupils are expected to obey without question, and they are ever watchful for students who might step out of line. This attitude creates considerable tension and tends to inhibit and upset the students, most of whom are not likely to pose a threat to the decorum of the classroom, if the teacher would only trust them and engage them in dialogue regarding their social responsibilities to their classmates and their personal responsibilities to themselves.

In addition, when teachers foster high levels of competition in their classrooms, pupils tend not only to be anxious, but also suspicious of each other. They fawn for teacher favors, they cheat to get ahead of their classmates, and they conspire with each other against their mentors. The wise teacher provides many opportunities for cooperative ventures, for children learn to cooperate and work harmoniously toward common goals only if they are given the opportunities to practice their social skills and can participate equally in the rewards system of the institution. It is therefore important in any school to maximize the means of honoring as many people as possible, rather than restricting the awards to only a select few people operating in just a few areas of competency. In the long run, it is probably more important that a person can work well with others, can demonstrate leadership, and can show sensitivity to the needs of others, than that he or she can get the best grades in school in the academic subjects.

Corporal Punishment

This is a controversial topic that is as yet not resolved in the minds of many professionals. While the traditionalists tend to cling to the custom of spanking children, there are others who question the usefulness of the practice, pointing out that massive evidence suggests it teaches the children the wrong things: physical power is important in solving problems; teachers can do things to children that children cannot do to each other; in American society only young, relatively helpless, mainly male pupils are paddled; adults sometimes lose control in ways that are counter-productive; and school personnel sometimes ignore their own policies with regard to spanking.

While most states in this country still permit spanking in schools, many nations have outlawed the practice. Similarly, many major school districts in America have also forbidden the practice. Most school boards have taken elaborate measures to protect those professionals who are permitted to spank their children, and in some cases the use of a paddle is accompanied by a long list of things to do beforehand and afterward.

Increasingly schools have begun to look for alternatives. Even though some professionals in exasperation claim they use the paddle only as a last resort, the research on the topic tends to contradict their claim. One study found that there are well over 100 possible alternatives to spanking students, but that teachers use only a few other weapons in their armory. It would be well for professionals to study this problem in considerable detail; and whether or not paddling is permitted locally, they should pursue some of their many options instead of striking children.

Correcting Mistakes

Children will be more comfortable in your classroom if they are led to believe that making mistakes is permitted and that errors are one way of learning. You will also do well to treat your own errors of fact or judgment with equal equanimity. Whenever it is important to help a child develop greater accuracy, however, you can aim for that goal. When the child is indisputably wrong, you can still send signals that preserve a sense of dignity while suggesting the need for reconsideration: "That was a good guess," "Is that what you meant to say?" "Did you forget to subtract the second number from the first?" "Did you remember about inverting the divisor?" "Can you think of a better answer?" "You almost got it right," "That was a good try," and "Would you care to change your mind?" are all good examples of how to get more accurate responses while protecting the student's sense of self.

Expressing Feelings

Make it clear to your students that human beings have an extensive repertoire of emotions, all of which emerge from time to time. Assure your pupils that negative feelings are a part of being human and, although it is appropriate to have these feelings and even sometimes express them, our purpose is to see how well we can redirect our feelings into constructive activities and habits. Let the children themselves discuss certain situations that engulf them from time to time and suggest ways each one could have been handled more effectively. Legitimize the need to express anger, jealousy, sorrow, frustration, and other negative feelings by letting them prepare stand-up faces to represent each one. Then whenever a child is feeling out of sorts, he or she may erect the appropriate sign on the desk to let classmates know. Similarly, some children might choose to prepare simple masks to wear when a given negative feeling overwhelms them.

Furniture Arrangements

Many behavior problems arise simply because of inappropriate room arrangements. For years teachers have been aware of the need to separate children who do not get along with each other or who get along almost too well. But not as many professionals are aware of the need to involve the children in deciding how their desks are to be arranged for a given unit of study or for a given period of time. Only too seldom are pupils asked for input regarding their study group and partners in certain tasks. So make a point to engage the children in discussing the optimal arrangements of the equipment and furnishings in your classroom; you will find that they will more likely respond to your expectations, having had a part in the deliberations.

Along the same line, see to it that materials are accessible, and that traffic lanes are free of feet and objects. Make sure the seats are comfortable, the lighting adequate, the heating and cooling appropriate to the season, and the air supply fresh. Have the desks and other work sites arranged so you have visual access to everything that occurs in the classroom. If it is appropriate to have private carrels in your classroom, have each one open to view from the top, and arrange these at the ends of radii extending from the center of your classroom. Children will thus be separated from each other visually but will still be visible to you.

Giving Compliments

Praising children rather than criticizing them is a more effective motivator of learning. However, not every teacher knows how to praise effectively. It is essential that, first, such praise be sincere, for children quickly see through flattery or pretense, and quickly learn to play the game based on artificiality. Second, a compliment is most effective when it is associated with one specific event or achievement. In this way the child can readily see the kinds of behaviors that are rewarded or recognized. Be especially careful not to make statements that might suggest the student should always be successful: "You are always so well-behaved" and "You did a perfect paper, as usual," although innocent in their intent, nevertheless convey the message that that child can never do less than his or her best, or can never make a mistake. In like manner, some teachers are either too lavish with their compliments, thereby overprizing a certain behavior; or they are repetitious. There are many ways to say, "Good job," such as a pat on the back. It would be to your advantage to find out what these are or to make up some of your own.

Giving Help

It is the wise teacher who knows how and when to give help and how much to offer. Some boys and girls grow as they struggle by themselves; others get quickly discouraged and give up; still others manipulate adults into providing them a dependency relationship. During the general activity period it is usually wise to be available to the students, asking from time to time, "Can I be of help to anyone?" or "Who could use some personal teaching?" You might want to suggest that the children make miniature "Help Wanted" signs to post on their desks when they require help. Such signposts would not call attention of the class to this need. Still another approach is to establish a panel of experts—volunteers who agree to spend a portion of each period or each week helping those persons who require assistance. In this case, let all the children have a turn in serving in at least some subject area, in keeping with their interests and their competencies. Do not make the mistake of "sentencing" the more capable students to being your helpers for the entire school year, for this puts them in a subservient role and curtails the opportunity for their own growth. A fourth possibility is to have for each row or cluster a "study buddy" who provides help upon demand. Here, again, the occupancy of this support role should be changed regularly during the school year.

Handling Aggression

Children who act upon their hostilities are easier to handle if you understand some of the dimensions of their feelings and the nature of their problems. As you interact with the members of your class, take special note of factors such as these:

- Some children's personalities from birth are such that they are naturally more asserting and more demanding.
- Where the rewards are limited to only a few pupils in class, much frustration and failure are experienced. Setting individual goals, varying reporting procedures, and diversifying grading are all recommended.
- Children often come to school suffering great stress due to the problems in their families, difficulties in getting up on time, missing the bus, forgetting books, and not completing homework. Their acting out in your classroom may simply represent the latest in a series of unhappy events that day.

- A child whose expectations are repeatedly blocked is likely to become frustrated; frustration leads to anger; and anger leads either to withdrawal or acting out.
- Aggression is sometimes a way to get attention when it has been denied. Look for many opportunities to recognize good behavior, however insignificant it may seem at times.
- Many children come to school from families where aggression and anger are the modes of living. Where a child has learned early that survival may depend on self-assertion, hostility, and anger, he or she is not likely to quickly conform to your expectations.
- Aggression is sometimes a mask for uncertainty. Some of the most hostile children are very insecure or otherwise see themselves as worthless. Find many opportunities to build your students' sense of self and provide security through predictable behavior.

Helpful Humor

Perhaps the single most important quality of a good teacher is a sense of humor. Readiness to laugh at funny situations as well as at one's own mistakes is a characteristic that both endears a teacher to children and models for them behaviors to imitate. Foster your pupils' appreciation by smiling readily at them and by bringing to class nonsensical words, poetry, jokes, riddles, and other items that show your students that you can laugh with the rest of them. Sometimes making gentle fun of universal foibles coaxes children out of a tight spot or helps remind them of their responsibilities to themselves and to others. For example, make a point to help the pupils think of names for inappropriate "diseases" that sometimes infest classrooms: "forgetfulcellus," "jitteritus," "pester fester," "messytosis," and "muddlemania" are just a few possibilities. Remember, too, to praise students for funny stories and displays of a sense of humor.

Making Allowances

Whenever a child fails to fulfill an obligation, treat the incident as if the pupil had forgotten, rather than deliberately disobeyed. Since it is less blameworthy to forget something than to deliberately misbehave, the benefit of the doubt is often appropriate. Casual hints such as "Do you remember how to walk down the hall?" are generally more productive than castigating the child for running indoors. A related suggestion is to deliberately forget or overlook most of the minor incidents that tend to occur, especially if you have made too long a list of things to remember about good conduct in your school. If you think you must notice, comment on, and judge every single event, you will find the day frustrating and filled with confrontations. It is also recommended at times to issue to the children a coupon book filled with slips of paper that will automatically forgive them a certain type or number of unsatisfactory behaviors. In this way the children will know and appreciate that there will be some latitude, even if they do fail to live up to your and their own expectations from time to time.

Making Comparisons

Many teachers are of the mistaken opinion that to compare one student with another is to motivate greater effort and therefore stimulate more learning. Psychologists tell us that, with certain exceptions, just the opposite is true. Even those older students who routinely behave or achieve at extraordinary levels do not like to be held up as the good examples, simply because this places them in the position of favorites and their peers quickly learn to resent or dislike them. (Note: Students, ages 6 to 9, do enjoy these demonstrations of praise. However, do not make them excessive.) Similarly, siblings are not happy about being compared with their brothers and sisters. In the same way, the students who are placed in ability groups early and without recourse are unhappy about being compared, directly or indirectly, with their classmates of greater or lesser abilities.

One ready solution to the problem of unfair comparisons is to diversify and individualize both the children's learning goals and their materials of instruction. If the pupils look to raise their own sights as they achieve more and more demanding tasks, they are likely to take considerable satisfaction in their progress, notwithstanding the fact that they and their classmates realize the class constitutes a group of people of varying abilities. Similarly, the child who is responsible mainly for his or her own progress can keep private and personal record of the attainments during the course of the year. And if you are successful in diversifying your instructional items, the pupils will have little opportunity to compare the growth of their peers, simply because they will be using many different sources of academic experience.

Managing Monitors

As a general rule it is not wise to place children in charge of each other, except in those rare situations where the very safety of the boys and girls may be at issue. Whenever a monitor is established for any important reason, however, make a point to explain the necessity of such protection, such as a patrol boy guarding the crosswalk. Also, make sure that you select only those persons who are sufficiently mature to understand the nature of their responsibilities. Try to avoid having children in charge of their same-age classmates. Train these student helpers to work from the positive aspect of controlling their young charges: looking for children to praise and reminding rather than remonstrating. To assess the effectiveness of the monitors, ask the children from time to time to respond to a simple questionnaire indicating the fair treatment and even-handedness offered by each person in a position of authority and responsibility.

Managing Upsets

There are many occasions during which children find themselves distressed. Be prepared to suggest many alternatives so the persons involved can more reasonably decide what to do about the situation. You might try these techniques:

- Ask an older child to talk into a tape recorder to tell or explain one side of a problem. Then ask the antagonists to listen to this explanation without interruption. Or, have both sides tape record their impressions and use these as a three-way conference.

- Use puppets or dolls as a way to act out what happened in a given situation. Allow the pupils involved in the conflict to manipulate the figures to express any feeling or offer any explanation.
- Suggest that the persons draw or paint a picture of an unpleasant situation and then, if appropriate, explain the picture.
- Let the children take a stuffed toy or mascot into a private spot and talk to that object.
- Tape record an actual outburst and then play the recording back to the person in private later on.
- Play soothing music when tensions run high.
- Set up an informal "office" where any person who has the need may withdraw until feelings are under control.
- Redirect the troubled child into a task in support of a younger or less capable person in class or elsewhere in your school.

Note-Writing Alternatives

If the passing of children's notes in the classroom disturbs you, take the initiative in redirecting these energies that will spare your children embarrassment and will conserve your instructional time. Announce early in the year that your students may write notes to each other, as long as other work is completed. Or, suggest that such notes may be used as a way of expressing language competencies that will be read only by the recipient. Stipulate that such missives should be in good form, should not degrade or embarrass anyone, and should be placed in a private mailbox maintained by each student in the classroom. Provide a pleasant example for your students by penning your own personal notes to the various members of your class from time to time, making sure that only the recipient knows the contents of each letter you send through this classroom post box.

Sincere Apologies

One of the least productive but most often used technique is forcing a child to apologize to an adult or to a classmate. Forcing a child to say "I'm sorry" to anyone simply shows that a teacher has the power to make a child do something he or she would rather not do. It also provides the student a model of insincerity: the words are the main thing, not the true feelings. Instead of making an issue out of a formal apology, make sure the misbehaving student understands clearly how he or she has erred, and how the offended party feels about it. If a child does indeed apologize spontaneously, it is more likely to be heartfelt. Of course, the most effective way to teach this habit and the concept that underlies it is to provide in your own relationships with your students the model for them to follow. Whenever any situation arises in which you have deliberately or unintentionally verbally wounded one of your pupils, make a point to sincerely apologize. This personal example will speak longer and louder than any number of words.

Withholding Blame

All too often teachers are anxious to find a culprit for a crime. Over the years entire classrooms of children have been unfairly punished for the faults of a few. Sometimes individual pupils have been singled out for punishment on behalf of the unknown criminal. Children question this practice with good justification, for the entire legal system of this nation is based on innocence presumed and on punishing the guilty party only. In addition, too hot pursuit of blame often leaves the genuine culprit with a sense of guilt that is not easily expunged later on. You are, of course, entitled to express disappointment that an unfortunate incident occurred. And while children should know the extent of their responsibility for their own behaviors, to force them to tell on each other merely produces ingratiating tattletales.

Calisthenics to a Beat

Encourage your students to bring popular records to class and make up calisthenics routines in time to the beat of the music. To simplify this procedure at first, suggest only a few basic movements to do in response to the rhythm. Then as the children gain confidence in their choreographic skills, permit them to devise more complicated procedures, encouraging two or more pupils to work together to invent their own routines. As a variation, suggest that the pupils devise series of movements that involve just one part of the body, such as the torso. Or, suggest that they think up a series of exercises involving just a single mode of movement; for example, jumping in various ways. If you have access to poems that also have a strong beat, have the children first read them aloud, and then repeat from memory short poems that lend themselves to movement. Encourage your students to assume different positions, prone, standing, bending, and the like, on the floor as they exercise. Introduce the production of original poems, such as couplets or quatrains, that give students directions for their fitness activities:

- Lie on your back, pretend to do a jumping jack.
- Face left, face right, touch your toes with all your might.

Choosing Partners

When the children are setting up groups or teams for game activities, make sure all children are chosen fairly with as little argument, confusion, and embarrassment as possible. You might say, for example, "Find two other people with blond hair and then sit on the floor," or, "Find one person wearing the same color you have on." Make it clear that when a person cannot locate a partner for such a game, he or she is to run to the center of the play area and there find partners from those who are left over from the pairing off. In the event you have one "odd" child left over from an "even" pairing or clustering, let that one child be the "IT" person or the judge or the game leader until at least several turns are taken, and then he or she can choose another person to be in charge of the activity.

Coping with Competition

High levels of competition in schools and classrooms tend to be counterproductive. The only people who continue to compete for limited rewards are those who have some reasonable expectation of succeeding or winning the rewards. The other people then tend to act out, withdraw from the effort, cheat to win, or resent those few classmates who time after time garner the few prizes offered. Maintain your students' interest in their tasks by making the competitiveness more appropriate to the age, capabilities, and expectations of your pupils. For example, if you are teaching young children, from time to time have the class compete collectively against your own performance in various physical tasks. For example, see if any student can jump rope more often than you can without missing. Or, have the boys and girls combine their performances to see if all the times they jump rope without missing is better than what you can do by yourself. Another possibility is to have the pupils compete against a clock rather than against you, against each other, or against a national standard. Any person who beats the time limit is a "winner." And when winners are being announced, make sure that there are "first winners," "second winners," "third winners," and so on.

An even better approach to physical training is to have the boys and girls of all ages compete against their own past performance. Physical education is one field in which the goals of achievement are clearly seen and the students can trace their own records without regard or knowledge of what anyone else is doing. You might have each student prepare charts in which a figure is indicated to represent him- or herself. The figure might be stapled or tied to a string that is strung through holes at the two opposite sides of the chart. Along the continuum of the chart an axis can show progress of that particular student. As the student masters a given skill, the figure, labeled and decorated appropriately to match that pupil, can be pulled along the axis to show the steady growth.

When the miniature figure reaches the end of the chart, offer that pupil some small reward or commendation in keeping with his or her effort, and then allow the student to continue to the next unit of instruction.

If the group is overly concerned with comparing and contesting, have each pupil keep his or her own progress in an individual booklet that only you and that pupil can examine. Your own attitude is, of course, a key factor in reducing the level of competition and the stress that so often accompanies it. Make sure the children are not encouraged to select only their friends for group activities or to choose only the best players for their teams. Make a point to focus on individual growth in a skill. Minimize the keeping of scores and center on cooperative effort toward a common goal. Try to avoid playing games that go on until only one player is left in them. Give the children ample opportunities to select the training activities for the group, and have many options so they can engage in those things in which they are most competent and therefore most secure.

Cue Cards

Vary the instructions for calisthenics and other simple skills activities by using visual cues rather than auditory ones. For instance, develop a series of flash cards showing a series of stick figures performing certain stunts. Mix the order of displaying these stimuli to the group. To give even greater variety to the exercises, distribute them individually among the pupils and have them perform the tasks pictured on each card, later finding someone else with whom to exchange cards. This procedure keeps all the children constructively active within a limited play area, makes the practice more interesting, and piques the curiosity of the pupils who must wonder what is coming next.

Instructional Helps

There are many common-sense suggestions for managing fitness experiences. Look at this list and then prepare for yourself a checklist which includes the most pertinent or most needed items:

1. Allow a practice period when you introduce a new activity or game, allowing the children to try it first before a score is kept, for example. If it is a running game or some other fast experience, let the children walk through the activity first, making sure they understand how it is to be done.

2. Stop your activities while the children's interest is still quite high. If they feel they have not yet been fulfilled the first time around, they will be more likely to request that same activity later on. Be sure you do not let the children participate to the point of exhaustion or boredom.

3. Involve as many pupils as possible in any activity. For example, if the activity involves a ball, instead of having only one or two students handle the ball while 20 or more boys and girls stand around watching, have many small groups and many balls. When any student has an appreciable time to wait for a piece of equipment, give instructions beforehand for each person to perform some simple physical stunt or exercise in the meanwhile.

4. Take precautions against having any one child become the goat or the butt of deprecating remarks. If there is a child who is appreciably less skillful than others, individualize the program or set up variable skill groups to introduce less demanding tasks.

5. Participate with your children in their activities, but do not monopolize them. Try not to show them the "perfect" way to perform the stunt or activity, unless such a demonstration is absolutely essential to the experience. Encourage the children for putting forth reasonable effort, rather than necessarily performing to your criterion.

6. As much as possible allow your students to choose the stunts and activities that will sharpen the skills you have in mind. At the conclusion of each instructional period, have at least a short time of free play with the equipment in the space you have.

7. Make a permanent chart of all the activities you introduce during the year. In this way the children will be im-

pressed with the number and variety of physical skills they have explored. And if you post prominently in the gymnasium posters on which all these activities are listed, the children will have greater knowledge when it comes time for them to select their own practice tasks.

8. Whenever you are explaining a complicated task, break it down into its separate parts and practice each of these before combining them. Ask various boys and girls to demonstrate the skills. Whenever you have completed your directions, start the group to work promptly so the children do not get bored waiting.

9. Whenever you need the complete attention of the entire group, forgo the usual whistle blast for the sake of either a visual cue, such as a red stop sign or a yellow caution flag, or a more pleasant audio tone such as a bell.

10. Begin an instructional period with vigorous involvement and gradually slow down the pace as the children tire and as they approach other school tasks that may require them to work quietly at their desks.

11. After the children have mastered a basic formation, vary the activity by changing one or more elements in it. For example, double the number of balls or beanbags in play, increase or decrease the size of objects and targets, increase or decrease the distances involved, extend the goal lines, or change the number of players.

12. After directions are given, ask one or more students to repeat their understandings of what they are to do. If, during the activity, one or two persons do not completely understand the procedures they are to follow, call them aside for a personal explanation. This will not stop the activity and will protect the feelings of those students who need extra support.

Motivating Fitness

Maintain your children's enthusiasm for fitness by tying in your instruction with their interests and with things that are happening elsewhere. For instance, festivals and play days stimulate participation by your children because they represent a variety of activities and also demonstrate for other children and for adults in and out of the school the skills your students have mastered during a particular unit of instruction. Do not try to choreograph a major production, but rather let these special events simply be the culmination of your instruction which reflects the things you ordinarily teach day by day.

No-Fault Fitness

Make a point to keep all your children constructively occupied at all times during your training period, not only to provide greater activity but also to help control their behavior while they are awaiting their turns. For example, never have a game that completely eliminates children. Rather, let them perform simple stunts or calisthenics to become reinstated in the game lineup if they are participating in a game that calls for some kind of forfeit or penalty. Similarly, when children are using apparatus at various stations around the gymnasium, have them perform some simple stunt on their way back to the group from the equipment at hand. This will tend to keep them from interfering with either the next person to use the apparatus or the other boys and girls waiting in line.

Playground Guidance

You can do a great deal to reduce random chasing and customary horseplay during recess if you paint on the playground surface a variety of games. Ask the children themselves to make suggestions of such games, and enlist their help in painting the lines on the hardtop. Such games can be as simple as "Four Square," hopscotch of several different kinds, and circles for dodge ball and other circular games. Make two or more concentric circles for various sizes of groups to use. More ambitious projects might include replicas of maps, checkerboards, and tic-tac-toe. For young children, make lines to resemble the lanes of a highway on which they can practice their driver's skills and pedestrian's skills while using the ride-on toys available in your school. Bicycle lanes for the older children are also appropriate, both to test rules of the road and to challenge their ability to ride a winding path, avoid obstacles, etc.

Safety Sense

Playing and practicing physical skills safely are certainly two main objectives of any program. Children need to be made aware of the importance of consideration for others as an essential goal. Encourage the children to think of themselves as each having a "space bubble" inside which they are all to be moving during movement exploration, during games, or during casual play at recess. If they should happen to bump into somebody else, explain that their bubble will burst, and they might have to sit down for a minute or so until the bubble grows again. In addition, simple common sense will help you avoid hazards to your children's well-being, so have the children all move in the same direction when possible. Note before a game begins where the potential problems might be in regard to safety. Provide sufficient areas for the games, and keep boundaries well away from walls and fences. Use deflated balls and other soft equipment where appropriate. Ask the children to remove sharp or hard objects from their hair and pockets.

Signal Systems

When the children are busily engaged in physical education, they get so involved that it is often difficult for you to get their attention for a change of direction or for additional explanations. While most coaches and instructors use a whistle, this is sometimes shattering to the ears of young children and is often overused. Explore the possibilities presented by visual signals rather than auditory ones in noisy gymnasiums. For example, a flashing yellow or red beam of light should attract the participants' attention. Or, simply flick the overhead lights. You have an opportunity outdoors to use large cartoon-type cue cards, particularly if you further instruct the children that the first one to notice your signal being waved is to sit down in place immediately, as a further visual attention-getter for the rest of the participants.

Skill Centers

Have a variety of stations in a large play area to involve the children in physical education. Such a method introduces and reinforces a wide variety of physical skills instead of usually stressing only one. Furthermore, the different pieces of equipment needed for this approach mean you can diversify your expenditures and seldom need many items of the very same type. The stations approach also keeps the children much more actively interested in what is happening and reduces the disturbances that often occur as pupils are awaiting their turns. Make a special point, however, to see that all pieces of apparatus are adequately explained, competently demonstrated, and appropriately supervised as the children use them. At each station you would be wise to prominently post a chart explaining the equipment's use, a stick figure or other drawing showing how the item is to be used, or a chart listing the kinds of stunts that might be attempted at that particular station. Where necessary, post responsible students to help explain and to oversee the use of certain items as a safety measure.

As a further motivator of the use of stations, ask the children to help you think of cartoon characters to embellish each position around the gymnasium or the playground. The boys and girls can make large figures to identify each one. They can also help you invent names for each character and each area of activity. The balance beam might become "Pirate's Plank," the side horse might be called "Silver" or "Trigger." A set of plastic hula hoops could become "Moon Craters," while the climbing rope is, of course, "Tarzan's Vine."

Skills Charts

Whenever you introduce a new game, stunt, or skill, record it on a chart using a simple stick figure and post this chart prominently in the play area. This simple device will enable your children and you to recall quickly the activities that are in need of practice. Also, as the students learn a new activity, maintain on a permanent chart the name of that ac-

tivity. The children will thus have a reminder of what they have already done. Whenever you want to review or reinforce a certain skill, or as you permit the students to choose a favorite activity to do for fun, you can look at this cumulative list and choose more intelligently from a wider selection, instead of merely naming something that the children tried just a few days before.

Squad Setups

When assembling your class for an activity that involves small groups, have the children already divided into squads of appropriate sizes. This will facilitate your taking the roll each time, for the leaders of each squad can help be responsible for the whereabouts of their members. Suggest that each squad choose a distinctive name for themselves and wear appropriate armbands, scarves, or headbands that identify each squad, thereby building group identity. From time to time change the structure and the memberships of these squads to prevent one group from dominating all the activities, and allowing all the pupils ample opportunities to work with all their classmates. If you have a situation wherein one or two students are so superior to their classmates that the competitions are always unequal, move these excellent athletes around to provide more equitable efforts from all squads. However, instead of just singling out the superior athletes, include their names in a much more general shuffling of groups.

Taking Turns

Many training activities have a person who is "It" or who otherwise must take turns. Make a special effort for all participants to have equal opportunity at a turn. You can do this in several ways, one of which is to issue to each child a marker such as a checker or a poker chip. Every time a person has a turn, that chip must be turned into a central collection point, continuing until no one has a marker. A second suggestion is to have a large spinner board with the names of all the children printed on it. Place this board flat on the floor and make sure the spinner rotates smoothly. The students can then select random leaders in this fashion. You might also have a list of all class members posted in the play area, and as each person has a chance to be in charge of the group, that person marks his or her name off the roll, thus providing a turn for every member of the group.

Team Selection

Sometimes the simple act of choosing up sides for teams presents subtle nuances of psychological distress that teachers are often unaware of. All too often the teacher gives the responsibility of choosing up sides to the most popular or the most competent members of the group. The same boys and girls are the team captains day after day, thus depriving the other children of the exercise of leadership. Furthermore, the pupils who are chosen by the teacher as the captains tend to choose first their best friends and/or the most competent athletes. Thus, the other students in the group are time after time passed over as the first-chosen or the early-chosen team members. The greatest insult occurs when one child is the last chosen, or when the team members collectively ask not to have a particular pupil on their team. Under such circumstances your students not only grow up disliking physical education as an activity, but also develop inadequate self-concepts based on their classmates' perceptions.

To prevent this type of thing from happening when you are introducing an activity where teams must be chosen, facilitate the fair and reasonable treatment of all pupils by varying the way teams are identified. Make sure that the roles of captain are passed out equitably day after day so everyone has a chance to choose. If this causes social uncertainty, resort to a variety of random selections that occur in terms of the alphabet, the section of the classroom in which your boys and girls are variously located, the digits in street addresses, the number of letters in last names, the neighborhoods in which your students live, or the colors of clothing worn to school that day.

THE ABC'S OF THE FIRST "R"

All-Purpose Advice

There are many bits of good advice to follow in any reading program. Examine this list to see if there are any items you might incorporate into your own reading instruction:

- Think of reading in terms of appetites, not in terms of lists of books. If the children do not read outside your classroom, you have wasted their time and your own.
- Share your own reading experiences with your pupils, thereby demonstrating that reading is as important and as interesting for adults as it is for children.

- Avoid insisting that your children finish the books they choose to read. After all, adults find dull books tiresome and put them down before completion. Just be sure, however, that this does not become a pattern with certain youngsters.
- Vary the time and the circumstances of reading. To have reading happen in the same way every day not only bores children but also makes reading seem all the more a part of classrooms instead of the real world.
- Keep reading experiences of your children as private as you possibly can when skills are being developed. Let most of this kind of sharing be done individually or in small groups.
- Avoid killing pupil interest that occurs by making them struggle for words or by overemphasizing certain skills. If there are selected items the children need to know, make a point to concentrate on these at a certain time of day.
- Introduce your students to the history of the language, its origins, its applications, and its uniqueness. Include a lot of nonsensical activities to further interest.
- In selecting library books for recreational reading, allow your pupils to choose books somewhat below their instructional reading level. No one cares to read for pleasure books that are difficult to decipher.
- Minimize the notion of covering material for its own sake. If the children do not finish a workbook they are not likely to be blighted for life, as long as they enjoy reading and continue to be immersed in the opportunities books present.
- Vary the number and kinds of books you have in your classroom. Retire some books off the shelves for a time, bringing them back later on.
- Avoid forcing your students to read what you think is a good book. After all, classics are being written all the time. Encourage the children to search for their own definition of a good book.

Book Clubs

A book club is one vital element of a successful reading program that deserves to be sustained throughout the entire year. In some situations the school librarian is able and willing to provide this ongoing service. However, if this approach is not possible, combine efforts with your colleagues elsewhere in the building, especially at the same or similar grade levels, and set up your own organization to offer your children quality books from one or more of the respectable commercial sources. You are thereby able to not only provide outstanding literature to your pupils at a nominal cost, but also to accumulate bonus credits that can be applied to related teaching materials, such as other book titles, charts, posters, maps, and records.

Boys and girls are always pleased to own books, particularly when these can be taken home to share with other members of the family, or used in the regular reading program in your classroom as a legitimate part of the daily activities. While the actual bookkeeping involved in such an effort is not a lot (and this can sometimes be tended to by the more mature boys and girls themselves), the advantages of a book club are beyond measuring.

Make a point to explain clearly to your parents that no child is pressured into purchasing even these outstanding titles. Inform them as well that all pupils will have access to new titles when the books arrive, at least on a free loan basis. Assure the children that a book order is sufficiently important to suspend all other activities in your classroom whenever it arrives at school; then carry out your guarantee and let the pupils account for the ownership of these books first, and afterwards spend considerable time examining and reading them in class, regardless of what else you had planned for that period.

Book Festival

In conjunction with a week of special emphasis, or just on its own merits, schedule for your children and for other persons in the school an event during which books are featured. As a part of such an event, schedule an appearance by a local author or illustrator. Ask the local librarian to introduce to your children some of the newest library acquisitions. Set up a schedule of movies about characters and topics prominently represented in your classroom collection or a central library. Suggest that some of your pupils present dramatizations of books through role play or puppet shows. Set up displays of the most loved books through the years, especially those well liked by the children in your school.

If there is sufficient interest, schedule a book sale in conjunction with Book Week. In some communities you can order books through a book wholesale house on the condition that books not bought will be returned intact to the source of supply. A parent-teacher organization, a student group, or some philanthropic or service group in the community can undertake this as a profit-making or a charitable venture, with the proceeds of the effort going to their own treasuries or donated for some special purchase for the school itself. Assistance from older and more reliable children in your school can be counted on for the routine operation of the display and the orders for books taken from it. As the books arrive at school, these same persons can reconcile the orders and distribute the books. Some schools find it advisable to order only single copies of each book, with the stipulation that the first person to sign up for that particular volume keeps the original when the sale is over.

To get the greatest benefit from such an effort, schedule it to precede by several weeks the holiday seasons in the winter, or have it coincide with a campaign for reading during the summer vacation months. Allow for ample time for the children in the school to visit the display and get some ideas as to the kinds of books they would like to order for themselves or have someone purchase on their behalf. Have an appropriate variety of items at hand, suitable for the various ages and grades of pupils who are invited to participate, representing many interests, types of bindings, and cost. Find some convenient place in the school where the display will be accessible to the pupils, but will be secure during the course of the exhibit.

Book Report Alternatives

Forcing children week after week to make the traditional book reports probably does more to kill their interest in reading than any other single thing done in the elementary grades. Many teachers find it necessary not only to demand a reckoning from everyone equally and alike, but also to insist that the students read only from an approved booklist, that mandatory areas be included in their reading, and that the reports of such reading follow a stipulated oral or written format. Teachers also unwittingly turn boys and girls away from reading by telling them that certain books are either "too hard" or "too easy," as if the children themselves were quite incapable of making such eventual decisions, even though these judgments might require a certain set of experiences with books over the course of the years.

The matter of interrogation in reading in general is much too exhaustive and too time consuming. The very act of reading in many schools is accompanied by a host of questions for which all the students are accountable. Unfortunately, these questions are both too many in number and too simplistic to generate much but contempt or distress for having to answer them. A child in school very often gets the idea that to read a book merely for fun is not encouraged.

A further consideration is that the traditional book report requires a child to make the same or similar kinds of presentations time after time. And while every pupil should have ample opportunities to report and share readings with classmates, such reports should be largely voluntary and mainly done when a genuine interest prompts a child to read a book. There is nothing quite as tedious as having to listen to 25 nearly identical oral reports over the course of a week or two.

There are many alternatives to the usual book report. Allow students to choose some kind of follow-up activity after reading a book. Such self-chosen ventures not only engage the children's creative thinking in the preparation of media related to what they are reading, but also further generate an interest in reading itself. As the students view the efforts of their peers, they are stimulated to select from titles that elicited such spontaneity and creative efforts.

Books in Comfort

One sure way to get your students interested in good books is to provide your own private reading center in the classroom. Make such a spot a comfortable and convenient nook, furnished with an easy chair or a rocker, a rug or carpet, bookshelves, a lamp, and a simulated fireplace made from a cardboard carton and commercial "brick" crepe paper. If nothing else, have several cushions available for relaxed reading in one corner of your room. If there is interest in a more secluded spot, assemble materials to make an Indian teepee, a cave, a nest, a den, a dog house, a rocket ship, a castle, a stage coach, a train, a jack-in-the-box, or any other cheerful accommodation suitable for one or two members of your class at a time. Enlist your students in locating large cardboard cartons that might be suitable for such a construction and further engage them in building and decorating it appropriate to the theme they have agreed upon.

Clever Containers

Motivate the curiosity of your children and spur their reading by using a variety of containers for your classroom book collection. You might assemble a mini-collection on a given theme from time to time and box them according to that theme. For instance, a suitcase might hold a set of books on distant places or on travel. A picnic basket would do nicely for volumes about foods or family fun. A backpack or a duffel bag would do as a repository of works about the outdoors or about nature. Engage your children in thinking about suitable containers as the year progresses, and when materials are not readily available to construct such items, contact your children's families for things that might be donated to your room or lent for a brief time.

Compatible Pairs

The use of the buddy system in reading has many advantages, as long as the members of the pairs can work well together, are at about the same level of competency, and can profitably use the time given them. Much time is saved as the buddies check each other's work, give each other practice help with flashcards, practice their own oral reading, and use each other as resource persons for spelling words needed in writing compositions. Make a point to ensure that all pupils remain with a buddy only as it is mutually agreeable. At the conclusion of the major units of study, make arrangements to regroup the partners.

Diversified Basals

If you are interested in individualizing a major portion of your reading program, provide a great number and variety of materials for your pupils. One way to do this is to get permission to invest the funds regularly budgeted for one basal series for your classroom in a different way: if you have 30 pupils in your classroom, for instance, you might arrange to purchase just 10 copies of the same titles in the basal program used by all the teachers in your school or your district. However, you could then spend the remaining money differentially, rather than purchasing 20 more sets of the same thing. You might decide to purchase 20 different books from many different suppliers, making sure that some are at your own grade level while others would be at higher levels and at lower levels of expectation. In this way you could provide each child several times as many appropriate reading experiences taken from many basal sources. If and when you find it necessary to have groups working from a single source, you could then use the 10 copies chosen originally or combine efforts with several copies of the same set chosen from various suppliers. Thus, your children would no longer be obligated to flounder through the same kinds of readers day after day, with no variety of topic or format.

Kits and Kids

Many schools invest heavily in commercially prepared reading kits. While most of these are well prepared and sequential in nature, and there is a certain professional security and comfort in having everything at hand, plans and activities alike, there is also the ever-present temptation to let the kit constitute the entire reading program. Children need and demand a wide variety of items in many formats from several points of view, however professionally prepared a certain kit may be. Furthermore, investing all the funds in one expensive offering may well curtail the possibility of purchasing other items. There is also a real temptation to teach to the kit as well, for once something is purchased, teachers tend to feel obligated to use it, however well or however poorly it may suit their children's instructional needs.

Libraries and Librarians

Use the central library in your school and the one in the local community to engage your students in reading on their own, a goal which is, after all, the ultimate objective of any reading program. It is unfortunate but true that some professionals treat the library as Fort Knox and the books as a horde of gold, not to be handled lightly and to be withdrawn only after adequate security checks for appropriateness of the reader.

Although some schools choose to schedule weekly visits of all pupils to the library, there is much to be said for having the collection more accessible during the instructional day, particularly to those more responsible and more talented students who warrant ready use of many different resources. The matter of going down the hall to take out a book should not involve the child in a federal case. And no child should be reprimanded for taking out an inappropriate book from time to time, nor for not completing a book that he or she found uninteresting or not useful.

In addition to the usual hardcover trade books, each librarian should make a point to have in the collection a representative set of paperbacks. There is something both appealing and convenient about these volumes, and some children will read them when they will undertake no other sort of literature. The central library is an ideal site for setting up racks of paperbacks for outright purchase as well. In addition, a paperback exchange is a handy idea, for the boys and girls can swap unwanted paperbacks of quality without regard for paying for their replacements.

Reading Group Alternatives

Children often become bored when engaged in reading around a group. You can vary the procedures by announcing at the outset of a group experience that the children will be asked pertinent questions about the content, either by peers or by you. This may help keep them more alert and thinking about the content of the story at hand. If your purpose in this oral reading is to check comprehension, set up the group so that as each person has his or her turn, he or she may move away from the group and back to his or her own desk, rather than necessarily waiting for the last child. Similarly, the other members of the group might well bring other work with them and complete other assignments as they wait their turn in the group.

If your purpose in oral reading is to focus on oral interpretation of the story, have the boys and girls try reading each bit of dialogue as if there were some other emotion present than the one indicated in the narrative: have these passages read joyfully, angrily, disgustedly, impatiently, sadly, and so on. You might further suggest that the children actually dramatize the story; as it is being read, they are to act out what they are reading. Or, you could collect a set of interesting hats or masks in keeping with the stories in your series and ask the students to wear these at appropriate moments and continue their oral interpretation of the narrative.

Reading Materials

The truly individualized reading program demands a veritable smorgasbord of reading possibilities. In addition to a diversified basal program, explore the kinds of reading matter casually acquired through a variety of sources. For one thing, explore what literature appropriate to the children's interest is available at home and at school. As boys and girls move through the elementary grades they acquire hobbies, join clubs, engage in sports, and reveal interests in many activities. Use journals and other materials suitable to these interests not only to show the children the legitimacy of their outside interests, but to also help stimulate those pupils who are not necessarily attracted to the usual basal program or other commercial offerings.

You would also do well to incorporate the newspapers and magazines that come to students' homes during the year, thereby tying in reading with current affairs and many other topics. The comic pages of newspapers are without equal in stimulating original stories that themselves can be included in things read for credit as a part of class exercises. Instruction manuals for machines, descriptions of inventions, and scientific data are other elements that might be included. Special journals and out-of-date magazines and books can be salvaged from second-hand stores, from professional offices and business, and from the families of the children themselves.

Reducing the Race

All too often teachers innocently turn reading into a competition that ultimately produces only winners and losers. While it is appropriate to encourage all children to read as much as possible and as well as possible, there is no excuse for making the act a competition with a prize at the end. After all, reading is never a timed activity, except rarely in classrooms, and adults do not compete with each other for recognition as a part of their own reading regimens. By fostering competitions, teachers unwittingly urge children to hasten through books, to choose only skinny books, to cheat in the accounting of their reading, to feel superior to their less capable classmates, and to look for extrinsic recognition from the teacher rather than deriving intrinsic joy from the act of reading itself.

Encourage reading by keeping a list of the Top Ten books in your classroom as the children report to you and their classmates the titles of their favorites. You might also make a poster to which you have attached pockets. Label each pocket to represent a different book and add the caption "Have You Read...?" Then whenever a student reads one of the books listed, he or she places a slip with his or her name on it inside the appropriate pocket. In this way the class members can ascertain how many people have read each title and can quickly find out which person has done so recently. That peer may then be consulted for his or her opinion on the nature and the quality of the book in question.

Reluctant Readers

The boys and girls who are either not as capable as their peers or are simply not interested in books, present a particular challenge to any classroom teacher. The problem is not ameliorated much by the usual shunting off to the remedial teacher, however gifted he or she may be at pedagogy, or however much fun the individual child so referred reports to his or her classmates.

The problem of the reluctant reader is in part a problem of professionals' unfulfilled expectations. Teachers are very eager to cluster children by so-called "ability groups," notwithstanding the fact that no such group is in any way truly homogeneous, and regardless of the research that shows teachers only rarely do the kinds of things in groups they think should be done with children of perceived similar abilities. While making only three or four preparations a day in reading is admittedly easier than making individual preparations for individual children, the success of ability grouping has been sadly overstated.

It is essential, therefore, that as much individualization as possible be used in classrooms at all levels. Grouping can be done, but on different bases, such as when several children need to work on the same skill, or when a cluster of pupils choose to share some of the things they have learned. The solution to the problem is also hastened as you deal with the self-concept of the pupil who may have arrived in a classroom already labeled as a failure or a member of a "dumb" group. In addition to individualizing instruction, provide opportunities for such persons to regain a sense of dignity and worth as they are allowed to practice some of their reading skills before other, less critical students elsewhere in the school, and as they are given an opportunity guaranteed by parents in some bedtime story hours.

A further consideration involves the assessment of progress at the conclusion of the marking periods. While most schools cling to the traditional grades represented by numerals, letters, or similar symbols, the reluctant reader demands and deserves a much more anecdotal approach to progress. Growth from point to point should take precedence over outright achievement as such, grade level accomplishments should be minimized in the reporting, and factors such as effort, appropriate study habits, and contributions to the entire group should be emphasized.

Sign-Out Sensations

To combine accountability for your books with strong visual appeal and an enticement for further reading, set up a sign-out spot in the most colorful area of the classroom. For instance, cut out a series of petals to complete a flower. As a child signs out a book, have this series of petal-shaped slips available, and ask each child to sign his or her name on one petal. This petal is then posted on the flower board. As the

Watch Our Garden Grow: Write your Name and title of the Book you read on a petal & tape it to a stem

PETALS for PAGES!

weeks go by, the spot ought to be heavily laden with visual reminders of how completely your children are involved with books. A leaf motif with a tree is still another idea, as well as fruits to hang on a tree branch embedded in a can of gravel. Adding spots to a leopard or a giraffe or a ladybug are yet other variations of the same theme. Further engage the interest of your students by replacing the customary sign-out cards with various colors of paper, each one cut into an interesting shape without regard for its use elsewhere on a display. Thus, as each child signs out a book, that card can be added to a collection of flowers, fruits, vegetables, vehicles, faces, and other items to compose a diversified assortment of tags or cards. Each such card may be decorated in some way by a child to suggest the theme of the book.

Story Hour

Perhaps the single most important way to motivate your students to read is to share with them an interesting book during a regular story hour. Make this a scheduled part of your day and do not fail to have it. Try to plan this early in the daily proceedings to set a happy tone for what is to follow later on, especially if your reading instruction is among the first important elements of your daily routine. Locate books that have been widely recommended for your students' age group and read a certain portion every class day. From time to time enlist capable student volunteers in this same activity as you join your students in listening to the narrative.

On other occasions devote an entire day to various story activities. Cancel all other assignments and obligations and just have a grand assortment of storytelling, puppet shows, dramatic productions, book movies, and other activities revolving around literature. In addition, once a week you might engage all your pupils in sustained silent reading of your own books or ones they have selected from the library. Many schools have sponsored a time each week when everyone in the entire building is similarly engaged. Promote this idea in your own school and see how many pages cumulatively can be read during one such period in your room or in your building.

Taping the Action

A tape recorder is very helpful in many different ways in a reading program. It intrigues boys and girls and enables them to work by themselves by operating the machine according to directions right on the recorder. Any time you read aloud a story to your students, tape the story. This not only gives the pupils something to listen to later on, but also allows them to follow along in the book you have been reading from. You can use a tape recorder as well in giving all sorts of directions to groups or to individuals. Children who are reporting on their reading can register their impressions of the books in this way so that you can listen to these recordings at your convenience. You can also use a tape recorder to capture your children's oral proficiency in preparation for sharing with the parents at regular conference times. Boys and girls also like to practice their oral reading skills, particularly if they can erase the efforts afterwards. Oral interpretation among older students is yet another application. Taping an entire story is invaluable for puppet presentations, for this frees the performers from thinking about the narration as they concentrate on the operation of the puppets. Pantomimed stories can also be done in this fashion.

Title Ticklers

There are several ways to intrigue boys and girls to read new books in your collection. Whenever a new story is introduced, read some of it aloud to the group, but stop reading at the most interesting spot; then challenge the class members either to finish reading the tale, or guess how the story ends. Some pupils might want to write their own endings before they have even completed the tale you provided. Another idea is to invent riddles and jokes that pertain to the characters or the plot. If appropriate, let the boys and girls review titles offered for addition to the central collection and recommend those they think might be most interesting. When examining catalogs or lists of such titles, ask the boys and girls to guess beforehand what each title might be about. Explore whatever book jackets are available in your central library and have a concerted effort to display and discuss them. Bring to the attention of your children the adage, "You can't tell a book by its cover." Challenge the children to guess what each book is likely to be about as they examine only the book jackets.

Workbook Woes

In all too many cases the use of workbooks not only curtails the possibilities of diversifying reading experiences, but also diminishes your children's interest in reading. While workbooks and worksheets are occasionally useful in developing certain specific skills, their misuse most often occurs when they are routinely assigned regardless of pupils' needs or interests. All too often, children are expected to fill in all the blanks on all the pages, whether or not this activity pertains to their capabilities or to their learning necessities. Even worse, these same pupils are then asked to turn in their workbooks to the teacher who then may require a day or more to check the adequacy of the students' answers, thereby denying these same pupils appropriate and immediate feedback on the accuracy and suitability of their responses.

Workbook pages need to be more selectively applied, particularly if your school has chosen the same consumable materials for all the students in your classroom regardless of reading levels and skill development. In some instances, it may be appropriate for you to allow the more capable students to take their workbooks home and complete the assignments independently, checking their work as they rely on your teachers' manual for answers. In this way the advanced pupils can move quickly through the materials mandated by the institution and can more readily get into a much more personalized reading program.

If the use of workbooks becomes a burden and a chore for either you or your class, consider putting them aside for a time in favor of using libraries, supplementary readers and other materials, skills-oriented kits, or learning aids that foster specific competencies in reading. Or, suggest to the children that as they work their way through the pages, they embellish each one in some unique way. Or, recommend that they make a fancy folder to use in filing their completed work. Always encourage the students to take their exemplary work home to share with their family. Consider eliciting from your class members questions, ideas, and illustrations that can be converted into original worksheets to be duplicated locally and distributed to classmates. The pupils can then review the story content and practice certain reading skills through the use of items they have helped prepare themselves.

THE CRAFT OF HANDLING ART

Assessing Art

All creative and expressive arts are difficult to measure fairly and are even more difficult to grade. Artistic endeavor represents a very individual effort, so the grade cannot be derived alone from the finished product. Rather, isolate those particular behaviors that are of value to any art and report the child's involvement in them and your opinion of his or her competency. Persistence, patience, uniqueness, motivation, and interest should be reported on and rewarded, along with one's willingness to try new things and to think unconventionally. Being aware of and using different elements in art are also important factors. Efficient and conscientious work habits are a third possible area of evaluation. Most important, each child should be assessed in his or her ability to relate art to the world at hand, to notice elements of art in the environment, and to make voluntary attempts at art outside the school setting.

Brushes in Use

When you need to purchase new paintbrushes for your class, arrange to have most of them not less than one centimeter wide, with many brushes wider than that. Most of the painting activities should use ample paint so the children will not feel restricted in their efforts. Have on hand just a few smaller brushes for occasional detail some students might want to do. Invest your funds in brushes that are of medium price; cheap brushes wear out much too quickly, while the more expensive ones are often abused. If your younger students find long handles too difficult to handle, cut these off and sand the ends smooth. Show the students how to rinse the brushes carefully after each use and stand the brushes upside down to allow them to dry without bending the bristles. Also make sure that your brushes do not stand in water or paint for long periods of time.

Chalk Hints

When you order chalk, explore the possibility of requesting it in bulk, which is usually cheaper than buying by the box. When using chalk, experiment by adding buttermilk to a rough quality of paper. This technique leaves an interesting texture when the liquid has dried with the chalk superimposed upon it. Another idea is to dip chalk sticks into a weak solution of liquid glue and water to keep the chalk from falling off the paintings. Or, you might use ordinary hair spray as a fixative of chalk. Still another notion is to mix powdered milk and water and spray it onto chalk paintings with an atomizer or a thumb-operated sprayer. Diluted spray starch in a bottle is also good for fixing chalk on paper.

Clay Helps

When ordering clay, try to get at least half a kilogram for each student in your group. While students should have some experience with prepared moist clay, the powdered clay is less expensive and easier to store, although it does require considerable mixing. If you have clay pieces that have hardened but are not fired, break these into small pieces, add water, and see if they can be reworked. Encourage the members of your class to explore many different possibilities of clay, such as scoring, punching, pinching, rolling, coiling, and attaching. If you have pieces to fire, be sure they are of uniform thickness appropriate to the heat to be used.

Clay Substitutes

As a variation of clay exploration, let the pupils examine the pliability of glazier's putty, which is available from a hardware store or a lumber yard. This putty will retain its pliability for a long time if it is carefully wrapped and placed in a sealed container overnight. Or, you might prefer to make bread dough or play dough from salt, flour or cornstarch. Consult any standard book on art techniques for appropriate recipes. Some of the products the children make can be hardened in the air, baked in an oven, or decorated with different kinds of paint suitable to the particular medium.

Discover natural clay in construction sites, fields, or quarry sites. Collect some of this clay and bring it to school. Pound out the lumps and sift it through various mesh screens. Then mix it with water to an appropriate consistency for the project at hand.

Clean-Up Time

Simplify your clean-up by helping the children keep ahead of the mess. For one thing, have at each painting station a container of rinse water. A plastic jug with a portion cut away for ease of emptying is one possibility. The children can readily rinse their brushes in this container. At the sink itself provide another plastic jug, this one with the top cut off and small holes punched into the bottom so the water will continue to drain out as the materials are rinsed in it. This kind of container will also catch the particles of paint and clay and other solid matter that should not go down the drain. If the boys and girls are working with individual cans of water, name two or three class members to circulate about the room collecting cans of dirty water poured into one plastic jug, replenishing clean water from another plastic jug as needed.

Crayon Melts

If properly supervised, older children can participate in crayon encaustic activities. (CAUTION: Do these encaustic activities only under teacher supervision.) One suggestion is to rub large crayons on a food grater and place the particles into different compartments in a discarded muffin tin. This container can then be placed on a warming tray to melt the crayons. Or, a small hot plate at a medium setting will provide the same effect. A second suggestion is to have candles placed strategically about a fireproof area of the classroom. Show the boys and girls how to take a crayon, unwrap it, and hold the tip of the crayon in the flame of the candle only until the tip is warm and soft. These crayons can then be used to make dots of color in an interesting effect.

Display Variations

A sense of the artistic is important in displaying children's art work. As each child selects something for public notice, make a point not to have the area cluttered with an overwhelming number or variety of products. Have these items displayed no higher than typical eye level of the average child in your classroom. Examine ways in which these items may be boldly outlined or framed to bring even greater attention to their merit. Suggest that some items be folded to stand upright on tables, or placed around a clean empty canister. Establish a small table labeled "Look Nook" for small pieces of sculpture and prepare an appropriate background for these items. Tie together areas of interest using lengths of yarn. Prepare bold letters to label the type of medium or the topic of study.

Fairs and Festivals

One effective way to stimulate pupils' interest is to schedule at least one day when the boys and girls can have on general display all their very best work produced by them during the year. This is particularly effective when all the other teachers in the school are similarly involved in an exhibit, for the variety of techniques and products can be spectacular. Instead of making this a competitive effort, give a ribbon or certificate for everyone who has something on display. Make sure each piece is labeled with artist, age, and grade. Set aside one portion of the display area for "This Is My Best," where each pupil may enter only one self-selected item. Encourage the children to make colorful posters to advertise the event, and if appropriate, to prepare cheerful and inventive brochures describing the display. Serve light refreshments to those who are invited, particularly if it coincides with a parent-teacher meeting.

Fingerpainting Surfaces

Salvage various discarded items to serve as appropriate places to spread fingerpaints. For example, use a discarded enameled baking or roasting pan, or a cookie sheet with a shallow ridge around it. In this way you not only confine the painting activity to a movable surface, but also make the matter of cleaning up afterwards much simpler, as all you do is transport the pan to the sink and rinse it out.

Another idea is to lay any smooth piece of stiff plastic on a tabletop. After the children have finished fingerpainting, the entire piece can either be rinsed off and rolled up or stored out of the way. Aluminum foil is also appropriate, for the foil itself can be displayed as a completed item after the children have finished experimenting with the paints on that surface.

Giving Assistance

There are several important things to remember when the students want you to help them with their projects. For one thing, you should remind them that if you do the actual work, the product is not theirs but partly yours. However, you can help the child to observe more carefully the process or the general effect he or she wants to attain. You could also demonstrate several possible solutions to a problem and let the child decide which one he or she would like to employ. Try not to demonstrate just one way because children discover soon enough that the teacher's way is the "right" way and their creative impulses are stifled. Make a special note not to ask youngsters what they are making. Often they are not sure themselves; even if they do know, they may be offended that you do not recognize the representation they have made. It is far better to ask, "Would you like to tell me about your project?" realizing that any pupil has the right to answer "No."

Handling Clay

Facilitate your work with clay by taking note of some quick suggestions. One idea is that if clay is too dry to work, jab holes in the top of the moist lump with a stick and fill these holes with water. Then wrap the clay tightly and in a few hours or days the entire ball of clay will be reconditioned.

If a kiln is not available for firing the children's work, decorate their products with watercolor or poster paint, and then cover with a layer of floor wax buffed to a shine. Cover this with a coat of commercial gloss.

If the students are making sculptured pieces, use large stones as the projects' bases to reduce the amount of clay required. You might suggest that some of the clay be lifted away from the stone, thereby producing a negative image of it in the clay.

When the children are using plasticene for modeling projects, keep it near a heat source, such as a sunny windowsill, to help in the molding process. In some instances where the plastic clay has hardened too much, add a bit of petroleum jelly to make kneading easier.

When mixing clay, place the ingredients inside heavy-duty plastic bags and let the children combine a kinesthetic experience with a practical exercise.

When the children are cutting clay into pieces, staple a short length of wire between two wooden spools; the wire can be used to make a clean cut while the children hold onto the spools. A discarded cheese slicer is also useful in carving small slabs of clay for medallions and other small pieces.

Make clay beads by rolling them into shape and impaling them on knitting needles for drying. When they are nearly dry, remove them from the needles; the holes will remain intact for stringing later.

Mess Made Less

Help the children contain the natural mess of art experiences by placing a recycled rug underneath the table where the pupils are to be using paints, water, and other messy items. When the rug gets wet, simply hang it up to dry. And when it gets too dirty, wash it in an ordinary washing machine.

A second suggestion is to have all the messy experiences near the water source, which will minimize the distance clean water and dirty water must be carried. You can also use only the tables in your classroom that have Formica, plastic, linoleum, or other surfaces impervious to water. If you would rather not do a lot of wiping up after art experiences, cover the tabletop with multiple layers of recycled newspapers. As these are covered with paint day after day, simply peel off the top layer to reveal a fresh surface ready for use. You might save some of these messy pieces for collage or montage activities.

Mini-Gallery

Encourage your students to examine popular current magazines for pictures of special beauty and set aside a portion of your bulletin board for a gallery of these pictures. Provide a temporary backing for these "classics" and let the students make interesting displays. Or, let them make easels of various sizes on which the items might be posted. If you have more than one art center or process under way, let the students find examples of reproductions to display in all areas of your room: replicas of clay and bronze pieces in the sculpture center, pictures of collages at the scrap table, and prints and paintings at the paint center. Such a variety will help the children to see that artists express themselves using many media, and each medium is uniquely experienced by each artist.

Mixing Made Easier

It is usually cheaper to purchase powdered tempera paint instead of liquid paint, although the dry variety is harder to mix. One possible solution to this problem is to salvage an old eggbeater and use it in making large batches of paint at one time. As paint is prepared beforehand, make sure it is stored in airtight containers. Another tip is to mix only the three primary colors. This reduces the number of containers and enables the children to experiment with their own color mixing as they use the paints. Since the powdered reds, oranges, and violets are sometimes especially hard to mix, you might try adding a few drops of alcohol to help the process. Powdered pigment sometimes settles to the bottom of the container, too. Try adding one part liquid starch to four parts water to help retard this settling out and to give a pretty sheen to the paint. Attach directions to each paint container instructing the students to stir the sediment before using the paint each time.

Paint Additives

There are many ways to enhance the quality and the consistency of tempera paints. For example, adding a small amount of either evaporated or condensed milk tends to enhance the glossiness of the picture after it has dried. Buttermilk added to tempera liquid produces a chalky effect. If the tempera is to adhere to a waxy or other slick surface, simply add a little thinned white glue to the paint. After the glue has been added to the tempera, the children might also use this mix for pasting paper bits onto a surface, such as an interesting bottle. Or, if you would like a thick paint without using up your entire supply, add wallpaper paste or cornstarch to it, stirring in the additive while the paint is being slowly mixed.

Paint Alternatives

Enlarge and diversify your painting activities with some of these handy suggestions:

- Salvage water-base paint discarded from a paint store or a hardware store, and obtain narrow roller edgers to make large paintings.
- Make an interesting watercolor wash by mixing a very thin solution of powdered tempera and water.
- Mix paints and other liquids in plastic bottles by inserting the ingredients, turning the cap tightly, and shaking the container vigorously.
- If you have felt-tipped markers that are completely dried out, soak them thoroughly in water and use them for watercolor experiences.
- Rejuvenate some kinds of felt-tipped markers by adding a few drops of duplicating fluid available in school offices.

- If you have paint that does not keep well, add a few drops of oil of cloves or peppermint or wintergreen. This will help keep it fresh. Try the same approach with papier-mâché mix and homemade clay mixes.
- When the children are using tempera paints, place cut-to-fit pieces of thin sponge in the bottom of a margarine tub, adding just enough paint to the bottom of the container to thoroughly wet the sponge. Then show the pupils how to press their paintbrushes down flat onto the sponge. This minimizes waste and prevents drastic spills.
- Assemble a collection of flat styrofoam or plastic meat trays, each with a shallow edge around it, and use these as painting trays. These can be left out to dry overnight, and since the paint is shallow it will dry out. When the tempera is to be used again, the students simply add a little water and mix it with the brush until the paint is once more usable.

Paint Instruments

Introduce unusual items to vary the children's experience with paint. For example, fill a waterproof egg carton with water. Let the children mix colors with an eye dropper and thinned tempera paints. After the mixing is finished, let the children make droplet paintings. Or, using a cardboard partition for protection, squirt colors at a paper target posted inside a large cardboard carton. Squeeze bottles or turkey basters are useful for this activity. Thinned tempera is also appropriate to pour into bottles that have thumb-operated sprayers. These containers are just right for making prints by misting the paint over cardboard stencils the children have made.

Paint Palettes

An excellent idea for a palette is a clean aluminum frozen dinner tray. The two or three smaller compartments can be used for the main colors, while the larger compartment can be used for mixing just the right tint or shade. A discarded ice cube tray or a styrofoam egg carton gives ten or more different compartments for those boys and girls who need even greater latitude in this explorations of colors. You can often salvage plastic inserts that are found in boxes of candy or plastic bags of cookies. Another idea is to acquire muffin tins along with foil liners so that each liner can be used for a different hue of paint. When a new set of colors is required or when one set of liners is muddied, the liners can be lifted out and replaced with a new set.

Paint Principles

Since good art instruction encourages the exploration of media, apply this principle by letting the students find out on their own what happens when any two primary colors are mixed; when any two secondary colors are mixed; and when all the primary/secondary colors are mixed. Let the children invent and name new colors by combining small amounts of paint left over from their regular activities. Have the children compare the results as they introduce white and then black to their hues. While making a color wheel is often a mandatory part of art instruction, this probably should be a voluntary experience. Some older boys and girls will be challenged to match the colors that appear on the prescribed color wheel, but other youngsters will find it very demanding and not terribly interesting.

Paint Storage

Tempera paints and similar materials have a tendency to dry out over long periods of time. One way to prevent this is to pour the paints into plastic lotion bottles that have been rinsed out. Have inside each bottle only several centimeters of paint at any given time, thereby avoiding not only extra waste from spills, but also keeping the ferrules (metal rings) of the paintbrushes cleaner. Choose bottles that have a cap and an opening just large enough to accommodate the size of brush being used. When the children are done with their painting each day, they need only to replace the cap on the bottle. Besides, if there is a flip-top dispenser as part of the cap itself, the children may be able to drizzle the paints out onto their paper as another painting variation.

Another useful idea is to mix your paints in small clean milk cartons that are open at one side of the top. Here again, the opening will accommodate one or two brushes only, and it can be closed with a large paper clip when the children are done painting. If you use small juice cans for liquid paints, insert a plastic baggy before pouring, and then twist-tie it shut when not in use. These can be conveniently discarded when the paint inside is no longer usable.

Paper Cutting

When younger students are just learning how to use the scissors, determine their dominant hands and have enough scissors for both right- and left-handed pupils. Where special techniques are being employed with scissors or other cutting instruments, first give the class members scraps of paper to practice with. If there are projects that would demand the children punch through with a sharp pair of scissors, instruct them to put the paper or other material down on a thick padding of cardboard or cloth. Otherwise, it is all too easy and painful to poke the end of the scissors into one's hand.

Paper Storage

Storage of paper should be convenient and accessible. One approach is to place the rolls of paper you use, along with waxed paper, aluminum foil, shelf paper, etc., on sturdy wire hangers. Tie a pair of scissors to this apparatus and hang it near the area where it will be most often used. A second idea is to place rolls of paper inside empty boxes that have metal serrated edges. The children can pull out an appropriate length of paper and rip it off without using scissors or knives.

When storing large amounts of flat paper sold by the ream, for example, make a simple set of shelves with flat rectangles of wood supported at each corner by a child's block or any other similar item. These shelves can be expanded or contracted conveniently simply by shifting the position and number of blocks. Thin plywood and pressboard are also useful as shelves. Larger versions of these shelves can be fashioned for the purpose of serving as drying racks for paintings, too.

Paper Uses

Children are sometimes wasteful of paper, especially when they are not quite sure how to approach a given project. Avoid much of this waste by giving the boys and girls scrap pieces of newspaper to practice on first. Encourage the children to salvage all the pieces of paper they would otherwise throw away. Have a special box or drawer for these discards and give the children permission to select pieces from this assortment for making collages or montages during the year.

Paste Mess

When children paste, they tend to make a considerable mess. Help control this problem by dampening paper towels and placing them on small squares of plastic at each desk or table. The children can periodically clean their fingers without going to the sink and making a mess there as well. Another good idea is to give each pupil a different copy of an old magazine. Ask the boys and girls to paste the first time on the first page of their magazine. When the pasting for that day is done, that page may be torn out and thrown away. Or else, simply fold the next pasting page over and a fresh surface will be available for the following day's activity. Similarly, when your children are pasting on a table, have the top surface protected with many layers of paper salvaged from the wastepaper bin. When the pasting for the day is done, merely remove the top soiled surface to reveal fresh space.

Paste Pointers

Paste is important in daily activities, but it can be difficult to manage. Simplify its use by ordering it in bulk and then dispensing it into smaller jars. Provide plastic jars that, first, will not shatter if they fall on the floor and, second, can be completely washed out from time to time. Place each jar at a paste center and have the pupils remove small portions on paste sticks, scraping off the excess into the jar when they are done. One central location for paste at each table is one way to consolidate the mess and prevent many little jars from drying out. Margarine tubs or ice cream cups with plastic lids, along with wooden spoons or tongue depressors, are good for paste, too.

Patterns and Models

Do not allow the use of patterns and the copying of models in your art instruction, since it is all too tempting for the children to imitate each other or your own representations. Individual expression and personal satisfaction are generally inhibited by patterns. If there is any legitimate excuse to have patterns, let the children make their own. Coloring books as such should not be widely used in classrooms for the simple reason that children get the notion all art work should be cartoon-like in representing elements in nature. While coloring in pictures may indeed provide casual entertainment for youngsters outside the art period, the use of such items should not be encouraged. Here again, if the boys and girls like to color in areas, let them make their own coloring books.

Personal Participation

Show your children a personal commitment to art. Join your students in their explorations of a given medium, but do not provide a model of a product they ought to make. Rather, you should present them with an example of a fellow-learner who also struggles with the problems and the possibilities of a medium. Bring to school examples of your own hobbies that reflect an interest in crafts, photography, and kindred arts. Bring in, too, local artisans who are singularly gifted in the arts, and arrange for your pupils to visit museums, galleries, festivals, and other settings where many kinds of art are presented and demonstrated.

Plaster Possibilities

Plaster of paris experiences are interesting and versatile because the plastic can be cast in many different ways and the finished product can be further shaped with sharp instruments. Several suggestions will make working with plaster easier. Since plaster of paris hardens quickly, you might want to add to the mixture a pinch of cream of tartar or a small amount of vinegar to retard this setting. On the other hand, small amounts of salt will accelerate the process. You might investigate the use of spackling compound available at most hardware stores. This medium can be used for casting experiences and sets up more slowly than plaster of paris. If you want to combine color with plaster, try swirling liquid tempera or food coloring in the plaster mix just after it is poured to produce a marbelized effect in the finished product.

Project Keepers

Maintain for each member of the class a separate folder where he or she can keep flat work that is completed. Each person's monogram or name can be designed to make this folder unique, and the children can further decorate them as a specific art project. If your purpose in art is to have all the children experience the same kinds of media during a given period, have a list inside the flap of each folder and ask the students to check off each project as it is completed. These folders can be used as a way to report progress in creativity to the parents during the year.

A second idea is to have the children punch holes in their regular-sized art projects and lace these together with yarn. Or, make an oversized laced-together holder from large pieces of discarded cardboard decorated by the children themselves. Yet another idea is to have the students produce scrapbooks for the small items.

Protecting Clothing

When the children are painting, cut sponges into small segments, one section for each pan of paint that is being used. Have a spring-type clothespin available for each sponge. As

the students are painting, they can clip onto any sponge that they want, replacing that sponge when they are done with it. You can further protect their fingers and clothing from paint and other messy materials by cutting from small plastic bottles pairs of cuffs that can be readily slipped over the children's wrists to keep their clothing out of the way. Have available as well a collection of small plastic bags, sufficiently sturdy for the children to slip over their shoes to keep these clean during paint and water activities. Furthermore, if you mix soap flakes with the tempera paint, the spills wash more easily from the clothing.

Random Reminders

As you have your children participate in various art experiences, keep in mind several important considerations. Make a note to check these points as you progress through the instructional year:

- Always have sufficient materials on hand to meet the needs of all students who are working on a medium. The boys and girls who have nothing to do will not only feel left out but will discover their own "activities" to engage in.

- Be sure to thoroughly explain the medium before distributing the materials. Children will not listen to your explanations if you have already handed out the items they are to use.
- Emphasize the process of exploration rather than the product they are to make. As you introduce paints, for instance, ask the boys and girls to suggest all the different ways a paint and a brush might be used.
- Always permit choices. If the children are necessarily limited to one medium on any given day, at least encourage them to find one way to use that particular medium, even if it varies from the way you have suggested.
- Provide adequate art experiences through encounters with the real world. Schedule many trips, movies, stories, and visuals. Encourage the children to recall and then to discuss their own personal experiences that might stimulate their imaginations.
- Incorporate art into other subjects of study. The children will thus begin to see the relationship between art and other areas of the curriculum and will further explore media appropriate to these areas.
- Be aware of appropriate interest spans. Begin the lessons promptly and allow for changes from one activity to another when interest begins to wane.
- Avoid planning too many small delicate experiences for young children. Instead, provide large surfaces and instruments and encourage the students to use large sweeping movements.
- Never use art as a reward for good behavior; art, like all other subjects, is something all children are entitled. Deal with misbehaviors on their own, but do not establish a connection between the problem and the right to study art.

Recycled Art

One challenge of teaching art is showing your students how to make things of beauty out of discarded materials. Throughout the year, ask your students to bring into class items that otherwise would be thrown out. Challenge them to prepare various sculptures, montages, collages, and other media incorporating elements they have rescued from the trash. In this way, they will begin to see the endless possibilities of commonplace items customarily found at home or in the neighborhood. They will also discover that art material need not cost a lot of money. Furthermore, they will find beauty in the everyday materials around them, and will be stimulated to look further for elements of art everywhere. In their efforts they will also be helping the environment by saving items that might pollute the environment or use resources unnecessarily.

Respect for the Artist

Creative sensitivities must be highly regarded and protected from possible abuse. It is important, therefore, that you display everyone's work. Challenge the students to select the projects they are most pleased with and have them do their own posting in your classroom or elsewhere.

Be aware that some children are reluctant to get dirty, perhaps because their parents are obsessed with cleanliness. You can sometimes successfully introduce these pupils to messy activities literally one finger at a time.

Do not insist on titles for work. Let the children make titles if they care to, or have them either dictate or write stories about their works.

Scheduling Art

Since art is often a messy experience requiring considerable supervision, you might want to set up your art instruction at stations in the classroom involving different clusters of pupils working on different media at the same time. This will give you an opportunity to localize those projects that need close supervision. Or, you might choose to have the art done by a few students at one time, with the other youngsters simultaneously working on other subjects or projects. If you elect to have your pupils working in groups, ask them to name one or two persons in that group to be responsible for getting supplies, for collecting materials, and supervising the cleaning up afterwards. This duty can be rotated from week to week. This approach cuts down on the traffic inside and outside the room, and relieves the congestion at the sink. Another good idea is to schedule art activities to end in an "open" period such as play or general study. Where there is no time pressure, there is no haste to finish a given project by an arbitrary time.

Sculpture Armatures

Involve the children in several different kinds of sculpture experiences by providing simple armatures that can not only support the medium but also be converted into interesting designs and representations in their own right. One possibility is to obtain discarded lightweight wire and bend it into shapes. The children can form clay, wadded foil, or other media around these after the wires are fashioned appropriately. Also encourage the children to use scraps of hardware cloth or chicken wire available from salvage sources. These can be useful in inserting bits of tissue paper or papier-mâché. Let the children also bring to class sturdy branches to experiment with winding wire or colored yarn around these to make abstract designs.

Smocks

There are several satisfactory substitutes for commercial garments to be worn during the messy art activities. Plastic is one obvious possibility. You can, for example, salvage plastic shower curtains and cut head holes in the middle to use the item as a poncho. Fashion a long rectangle of plastic, of double-folded length, to fit the front and back of the typical child in the classroom. Cut a simple head hole in the center fold and staple sturdy twine ties at the sides.

Old plastic or rubberized raincoats can be cut and adapted to your children's needs, as well as plastic or paper bags in which dry cleaning is returned. Old shirts and blouses from brothers and sisters are useful, too, particularly because the garments that are just a little bit larger than the child are not as likely to drag in the paint and paste. In a pinch, tie folded newspapers around the waist and the chest to provide temporary protection.

Time and Space Considerations

Allow enough time for the children to formulate their ideas about an art process. Do not spring art assignments on them the last period on Friday simply because that is the time you have set aside for it. Instead, earlier in the day or the week, lead the children in discussing possibilities of a medium to explore. Creative ideas are hard to develop, so time is needed to think of ideas. Similarly, allow sufficient time to finish projects. Once children are well begun on a task, let them put the projects aside without penalty and without being interfered with later on. Try to schedule art periods so they open onto free time, such as activity time, play time, or study time.

Children need to have a lot of space for their efforts, to keep them somewhat apart and to discourage them from copying what classmates are doing. Make sure your students feel free to work indoors or outdoors, on the floor, or at tables and desks.

Water Source

Add interest and portability to your water supply for painting and other activities in art by obtaining a discarded picnic jug that has a working spigot. The water can be safely carried to where the children are working. They can draw the water they need from the tap. When their experiences are done, they can pour their individual containers of dirty water into the jug again for transporting to the sink. Other salvaged items are appropriate for this same purpose. For example, plastic juice containers of the one- or two-liter size have lids that snap into position to prevent spilling in transit, and that snap off to pour into and out of. Some of these lids have pour spouts that similarly snap off and on for safety and for convenience. Survey your parents for such items, or scour second-hand stores for them.

Ways with Paints

Here are some good suggestions for working with paints:

- If you are using tempera paints in solid cakes, be sure to add water to them well ahead of the experience so the children will not be tempted to scrub their brushes against the cakes, thereby damaging the bristles.
- When waxed surfaces are being painted, roughen them first with sandpaper to help the tempera adhere.
- Make miniature palettes for fingerpainting by cutting out a small cardboard oval, incising a thumb hold for holding on, and then adding dabs of primary colors at different spots along the edge of the palette. Let the students experiment with using only their fingers as brushes when they apply the paint to paper.
- If the children are using thick pigments to make their paintings, such items take a long time to dry. Aid the drying process by pressing carefully discarded newspapers onto the surface of their paintings, thereby absorbing some of the extra pigment.

4

Organizing Classroom Equipment for Easy Use

Teaching has traditionally been thought of as a profession demanding as much housekeeping and clerical work as actual instruction. It is unfortunate but true that considerable teacher time and talent are squandered each year in preparing, storing, locating, and arranging instructional materials. Students themselves are also frustrated at times in not having needed items handy. There are many convenient ways a teacher can structure the classroom at the very beginning of the school year to allow students to find and use the equipment they can best benefit from, and help in the distribution and collection of these materials.

In addition, the wise teacher appreciates the need for routine changes from time to time. After the first few tentative weeks of school in the autumn, students too often settle into schedules that become deadly in dampening enthusiasm for learning: the same arrangements of furniture, the same drab walls, and the same kinds of groupings, day after day after day.

A teacher who is alert to the psychological needs of students introduces many variations to the traditional classroom themes: various uses of colors, unique pieces of furniture, devices the children prepare themselves, comfortable centers of interest, bright corners for small groups and private work, and many other methods of creating an atmosphere that invites relaxed but businesslike pursuits of learnings.

The time and care a teacher spends on such efforts is well invested, for in the long run pupils are glad to attend, eager to learn, and more proficient in the competencies they are exposed to as the year progresses.

ORGANIZING SPOTS AND SPACES

Ceiling Brighteners

Many older schools have high ceilings that are both unattractive as well as acoustically unsatisfactory. Brighten up such spaces by painting the ceiling and the upper walls a dark color and the lower wall a bright complementary color. Or, if there are pipes, vents or other apparatus visible on the ceiling, paint these to make an overhead rainbow of color.

Explore the use of directional lighting that focuses attention downward. If the overhead lighting cannot be changed readily, set up small areas on the work level that are illuminated with spot lighting of an incandescent variety.

If reverberation of sound is a problem in a high-ceilinged room, dampen the echoes by salvaging scraps of acoustical paneling from construction sites or from other supply sources and suspend these from the ceiling at irregular angles. Some of them may need to be painted to add to the color, as long as the painting does not impair the absorption of the panel. Still another suggestion for this difficulty is to use lengths of fabric to make colorful class banners, site labels, directional signs,

and mottoes which not only help control the noise but also add color to the room.

Desk Arrangements

When children's desks are arranged day after day in the traditional rows, several difficulties may arise. First of all, the children occasionally tire of the routine. In addition, the arrangement removes from the focus of activity many of the more distant pupils, in part because they cannot see what is happening, and because teachers tend to call on students who are seated close to the front. A definite "back" and "front" of a classroom also prompts teachers to talk at students and to present their classes as lectures more than they otherwise would. One alternative is to have the children arrange their seats in a circle or a semicircle. In this way every person has a front-row seat. If the classroom is too small for a single circle, try a double-rank circle. A large U-shape is another possibility that gives the students equal and ready attention to the teacher and each other. At other times, of course, you will want the boys and girls to make clusters of desks for special group projects. Invite the students themselves to suggest yet other arrangements of furniture.

Display Surfaces

Flexibility of display space is important in congested areas. One idea is to have your display boards hinged so they will swing out perpendicular to the wall during use and then be folded back against the wall when they are no longer needed. Chalkboards, corkboards, magnet boards, and flannelboards can be similarly attached to swing out of the way. Another idea is to adapt such a hinged display surface for more than one purpose; for example, one side a chalkboard, the other a corkboard. Another notion is to make a freestanding double display surface that is hinged at the top. This item can be placed vertically on the floor in an inverted V-shape. Or, you might be able to put it horizontally on a table or a countertop. When not in use, it can be collapsed. Yet another quick way to conserve space while providing display places is to attach a lot of colored spring-type clothes-pins to your venetian blinds, drapes, or window shades. As the children have things for posting, let them clip each item to the window area with a clothespin.

Doing Doors

Doors sometimes swing shut and close or lock, making it difficult for small children to open them. If this is a problem, cut cross sections of rubber inner tubes and slip these giant rubber bands over both door knobs, and across the latch as well. When the door closes, the width of the rubber should keep the door from closing completely.

A second problem of doors has to do with their projecting into a room when the inside space of the classroom is already cramped, making it impossible to use the floor space fully. One obvious solution is to remove all the doors you can and paint the interior of the space formerly enclosed. Use light bright paint to enhance the visibility of the space you have now opened. Where doors cannot be removed, exchange them for sliding doors that do not interfere with floor space. Or, where this too is impossible, use your doors for more than merely enclosing space—convert them into ready display space and chalkboard space. If you have need of a sight screen for open shelving produced by removing doors, make sliding curtains on rings and rods.

Dual-Purpose Items

If you have cramped storage and classroom space, try to maintain only those items that can be used for more than one purpose. For example, obtain a large panel of galvanized sheet metal and paint it with blackboard paint available at a hardware store. Cover the reverse side of this panel with corkboard or fiberboard. Attach to the top edge a large sheet of flannel. Just this one item can then be used in several different ways without necessarily occupying any more space than a single-purpose item. Similarly, if you have in your classroom pull-down shades, convert these into charts and posters that will help to inform your pupils and enliven their days while shutting out the sunlight. Convert the back sides of filing cabinets into magnetboards by placing them conveniently in your classroom and obtaining a set of small magnets and/or magnetized numerals and letters.

Easel Ways

Easels occupy a lot of floor space and are sometimes difficult to work around during the day. You can avoid this problem by having desktop or tabletop easels made from some folded cardboard you have cut from large cartons. The children can then sit down to paint and thumbtack their papers to the easel. When the pupils are done with their painting, these easels may be folded flat and stored away. Such an easel can also be readily converted into a flannelboard, a bulletin board, or a pocketed card holder.

Foldaways

Several methods of folding things help make limited floor space more efficient. One is to use folding tables, such as card tables, for these can be stored out of the way when the floor is needed for large group activities. A drop-leaf table is yet another possibility. You can also convert large cardboard cartons into privacy areas for individual students to use and, if you have young pupils, one or more of these can be converted into a doll house with very little effort. Do not attach a permanent top to any of these constructions, however. This will allow you to fold the object flat and store it out of the way when the activity is done. You can use a folded piece of cardboard laid across the top of each item when the boys and girls are inside it.

Glare to Spare

Some classrooms face direct sunlight for a portion of the instructional day, creating unwanted heat as well as disturbing glare in the eyes of the children. Instead of drawing shut the blinds or curtains, suggest that the children create interesting cutouts from aluminum foil and place these in the windows, fairly well covering each pane. In this way the glare and the heat are dramatically reduced and the passers-by out-doors are treated to a sparkling menagerie developed by your children. Have the students use various colors of foil. Other ideas are to make a foil battlement to convert your classroom into a silvered castle, or change it into a space ship or a sub-marine with the addition of portholes covering certain panes.

Lightening and Brightening

If your classroom is dark and dingy, brighten things with inexpensive mirrors placed strategically to reflect the natural and the artificial light. Where appropriate and economically feasible, attach to the walls bullet lights or spotlights to focus on particular areas of interest or importance. Add other ele-ments of cheer and color by suspending from the ceiling bright play items and streamers of yarn, tissue disks, balloons, flags, and other items that move slightly in the air currents. Re-move and place in permanent storage any heavy curtains or drapes that are not needed to shut out the noise. Where sun-light is a problem, on the other hand, exchange any dark cur-tains or drapes for light material (such as tissue paper or stained glass panels) of half-length that will curtail the direct sun without shutting out all the outside light.

Mobility Management

Whenever your pupils are working at different centers in the classroom or at other times of day when they are working at their desks, you will need to check their progress without requiring them to come to your desk and form a line. One suggestion is to have the centers located and the desks situated so that there is ample space for you and your students to move about the classroom. A second suggestion is to obtain a swivel chair that has casters large enough to allow you to move conveniently about the classroom to help each group. A low stool with casters also serves this purpose, permitting you mobility in the classroom, preventing back problems from bending over desks all day, and keeping your contact with the children at appropriate eye level.

Poles and Posts

Many older schools have posts and poles in the middle of classrooms. You can convert such an obstruction into a central study area by making a shelf-like table that surrounds the pole, sawing out two semi-circles or squares of plywood with an opening in the middle to accommodate the post or pole. These two pieces can then be bolted together and supported by legs that go down toward the floor at an inward angle so as not to interfere with the children's feet as they sit around the pole area. Low stools can be pushed under the table when they are not in use. You can also decorate such places by converting them into Maypoles consisting of plastic flowers and streamers. Another idea is to convert the post into the center pole of an Indian teepee with muslin panels cut into triangular shapes and fastened to a wire attached to the top of the pole. This area could also be spread with rugs to resemble bear hides or buffalo hides and be used as a reading or a study center.

If nothing else is considered for center posts, cover them with carpet samples or heavy fabric scraps to keep the children from injuring themselves. Such fabric could be sewn together with strong nylon thread. This surface can then do

double duty as a display spot for children's work as you attach with Velcro an attractive array of colored clothespins. You might also choose to open up discarded cardboard cartons that fit around the circumference of the post. These cardboard items may be gaily decorated on a theme and serve as cheerful roofing to an attractive focus of action in the room.

Privacy Carrels

When the children have work to be done without distraction from others or whenever they simply want to have some private time, prepare a set of several three-panel cardboard screens that the children have decorated themselves. These can either be set up on an individual desk or on the top of a table. When they are no longer needed, fold and store them in any narrow spot. Another approach to the privacy problem is to have on hand large scraps of interesting fabric to drape over small tables or individual desks to give space underneath. If the fabric is sufficiently light in texture, it will permit some light to shine through.

Room Dividers

Save and thoroughly rinse out the disposed styrofoam cups customarily used at coffee hours. Show the children how to paint these or to make interesting designs on them. Add liquid detergent to tempera paints to make the paint stick to the cups. Do not use non-water base markers as they make cups disintegrate. Then punch a hole in the exact center of the bottom of each one and thread a colored length of twine or yarn through them to make a hanging of cups, each cup suspended above a knot in the twine. Other more colorful dispenser cups are also appropriate for this, especially if you show the students how to cut down into the cup around the lip, from the lip to bottom, and open the cup to resemble the petals of a flower. When these daisies are attached in vertical rows, such hangings can be combined to make a partial sight screen to identify particular areas of your classroom.

Another suggestion is to salvage an old volleyball net or a fishing net and use this not only to divide classroom space but also to display, with the aid of clothespins, items the children have produced or have brought from home to share with their classmates. Paper chains are a third possibility. The students can make them from strips of colored paper cut out of discarded magazines. Or, they can use this same paper to make flower shapes and construct a daisy chain.

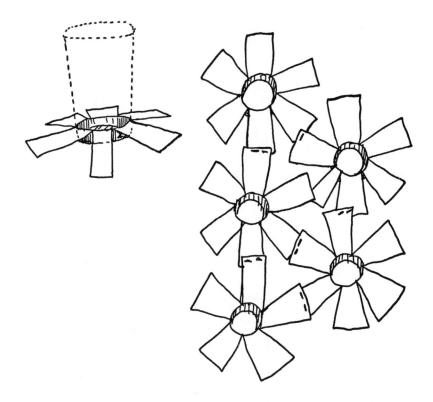

Large boxes and cartons are also useful. These can be collected and painted or decorated by the students in their spare time. If these containers are carefully selected, you may be able to arrange them one inside the other whenever you need to store them. To convert the nested group into a room divider, simply invert them all, the largest on the bottom and the smallest on the top. Such dividers can also be used as display boards.

Egg cartons have many possibilities in this regard, too. Ask the children to collect the pastel-colored styrofoam ones or paint the cardboard ones. These can then be cut apart, leaving only the indented halves of the boxes. String these halves to each other using chenille pipe cleaners and suspend them from the ceiling. The styrofoam or the pressed fiber will also help absorb the sounds in the classroom.

If you would like a more permanent room divider, set up a frame made of lightweight wooden strips, floor to ceiling in size, and then string the entire frame to resemble a loom. Twist or tie lengths of yarn from floor to ceiling around the cup hooks or eyelets inserted into the wooden frame. The students can then be invited from time to time to interweave the strands of yarn or twine their own papers or other decorative details of paper or yarn, all of which can be removed from the frame when everyone wants a change.

Space Conservation

If you have a small classroom, make your present furnishings more efficient. Do without the larger pieces of furniture, such as replacing a piano with an autoharp, thereby saving a lot of floor space. Or, if you have a piano that cannot be moved out, use a large sheet of fiberboard to convert the back into a display space for the children's learning products. The teacher's desk not only requires a lot of space but also tends to form an artificial and arbitrary barrier between teacher and students. This item can also be removed from the classroom in favor of storing the adult materials on high shelves away from the children. Here again, if the desk cannot be removed from your classroom, convert it into an interesting piece of learning equipment by adding bright paint and relabeling the drawers and other compartments as receptacles for children's materials.

If possible, try to convert large items into wheeled pieces. Explore hanging things on walls rather than standing them on floors. Think about having some of your materials on wheeled carts that can be moved just outside the classroom door during the more active periods of the instructional day. Dispose of long cumbersome tables and in their place attach shelving to the wall; shelves can be raised or dropped as needed, thereby saving precious floor space.

Look into the possibility of purchasing chairs that stack in neat vertical piles. If you have old wooden tables, convert them into trundle tables by cutting off some of the legs so tables will fit underneath each other.

Special Spots

Set up places that are labeled for special purposes. These will attract the children and remind students of their primary use. Label each spot according to its function, such as Art Part, Think Tank, Math Path, and Book Nook. One way to make each place is to convert a large cardboard carton into a cubicle just right for one or two persons to occupy. Have the boys and girls decorate each carton appropriate to its purpose. If a station is to be occupied only on certain occasions and under certain stipulations, include a cardboard replica of a clock showing the next time it is to be occupied and/or vacated, and have available a "do not disturb" sign if absolute privacy is necessary for the occupant.

Table Flexibility

In considering appropriate tables for your classroom, you might include several factors. Two small tables provide greater flexibility than one large one that provides the same space, and a set of trapezoidal tables combine into many different arrangements that are not conveniently formed with rectangular or circular ones. A circular table allows group work in a psychological climate of equality. A semi-circular table allows you to interact with a group of children on an equal basis; two semi-circular tables can be pushed together for a different configuration. Contact the parents of your children for small sturdy tables that can be repainted in a variety of colors cued to the specific activities that are to occur at each table.

Table Ways

Tables can make your use of space more versatile and more effective, so try not to have any table that serves only one purpose. Have a pressed fiberboard that can be laid on a table for construction work and other activities that might otherwise mar the table's finish. If you have a water table or a sand table, make a cover for it that will let the children use it for one of several kinds of activities. Any table that is light enough to handle can be inverted and thus changed into a study spot with the addition of some cushions, and a drape over the upside-down legs. Tables can also be combined to double the actual floor space. Push together two or more tables of comparable height and tie them together so they will not slide apart. Some children may then climb up on top of these tables, particularly if you have covered them with a rug you have salvaged. Other pupils may crawl underneath the tables and have their own private areas, also carpeted or covered. For a dramatic production, two or more tables of different heights can be tied together securely to produce a stepped effect for either performers or the audience.

Work Space Markings

Some classrooms are used by more than one teacher or for more than one purpose. If it is necessary to move furnishings in your own space, have the children mark on the floor with washable felt-tip markers or with removable fabric tape those spots where major pieces of equipment and furniture would ordinarily be located. A circular arrangement could also be indicated in this way.

LESS OF A MESS WITH STORAGE

Aprons

Add interest to the storing and distributing of school items by investing in a carpenter's apron, complete with a variety of pockets and loops. These can be filled with crayons, pencils, scissors, and other materials. Name one child to be in charge of wearing this apron every day. If you have an active and supportive group of parents, suggest that they make a set of several such aprons. Each can be identified distinctly, and the contents of each compartment labeled with stitchery or liquid embroidery.

Bags and Baggies

Make a collection of shopping bags with handles and give one to each child, asking him or her to decorate and label it according to interests and contents. The students can use these bags to carry things between home and school, and to store their own materials. Scraps of plastic can be stitched together by parent volunteers to make bags that are more durable for transporting items between home and school regularly.

When it is necessary to store many small items in a collection, assemble a group of sturdy transparent bags that have reusable locking tops. Place the items inside the bags so that the children can see at a glance the contents of each one. Attach the bags to a clothesline with spring-type pins.

A third idea is to obtain from an auction sale or a garage sale an old shoebag that is designed to hang on the back of a door. Clean this and decorate it with labels for each compartment appropriate to the materials you want to store. Place the bag on the back of any door in your room, or simply hang it on a hook at a level convenient for your children to reach.

Boxes and Cartons

Use an expanding file box for storing letters you use for bulletin board displays. Let the children not only be in charge of cutting out and attaching these letters as they are needed, but also have the responsibility of filing them back in the suitably labeled file compartments.

A storage place for charts, posters, and pieces of posterboard and cardboard may be made by cutting a large cardboard carton on the diagonal. Cut notches in the sides at regular intervals, and make notched dividers that match these notches. Label each divider to identify the contents of each section of the carton.

If your classroom has toy vehicles, prepare from salvaged cartons a set of "garages" in which each item is stored. For example, small cars and trucks can be decorated by the children and stored on a counter or a shelf. If there are ride-on toys, however, these can be "parked" overnight in boxes in which you have cut doors that swing open for end-of-day storage.

Cans for Keeping

Collect discarded juice cans of various sizes, wash them thoroughly, and remove both the tops and the bottoms. Depending on their sizes, use them as storage wrappers for rolled-up maps, charts, posters, and art work. Large pieces of newsprint can also be stored in them. Label each can with its contents just in case the item stored cannot be identified. Use comparable cans as carriers for the children to use in transporting their rolled-up projects home. Or, attach wire handles to some of the cans and hang them on the branches of a tree you have brought indoors and planted solidly in a bucket of gravel or cement. In this way small cans can contain the daily papers and other items you return to the children from time to time.

Cardboard Carriers

The heavy-duty carriers that accommodate six or eight bottles of carbonated beverages are especially useful for storage in the art center. You might place in each compartment an empty can for a different color of paint. Have only those cans that come with plastic lids to keep the paint from drying out. Or, one carrier might be used for storing brushes of various sizes. Still another idea is to convert a carrier into a handy way to transport the many consumable items used during the day, such as crayons, pencils, pens, paper, and scissors.

Clotheshanger Reels

Obtain wire clotheshangers that have a thin cardboard tube on the crosspiece. Remove this tube and thread it through the openings in a collection of spools on which you have wound yarn, ribbons, string, and other items. Tie a pair of scissors to the neck of the clotheshanger and hang the item near the art center. When the children need these materials, they can pull off a length and cut it.

Cubbies

Children, especially younger pupils who do not necessarily work at individual desks, like to have a special spot of their own for storing personal materials. Provide "cubbies" for these children by salvaging uniform-sized cardboard boxes, plastic dishpans, and transparent plastic storage boxes with lids. Encourage each child to decorate his or her cubby appropriately. To prevent much of the clutter inside individual desks, obtain a set of flat boxes. Here, again, have each child label a box appropriately, and then place in the container pencils, scissors, crayons, erasers, paper clips, and other small items. When their desks need to be cleaned, the children can simply lift out the boxes.

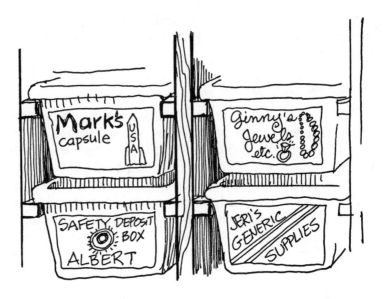

Gym Shoes

When your students must store their sneakers in the classroom, instead of having them cluttering the coat racks or the lockers or the desks, provide a set of matched shoeboxes salvaged from families or from a local shoestore. Each box may be decorated attractively to identify its owner, and then assembled in an interesting and compact stack. These may also be numbered like a post office letter sorting space, with each child responsible for returning his or her box to its appropriate spot in the collection. A similar suggestion is to obtain from a store a set of cardboard inserts, such as those used to ship heavy bottles or jars. The boxes can be placed on their sides with the inserts in place so the children can use the many compartments to store their shoes when not in use.

Handy Hints

There are many quick and easy ways to simplify your storage problems. Here are some to consider.

- To store pointed items, such as thumbtacks, pins, and scissors, use a styrofoam cone or cube salvaged from the winter holiday seasons or obtained from a crafts center.

- Make a temporary bookend for a few books on display by pulling a wire coat hanger on its crossbar until it forms a long flattened oval. Then bend both ends of this oval up, and place the books in the U-shaped space you have created.
- Run a dowel rod through a series of heavy-duty "bulldog" or "gripper" clips you can purchase in a stationery store or a department store. If you have a rod that is small enough, the grippers can be operated freely while they are so impaled. Each gripper can then be used to store something that should be suspended.
- Fold a stiff piece of paper into a shape that looks like an "N," a "W," or an "M" when viewed end-on. These holders can then be used to hold flashcards, cards used in a game, pieces of a puzzle, or other items.
- Use accordion-folded paper for pupils to put on top of sloping desks. If they place their crayons, pens, and pencils in the slots created, the problems of such items rolling off onto the floor will be dramatically improved.
- Sometimes, bottles of glue and containers of paint dry out between the times they are used. Store certain containers in an inverted position to prevent the problem.
- Since thumbtacks are difficult to store in drawers safely, have available near the bulletin board a double thickness of cardboard or a slab of styrofoam and instruct the students to store all tacks there. A piece of cork or a scrap of pressed fiberboard is also appropriate. Encourage the children to use the tacks to make outlines of interesting faces on this item, thereby ensuring that the tacks remain handy.
- Try storing glitter, powdered paints, sand, and other fine materials in large salt shakers.
- Obtain discarded egg cartons and use them to store small items such as rice, confetti, eggshells, sequins, buttons, macaroni, cereal, and other items for art ventures.

Homework Holders

As the children prepare their homework each day and as they need to take it home, prepare for them sets of envelopes. These might be of uniform size and decorated and labeled by the individual pupils. Holes can be punched to let the students string the envelopes together for safekeeping. If such envelopes are stored in a box in the classroom, the children might write their names on the flaps. Then if you have something to call to a child's attention, simply lift the labeled flap so it will stand upright.

Interesting Containers

By varying the type of containers in which materials are stored, you will be able to stimulate the pupils' interest while they clean up the room or maintain proper storage of supplies. One idea is to hang up old pairs of jeans that have been sewn shut at the knees after the bottoms of the legs have been cut off. The boys and girls can store items in these pouches and in the pockets. Similarly, old pairs of bib overalls can be decorated with colorful patches using a whip-stitch, and the pockets filled with pencils, crayons, rulers and other implements used in your classroom.

Irregular Materials

Toys, materials, and equipment that are irregular in shape are sometimes difficult to store, but you can solve this problem. Have the students save some net bags, the kind used to merchandise grapefruit, oranges, potatoes, onions, and other produce. Then attach ordinary wire coat hooks to a board on an empty wall. The bags can be suspended from these hooks, two or more at each spot. A label above any hook will identify the bags that belong there.

Labeling Containers

Whenever you designate a given container for a certain type of material, label all its sides. In this way the children can easily determine the contents in all compartments. Where feasible, store supplies inside large clear plastic boxes that will further assist the children in telling what is inside. Label, too, all your equipment and containers with your name and room number, so that materials shared with other classes or taken out of the classroom can be brought back to you without loss.

Large Flat Items

Sometimes it is necessary to store large flat pieces, such as huge art projects or pieces of cardboard you are converting into different things. One suggestion is to place a child's chair upside down on the edge of a table and stand the items upright inside the legs of this chair. Another idea is to salvage a carpenter's sawhorse or make your own using rough lumber and brackets. Invert this sawhorse and prop it up so it will not fall over. The flat items can then be stored in the V-shaped opening.

Paper at the Ready

When storing rolls of paper, place them inside perfectly fitting boxes. The children will then be able to unroll the exact amount of paper needed and cut it off.

If paper is stored at the easel for painting activities, take a large number of sheets and pound small finishing nails through all the sheets at the top of the easel. Whenever any child needs a sheet, he or she simply flips the first sheet over the easel, paints on it, and rips it off the nails when the painting is done. Thus, there is always a ready supply of paper for the next painter, out of the way of being splashed upon by the painter who stands on the opposite side of the easel.

Paper in Boxes

Salvage a collection of boxes of uniform size, each of which fits exactly one ream of paper or any other uniform packet of paper you customarily use. Attach the tops of these boxes with glue and, when the glue is dry, cut out one end of each box. Inside the box place one ream of paper. The children can then see at a glance the kind of paper they have without disturbing the other boxes that are also in the pile. As space demands it, experiment with storing these boxes vertically or horizontally.

Pegboard Possibilities

Save panels of pegboard or make your own by drilling holes at regular intervals in salvaged sheets of plywood or cardboard. Paint each panel an interesting color or have the students decorate each one with motifs appropriate to your classroom. Obtain hooks that are designed to accommodate various sizes and shapes of equipment, and then use these panels as display panels. Or, use them to store items. Simplify the return of tools and equipment to each panel by having the outlines of the items on the boards. Then as the children return the materials, they merely have to match the shape of the tool with its outline.

Phonograph Records

Records and albums are sometimes difficult to locate and easy to damage when they are placed in an indiscriminate pile. To solve this problem, find an old dish drainer to keep the flat objects upright and allow the children to leaf through the albums more readily. Another suggestion is to solicit from the children's families unwanted covers for records and albums. Discard the records that you cannot use, and have the students make their own decorations for each cover. Label each one appropriate to the records that are stored inside.

Plastic Drawers

Visit secondhand stores for sets of small plastic drawers that are used for storing nails or sewing items. With colored fabric tape label each drawer for a different kind of art supply, office supply, or other small items. Or, you might want to convert these compartments into a center to serve as a point of interest in the classroom. Invite the children to bring for display their most interesting stones, feathers, stamps, marbles, or other comparable items.

Plastic Jugs

Ask your students to bring to school clean plastic jugs in which bleach, milk, and fabric softener are sold. Cut out a section from the side of each jug and label the jug in keeping with its contents. If you leave the handles of the jugs in place, the children will find it easier to move these containers from place to place. Or, cut all the tops off and staple their sides together to make a long and permanent array of containers. This same array can be attached to a vertical surface as well as a horizontal one. The jugs can then serve as personal mailboxes for the children to use in distributing worksheets, notices, or other items. Still other sizes and types of clean plastic jars, jugs, and bottles should be carefully investigated for storage possibilities.

Puzzles Places

Simplify the acquisition and management of puzzles in several different ways. First, when using large wooden puzzles with thick edges, store them in a horizontal wire rack and label the edge of each puzzle so the children can readily see the contents of the rack. Then, on the back of each piece in that puzzle make a symbol, color, or letter to indicate which piece goes with what puzzle. If you have large lift-out pieces, make holes for the children to use in punching the pieces out of position when the puzzle has been reassembled. Or, convert wooden puzzles into lift-out items with the addition of small knobs for fingers to grasp more readily. If you have puzzles that might be too difficult for your students to solve, outline each piece in its proper position using a felt-tip marker. Then the pupils can reassemble the puzzle matching the pieces with the outlines you have made on the puzzle board.

Safe and Handy Scissors

For safe storage of pointed scissors, rinse out a large coffee can or any similar metal container and, using a triangular can opener, punch out a series of triangular holes around the circumference of the bottom of the can. Then turn the can over so the bottom becomes the top and place the scissors point-down in the several holes you have made. Another safe suggestion is to punch holes into each segment of an egg carton; the scissors will stand upright in these slots.

Yet another idea for scissors storage is to drill a series of holes in a wooden box, with a child's name by each hole. The children can then have access to their own pair of scissors at any time. If tangling has become a problem, make a board on which two dowel rods have been inserted and glued. (The dowels should be of sufficient length to hold all the scissors intended for it). As the children put away their scissors every day, they merely slip the ears of the shears over the two dowels to let the scissors hang safely.

Shelving to Shift

To make inexpensive shelving easy to move, invest in some concrete blocks and boards or salvage some from building sites. The shelving can be built to various heights and serve many purposes. Let the children also use the holes in the blocks as their own private places to file papers or other materials.

Partially filled bookshelves of any type permit books to fall over, so the children are less likely to read the books that are not straight. One suggestion is to cover a set of ordinary bricks with colorful fabric and use these as bookends. Another suggestion is to arrange your temporary shelving in such a way that the shelving slopes gently downward. The books will then lean into each other and thus remain upright.

Small Hooks

When you need to make hooks that hold lightweight objects such as cards on a poster, use brads. To make a hook on a poster, punch a slot in the poster where the hook is to be and insert one prong of the brass fastener through this slot, bending it back upon itself so it will not pull through. The other prong of the brad is then bent up, making the hook. Be sure you do not punch a round hole in the posterboard because if you do, the hook will simply rotate in the hole and be more difficult to handle.

String

When you have a lot of balls of string, yarn, or roving for art projects, place these inside a shoebox or a gift box or any other comparable container. Then punch a hole in the lid for each ball inside the box. Thread the string through the hole and pull out just enough for the children to see what color and type it is. As these materials are consumed during the day, suggest to the pupils that they cut off their pieces in a way that a short length remains exposed, thereby helping the next person to see what that box contains. Attach to each box a pair of scissors for the children to use.

Study Papers

Facilitate the storage of worksheets or other regularly distributed materials by salvaging from your school office a set of manila envelopes that are in good condition and uniform in size. Find a box that fits these envelopes exactly and cut this box on an angle, providing the children easy access to the envelopes as they are stored. Label each envelope on the front or on the flap, and color-code them by subject matter, by time of year, by difficulty, or by any other appropriate criterion.

Tubes

Discarded wrapping paper tubes can be used to store large rolled-up pieces of outlines, drawings, and bulletin board displays. Another tube might contain paper maps the children have made for permanent use in their social studies. Still other sets might incorporate charts and diagrams made for a better understanding of mathematics, science, or any of the other subjects. Some children might want to donate their murals and other major art efforts to decorate the classroom when a new class has enrolled in some subsequent year. Whatever purpose these tubes are put to, however, color-code the ends of each according to their contents, and add a label of the exact item inside. Such tubes can then stand behind objects in out-of-the-way areas of your classroom. Or, you can place a piece of twine around them and make a cluster of tubes.

Worksheet Extender

Extend the usefulness of your everyday worksheets by covering them with clear Con-tac. Give the students grease pencils or washable felt markers so the students can write their answers directly on the Con-tac. Students can check their answers by obtaining the answer key from a decorated box in the classroom.

LEARNING STUFF AND STATIONS

Adjustability

Whenever you are ordering new furniture for a classroom or supplementing the furnishings you already have, check them for adjustability. Since the children entering your classroom are of different shapes and sizes, and since they continue to grow during the school year, see that the desks, tables, and chairs are easy to modify. It is a burden on the custodial staff to continually change the furniture, especially if the items can be adjusted by the children themselves. Adding or removing blocks underneath table legs is one simple remedy to this problem, especially if these items are donated by members of the community or are obtained from secondhand furniture stores. If the equipment in your room demands more sophisticated adjustments, have a set of tools handy for modifying and engaging the children to do the work themselves. Most groups of any size have at least one person who is particularly clever with mechanical things and is glad to contribute time and expertise to this recurring task.

Book Bus

Whenever it becomes necessary to share library books, textbooks, or reference works with other classrooms in your building, convert a coaster wagon or any table with large wheels into a bus or a locomotive appropriate to the age of your children. Simply cut from cardboard the shapes you desire and paint them appropriately. Or, you might purchase or repaint sturdy shelving either yellow, orange, or red. Add a wooden platform to which you have attached wheels or casters, and put an elasticized rope around the shelving to prevent the books from falling off. Add decorative motifs cut from colored cardboard or from colored fabric to resemble an emergency vehicle or a schoolbus.

Bulk Orders

It is possible to save quite a bit of money by ordering school supplies in quantity. You may be able to combine orders with your colleagues, for example, sharing the cost of the materials you requisition for the year. Try to plan your expenditures well enough in advance to avoid making several small orders of the same type during the year. If large paper is appreciably cheaper than smaller pieces, order the larger and have the children cut it to the various shapes and sizes you might need during the year. Sometimes it is possible to order chalk and crayons in bulk, too, at considerable savings. This collective ownership of supplies in your classroom not only makes more crayons, chalk, and other items available to your pupils, it also eliminates the question of ownership as well. It is, of course, possible for the students to divide into individual portions any materials that are purchased in large quantity.

Checking Out Items

Whatever toys, games, records, books, and small items of equipment you may have in your classroom, attach to each one a circulation number by category and then have in your room a series of sign-out cards, one for each piece. Encourage your students to sign out these pieces for a predetermined period, returning them to the classroom before the agreed-upon deadline. Have the children's textbooks registered as well under this system, with the idea that if the children think they are truly borrowing something, its importance will be enhanced. Furthermore, a loan system for textbooks means you will not be so inclined to give all the children at the same time the same assignments; in addition to diversifying their instruction, you will need to purchase fewer textbooks. In addition, if students have free access to borrowing their instructional materials, they will be more likely to want to work ahead and learn as much as possible on their own.

Color-Coding

The wise use of colors can help simplify your record-keeping and other procedures. For example, the materials that are graded by difficulty might have attached pieces of fabric tape or varying degrees of colors that indicate the level of expertise needed for mastery. Colors are convenient for identifying groups of children or for labeling interest centers you have established in your classroom. When you are teaching more than one subject during the day, set up different colored and pocketed folders for each class or subject; this will enable you to keep in each folder only those papers and projects that pertain to the label on the front cover. To keep the children's assignments in order, instruct them to write their names for math papers in red, for example, science in green, language in blue, and so on.

Still other applications of color coding have to do with the kinds of things you send home to parents. General notices might be printed on yellow paper for greater visibility. Or, yellow paper might be utilized for "happygrams" that convey to your parents compliments about their children. Blue paper might be used to note areas needing added assistance at home.

As the children complete their assignments during the week, suggest that they use different colors of crayon to underline answers in their workbooks or on their worksheets—one color might indicate a correct answer and another color might underline an incorrect one. This use of colors makes the checking of answers easier and helps establish a visual pattern of responses. Also, instead of using letters or numerals in your assessment of pupil progress, use red, yellow, and green to show relative growth: green might indicate mastery and the ability to proceed to the next unit; yellow could suggest a casual review is recommended for mastery; and red should signal danger, a demand for more intense relearning of an essential concept or skill.

Distributing Systems

You can reduce the time and effort expended on the routine distribution of papers, projects, and supplies if you follow these suggestions.

Consider handing out items in the order in which they are to be used, but do not overwhelm your pupils with too many items and complex explanations for their use. Remember not to hand out an item before explaining its use, because children tend to be distracted with the process of handing out and making sure they have one that they might not be listening to you. Make at least a brief explanation of what the item is. Then, as the children need further explanation, distribute them and clarify, making sure all questions are answered appropriately.

An element of fun is added to the passing out of items if you have the children pretend to be a gigantic robot or other machine that passes one item on to the next robot in line.

If you choose to use an in-basket, position it near a large replica of a clock and/or a calendar that indicates when the requested items are due. Add a label, such as "Put Your Best Work Here," to encourage the children to check the accuracy of their work beforehand. Still another suggestion is to obtain or make a large rural mailbox with a red flag. Whenever there is something for general distribution, raise this flag to attract the child whose job is to distribute the material. A set of sturdy bags, each with a handle and labeled with a child's name, is yet another way to have the work categorized each day. An array of clean plastic cartons or jugs is also appropriate here. The children can take turns being the postal clerk in charge of sorting and handing out the papers that are to be placed in the compartments. For the sake of the children's confidentiality, however, make a point not to let classmates hand back any papers on which a grade or a point total is written. Yet another container for papers and supplies is made by cutting one sturdy paper plate in half and stapling that half to a second paper plate, face to face. This makes a neat compartment for papers. Each holder can then be taped to the individual's desk.

Duplicating Economies

If your budget for duplicating paper is on the wane, investigate the possibility of procuring a quality of paper just a little heavier than the usual, and then printing your items on the front and the back. In addition, many informal worksheets can be reproduced on the plain side of discarded paper from the school office, the teachers' workroom, as well as local offices and industries. As an added point of interest, collect from colleagues discarded worksheets that might be within the capabilities and needs of some pupils in your classroom. Students are often challenged to try tasks that come from the higher grades in school, while others might be enticed to try the less demanding tasks associated with the lower grades.

Free-Fashioned Furnishings

There are several ways to add to your seating without spending much money. For instance, collect a discarded child's mattress and cover it with a new plastic cover. Use this as a reading lounge area, topped with a rug or a carpet sample. A salvaged seat from an old automobile is also appropriate for this same purpose. Contact a telephone company to acquire empty spools used for cable and wire, and enlist your parents to make cushions that will fit each stool. Sand and paint some large wooden spools to serve as tables indoors or out.

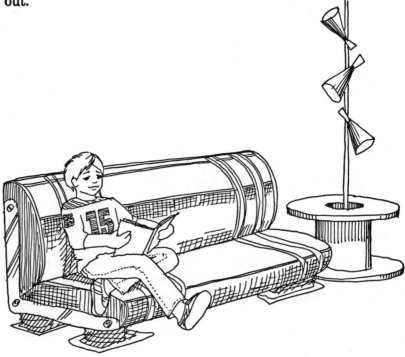

Small sturdy cardboard boxes are often available at liquor stores; their inserts make a firm seating or writing surface, particularly if the boxes are repainted in cheerful colors. For seating on the floor, consider salvaging oilcloth or heavy shower curtains and sewing them together after you have padded each one with a square of foam rubber.

Oilcloth Covering

If you need a protective covering for desks or tables, obtain colorful oilcloth from a department store or obtain it from the children's families. Use a permanent felt-tip marker to outline gameboards and game pathways, such as checkerboards, on these scraps. In this way your pupils not only protect the working surfaces but can also have fun during free time. Whenever you need the desks or tables for other activities, the oilcloth or plastic can be rolled up and stored out of the way. A similar suggestion is to obtain from a hardware store heavy-duty plastic covering. The pupils can use this for many purposes, including drawing erasable pictures, fingerpainting, and constructing see-through tents.

Panels and Partitions

You can make inexpensive room dividers by framing panels of fiberboard or pegboard with ordinary lumber for rigidity. If you want the partition to be free standing, hinge sections together, two or three at a time, with screw eyes and nails. Such panels double in service as display boards, storage boards, and sight screens. To protect the floors and to make their transfer easier, pound small metal ball-type casters into the bottom of each frame.

Paper for Backgrounds

There are many ways to make backgrounds for bulletin boards and other display areas. Consider using the classified advertisements from old newspapers. Their uniform gray surface is appropriate for displaying black and white items, for setting up a news events corner, and for silhouettes. The colored comics pages add a note of cheer to a corner devoted to cartoons, jokes, riddles, poems, and funny stories. Plain gift wrapping paper is most suitable for the holiday seasons; it can be requested at the conclusion of any major holiday, for it is readily available from most families who exchange gifts.

Different kinds of aluminum foil, whether silver or colored, can be useful for making backgrounds that relate to water and ice themes. This, too, can be saved as parents and others discard it from time to time. Commercial kraft paper that is available by the yard in most schools is convenient and easy to put up and store afterwards. If you choose to use the traditional construction paper for your backgrounds, you will discover that as it is exposed to light over the course of several weeks, it has a tendency to fade. Therefore, as you remove it, stack it with the good side (the bright side) up, and it will still be appropriate for other art projects.

Sending Notes Home

One of the ongoing responsibilities of teachers is to see that notes are promptly taken home at the end of the day or the week. One helpful hint is to have a spot set aside near the door for this purpose. As the children pass by this place they are much more likely to remember to pick up their notices. Convert small plastic jugs into carriers by thoroughly cleaning them out and cutting a large slot for the insertion of important papers. As the child's name is added to such a carrier, he or she is more likely to take charge of it by clutching the handle securely. A covered and colored oatmeal box is yet another kind of carrier, particularly if strong twine is run through the lid and the side of the carton so the top does not get mislaid once the box is opened.

Older children typically prefer a carrier that is more sophisticated. Ask them to explore unwanted office supplies and bring to school a large manila envelope with a clasp top, for example, or some official-looking folder that can be securely closed. Sturdy flat boxes are also appropriate for this purpose, particularly if the students are encouraged to letter them or otherwise label them for the importance of their contents.

Stepped Effects

If you have parents who are handy with tools and who are willing to spend some time in a worthwhile project, engage them in locating scrap lumber that can be smoothed and painted and incorporated into a series of steps, very much like a staircase. Depending on your needs, the size of your classroom, and the lumber at hand, make a set of stairs the children can sit on to study, after having covered them with carpeting or a rug. Such a set of steps is ideal, too, for viewing puppet shows or other presentations. And the space underneath is ideal for secure and secluded study on an individual basis.

Stuff and Junk

Many usable pieces of furniture can be found in second hand stores or at auction sales. An old-fashioned bathtub can be padded with cushions and converted into a reading center for one or two. A discarded easy chair or an old rocker not yet qualified for antique status can be cleaned, painted, or recovered for a reading center. You may be successful in involving your parents in reconditioning such items for their children to use in your classroom. Make a point to scour sources of junk furniture regularly, for in some cases if the proprietors of such establishments know you are looking for things to use with your children, the items may be either donated or sold at a reduced cost. Unusual furniture not only involves the parents, the children, and the community, its very uniqueness may attract attention to the extra effort you spend on behalf of your pupils. There is no doubt that your students will be more motivated to learn in a classroom that is cheerful, comfortable, and just a bit unusual.

Substitute Materials

There are occasions when you need to save money by using materials that are cheaper than their more expensive equivalents. For instance, examine the relative costs of

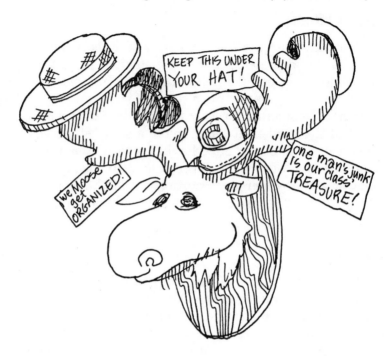

gummed brown tape as compared with other kinds of tape. Make a point to collect all kinds of scrap materials for various art projects, as well as for practice experiences. Engage the children in putting the residue from their own projects into transparent plastic containers which readily reveal the contents. This will save on expenditures for paper, as much of the waste will be eliminated. If nothing else, let the youngsters punch out holes from paper scraps and use these dots for still other art projects later on. Similarly, scraps of crayon can be melted in small tins and used with cotton swabs for encaustic art experiences. When colored chalk gets too small to be held in the hand, let the students grind it to power and use it sprinkled onto wet surfaces or incorporated into sand paintings.

Tabletop Treatments

You may have tables or desks with tops that are rough and scarred from years of wear. Renew these surfaces by simply painting a piece of plywood after having sanded the edges, and screwing it into position. A scrap of Formica, pressed fiberboard such as Masonite, linoleum, vinyl sheeting, or any other smooth material would work equally well. If you need a less elaborate treatment, just obtain a piece of oilcloth or plastic by the yard. If you notice pupils who like to write in and on their desks, ask them to tape onto the desks a piece of colored paper that serves as a blotter. The children can then decorate this piece whenever the urge occurs. Then when the piece is either worn out or filled up, a new scrap piece can be substituted. Where it is possible and appropriate, paint at least one tabletop (or its plywood or Masonite substitute) with blackboard paint, thereby providing at least one spot other than the chalkboard where pupils may practice arithmetic computation, spelling words, and handwriting skills.

Worksheet Ways

If you have students who are having difficulty with a certain skill or concept, duplicate several extra copies of worksheets. In this way the less able children can practice the item at hand more than once, and attain a high level of proficiency on the item they ultimately hand in for credit. Extra copies might also be generally available from past experiences for redoing later on just for the fun and the security of doing something familiar.

5

Simplifying Routine Classroom Tasks

If there is anything that teachers lack, it is time. Classroom responsibilities are so numerous and pupils are so diverse that there are never enough hours in any day to do all the things you want. In view of the tyranny of the clock, there is sufficient reason to find ways in which the classroom routine activities may be simplified. For example, the matter of cleaning up the premises at the end of a busy day can become a joy not a job as dozens of hands work together to restore the environment to an acceptable condition.

In addition, other problems sometimes intrude. Emergencies inevitably but unexpectedly occur. To be prepared for such situations before they arise not only reduces the degree of interruption, but also helps the children confront their own problems calmly as they model the behavior after that of the adult in charge. Even the simple matters of managing light, noise and distractions can be reduced to their easiest terms as the teacher applies special techniques.

Of all the other classroom responsibilities besides teaching, the most important elements are those of handling time and accounting for the whereabouts of boys and girls, keeping track of a host of tasks, taking attendance, and relating the calendar to daily events.

However much activities such as the ones in this chapter may simplify your daily routine, the added benefits of these ideas accrue to the children themselves, for they are deeply involved in the direction of much of their own experience. This act of trust endows pupils with a sense of satisfaction and self-worth, and builds within themselves a measure of responsibility for making their own decisions. As students cooperate and manage their own sessions, such collective efforts cannot help but make the days go more smoothly and produce greater academic success.

TECHNIQUES FOR TIME AND TASKS

Activity Signals

Instead of calling out to your children when it is time for them to change activities, use an imaginative signal system that will be less intrusive. One possibility is to teach the boys and girls some of the basic signs used by deaf persons. The children will need to be alert to your gestures in order to note the new directions they are being given. Similarly, teach the class members some of the basic signs from historical Indian sign language. Another idea is to procure a set of tone bells; use a different chord or note progression to send various signals to the class. Another idea is to have a spotlight in each area of the classroom to which you want to transfer the students' attention.

Appointments

When your students have appointments during the week for special help in areas such as speech therapy, remedial reading, work assignments elsewhere in the building, or any other engagement, let the involved students make miniature clocks they can place prominently at their work places. At the beginning of each day ask these boys and girls to set the hands of their personal clocks to the times at which they are to leave the room. When certain students have trouble remembering this visual cue, let some of their peers also make clocks to serve as friendly reminders. Or, suggest that the more forgetful class members use an ordinary kitchen timer that is set to ring at the appropriate moment.

Before-School Privileges

In some schools the children are not encouraged to arrive inside the school before a certain time. Where it is possible for you to do so, allow your students to come into your classroom ahead of this mandated time, especially if it is convenient for them to enter the room through a nearby door. This procedure not only cuts down on the ganging up to enter the main door when the bell rings and the subsequent noise in the hallway when the rush occurs, but it also lets the children make a smoother transition from home to school and gets them into a frame of mind for the day's tasks. It also allows you a chance to get acquainted with your pupils informally as individuals, and permits them to work together on things of high-interest before the regular instructional day begins.

Have available for these early-comers self-selected educational puzzles and games, riddles, jokes, story books, and manipulative items that entice their interests and tie in with your curriculum at the same time. Or, permit them simply to begin on their assignments. Whenever it seems convenient after the official starting time, take a few moments to take attendance and see to the general business of the day.

Dismissal

Instead of requiring children to line up before being dismissed, spark an interest by using different cues. For one thing, you might say something like this: "As soon as your work space is clean, you may leave the room," or, "Anyone who can walk to the bus safely and quietly may go now." Another, more controlled, procedure is to pose a quick and simple cognitive question for each student randomly in turn. This might consist of an inquiry into one of the concepts or skills that were learned or reviewed during the day. Fashion each query to fit the ability of the child asked to respond to it, thereby assuring a high degree of success and personal satisfaction.

Movement

Whenever a group of children must move through a crowded area en masse, ask them to line up either in numerical or alphabetical order. This technique will eliminate the usual pushing and shoving that otherwise occurs as children strive to be the first in line. Make a point to rotate the leadership of your lines daily so each person has a chance to serve as line captain. Designate as one other point of honor the last pupil in the line; the duty of this last person is to see that no stragglers are left behind, to turn off the lights, and to close the door. Give the directions to the line leader before you leave your point of departure and ask the rest of the group to "follow the leader." To add variety to their travels from place to place, suggest that this leader perform some simple stunt that every other child in line is to imitate as they walk in order. You might give each of the duty persons a special name, such as "Engineer."

Quiet Signals

To change the mood of your class, especially if they are being unusually noisy, convey your needs and your directions through the use of a "silent spot" at which time the class members understand they are to be communicated with only through hand signals and written notes on the chalkboard. Your pantomimed needs ought to engage their curiosity for the time needed to get the message across to them. A quite different signal is a bicycle horn, bell, or any other unusual sound. A still different approach is a string of colored lights salvaged from a family's Christmas discards. The children are informed at the beginning of the school year that whenever these lights are illuminated, something special is about to happen.

Scheduling Cycles

When you set up your daily schedule at the beginning of the year, remember that children need a cycle of activities that fits in with their interests as well as their physiological needs. For example, they require an alternation of active experiences with quiet ones and closed or structured ones with freely flowing or self-chosen ones. Where your morning sessions might be filled with subjects such as reading and mathematics that often involve seatwork, books, and quiet study times, plan a mini-break at mid-session with a game or some other high-interest activity. Make a point to announce this break time without predictability, so the children will always be looking for it to happen unexpectedly. If you have groups of boys and girls working on various projects at the same time, plan the day so that all the noisy activities are conducted simultaneously, and all the quiet ones at a different time. This will avoid disturbing those students who require an environment relatively free of noise and distractions.

Share and Tell

In the event the children bring in things to show and talk about with the class as a whole, vary the sometimes boring procedure by suggesting that only one group of children may do so on any given day. You might have these boys and girls bring to class just one kind of item: newspaper clippings on a pre-announced topic, items pertinent to an aspect of science inquiry, evidence of recent trips taken, or artifacts and souvenirs from a given holiday or season. Increase the usefulness of this sharing as a learning experience by designating a special table where items may be placed for examination later in the day. Encourage the children to write about these items, or to use them in their play or other learning activities. As appropriate to your purposes, set up several such tables and have small groups cluster around each one, reflecting their interest in the materials being shown and explained. Thus, you might have three or four small groups operating at the same time.

Signal System

Make visual cues to regulate behaviors by converting two flashlights into signal lights. Cover one with yellow cellophane to produce a "caution" marker and a second one with red cellophane to communicate "stop." When the noise level becomes too loud, or when certain pupils are misbehaving, simply flash the warning signals. A related idea is to construct from colorful cardboard certain shapes on which you write slogans or clever directions for the next activities, each of which is indicated with a symbol appropriate to that experience. As it becomes time for you to shift attention from one part of the room to another or to change subjects of study, simply begin waving these attractive sign boards.

Start/Stop Symbols

Instead of using verbal signals to tell your children how to respond to certain classroom situations, prepare a series of colorful cartoon characters that are attached to long sticks. These can be raised at appropriate times to indicate the desired response: "Clam Up!" featuring a bi-valve suggesting the group members are too noisy, "Be Handy" starring an octopus to indicate they should take turns by raising their hands, "No Butting In" representing a goat to remind them they have been discourteous to their peers, and "Freeze!" picturing a snowman asking them to stop in place. If you prefer to use auditory cues, tell your students that when you begin to whistle a certain tune, that will be the signal for a given activity or for a certain group response. Or, use a set of tone bells or a child's xylophone for the same purpose. A popular record works well as a signal, too. Or, make up a parody of a song related to the next task you have in mind. You might ask the boys and girls to help you invent the words of this silly melody.

Taking Turns

"Whose turn is it?" is often a bothersome question asked in classrooms. When you are trying to find a fair way to decide the answer to this query, use one of these ideas. Let the children randomly draw number cards from a hat to tell the order in which they will have turns. Or, have them each hold a bottle cap or a poker chip—when each person in turn is called on, he or she must toss the cap or chip into a basket. Or, when choosing sides for a game or a team, stipulate that you will set a timer randomly and hide it in the classroom. Then the child who is answering your question when the timer rings may be the leader of the next activity.

If you teach young children, tie in their turn-taking with certain cognitive—and listening—skills. "The boy with the blue shirt may come and move these flannel figures now," or "The girl whose name begins with 'D' may be the leader of this activity," or "The person whose name is spelled 'A-L-E-X' may be the line leader today." When dismissing children from an activity, toss a beanbag to any child randomly, and let him or her then toss it along randomly, until the last person in order then tosses it back to you.

Time Cards

Engage the children in the use of "time cards" to serve several purposes. For one thing, time cards promote the notion that students' work at school is their job, just like a job performed by their parents. A time card can also be used as an attendance device. Each day the boys and girls can mark their own cards to report the date and their time of arrival, turning each card over in its appropriate slot provided somewhere for that purpose. The students who find it difficult to get to school on time are thus prompted to be more punctual. A third application of the time card is that of keeping in order the priorities of the children who want to use a particular high-demand game or piece of equipment. The time card can indicate the times the children may begin and the times they are to conclude a particular activity.

Timely Reminders

To indicate the main activities you plan for the day and to satisfy those children who seem always to ask, "What time do we . . . ?" post prominently on the wall in your classroom small clock replicas located near the real clock. Label each miniature appropriately: "Time for gym," "Time for lunch," "Time to leave," and so on. Younger children who cannot yet read time may be able to compare the positions of the hands of these several clocks. You might also add a set of symbol pictures to each clock to aid in this association: a large musical note for music, an item of food for lunch, or a ball for gym.

Timing Turns

To settle arguments concerning how long students can do certain activities, consider using a timer. At other times, when the boys and girls are engaged in calling on each other for answers, give the person whose turn it is an appropriately decorated "magic wand" to tap the person who has the next turn. Or, when a group is reviewing flash cards or any other card activity, shuffle into the deck of cards another set of cards on each of which you have written the name of a child in your class. The person who is in charge of the activity shows the cards to all the persons who are participating. That person called upon continues to respond to the cards flashed until another name is randomly drawn from the stack of cards. At that point the person whose name is shown next on a card takes over and continues the activity, either as the questioner or as the respondent, depending on how you have structured the activity.

Traffic Lines

Whenever you have a group of young children moving anywhere in line, designate one person to be the lookout in front and a second person to serve as the observer at the rear. You might garb each of these persons in the cardboard hat of a police officer. Explain to the children that moving in line in a building is very much like traffic flowing on the highway. The children are to look carefully at corners and also keep to the right. You could even make and post heavy-duty and colorful "Yield" and "Caution" signs at heavily traveled intersections inside the building or on the playground. The child who serves as the head of the line might carry a replica of a stoplight or a stop sign to give the rest of the group a visual signal of when to stop. Other replicas of traffic signs, such as "Keep Right," "Slow," and "Children at Play" may be similarly used by the leader of the line.

Transitions

Make the flow from one activity to another easier by alternating open activities with closed ones during the day. For example, whenever you assign a task to all students and expect them to work on it until completion, assign an activity such as free reading, art exploration, or play to follow the more structured activity. In this way, as the children complete their assignment, their work can be checked individually, and then they may move into the open-ended activity to follow. Also, by having a high-interest experience to follow a demanding work assignment, you will help to motivate your boys and girls to complete their work promptly and to do it well.

Waiting for Responses

Sometimes an activity that ought to involve many students engages the attention of only a few. You can stimulate greater participation by being less anxious about waiting for an appropriate response after, for example, you have asked a question of the class. Research studies suggest that teachers ordinarily wait only one or two seconds before going on to someone else or rephrasing the question. Try to give any child you call upon at least six or eight seconds to formulate a reply. If a child cannot answer your query, let him or her choose another class member to respond, but structure this by insisting that a boy must call on a girl, and vice versa, until all pupils have had a turn. Try not to repeat your questions, if this repetition can be avoided. Speak clearly and slowly. Interject into your stream of conversation the name of any child who is clearly not attentive to you. Engage more students in the discussion by redirecting a pupil's question to you back again to the group as a whole.

Waiting in Lines

There are many situations where boys and girls must wait for something to happen: the lunch line, the bus line, the line to enter a building, or the line to go out of the building. To make better use of this waiting time and to minimize misbehaviors that may arise, provide high-interest materials at those stations. A portable magazine rack, for instance, might be filled with crossword puzzles, collections of cartoons, jokes, riddles, short stories written by the children themselves, original drawings and paintings, or a set of paperback books which are constantly being renewed and recycled as the members of your class donate unwanted volumes. Or, install a portable chalkboard and encourage the children to practice their creative skills in the form of pictures, fancy lettering, original graffiti, and other items.

MAINTAINING ORDER IN THE COURSE

Art Clean Up

Caution your students not to dump plaster, sand or clay residue into the sinks, as very few basins are built to accommodate this kind of debris. Instead, provide a separate dishpan in which the children are to rinse off their implements and their hands, and then dispose of the waste water appropriately. You might also have in the sink itself another dishpan into which tiny holes have been punched, just large enough to let the water seep out. In this way the bulk of the residue dumped into the sink by mistake is automatically trapped without damage to the drain itself.

A second suggestion is to have at the sink a squeeze bottle into which you have put detergent solution. Encourage the students to use this container in washing their hands and in washing up the tables and counters that are painted on during art class.

Assigning Jobs

The very simplest solution to the question, "Who does what?" is to construct two large concentric circles cut from heavy cardboard, one considerably larger than the other one. Subdivide each circle into "pie" wedges. On one set of wedges print the names of the children in your class, and on the other set print the titles of the tasks that need to be done, one for each section of the circle. If there are more children than jobs, some of the students will have an occasional day off. On the other hand, if there are more tasks than children, let the pupils draw lots for the extra duties. When children are absent from school for any reason, teach your students some new counting out rhymes and use these to select randomly the substitute work for the job left unattended by the absence of that particular child.

Bad Weather Tips

Several suggestions help to make rainy and snowy days more bearable. For one thing, always have on hand some high-interest activities that your children can have access to only when the weather is bad, particularly when they are required to stay indoors all day. Make a point to have a plastic tray or a cardboard box at your exterior door to hold boots or galoshes. Also have on hand clear tough plastic bags the children can wear outdoors over their shoes, especially when they come to school without appropriate footwear. Plastic bags are also helpful to slip over shoes when the children's boots are a little too small to be pulled on over the shoes.

Clean Up Campaign

Sometime every spring have your students clean up the school grounds. Take the initiative in picking up debris, repairing equipment, and organizing materials. This not only saves money and beautifies the school, but also helps your students develop a sense of responsibility for their environment and the communal property. Also, when your pupils take the lead in such matters, other students are likely to follow the example. Tie such efforts into an anti-litter program which might involve a walk around the neighborhood during which the students pick up scrap material. Let them make collages or posters to dramatize the variety, extent, and potential of the materials they have recycled.

Whenever your children help with clean up, let them use cans, cartons, and other containers that are painted or decorated attractively to generate interest in the project. For example, a garbage can may be painted to resemble a trash monster, a big box can be converted into a garbage truck, and a wastebasket is handily changed into a silly clown with a conical cardboard hat. To make any of these clean-up efforts especially attractive, schedule them for bright sunny days, and offer the children a special snack or an extra surprise if they work well at their tasks.

Clean Up Concepts

Engage your students' interest in the end-of-day tidying up by referring to the clutter as "our clutter" rather than "your clutter." Set a good example to your pupils by participating yourself in this daily act. Be prepared to expect no more neatness of your students than you display yourself. Suggest that each person clear his or her own work space first, and then put away, for instance, as many other items as there are days in a week or as many things as there are letters in a given student's last name. Stress the need for a clean environment, not only as an esthetic necessity, but also because neatness simplifies the work of the custodian after school. Point out, too, that a clean room is a safer room and makes it easier for the pupils themselves to find their materials the next time. You can also drum up enthusiasm for student assistance by displaying a colorful "Help Wanted" poster and asking the children to sign up to indicate their willingness to assist with specific tasks you have identified on the poster.

Clean Up Roles

Designate the clean-up tasks in your classroom by specific roles related to community activities and helpers. For example, the "Plumber" is in charge of the washroom area, the "Engineer" is responsible for the movement of lines through the building, the "Inspector" can monitor the general condition of the classroom, and the "Environmentalist" can see that the trash is properly disposed of. A related notion is to equip each child with hand puppets, who give instructions to the other class members engaged in tidying up the site. Be sure that each child in your class has an opportunity to fill the various roles you invent.

Distraction Reduction

One of the main distractions during the day is the constant sharpening of pencils. To minimize this problem, designate one child each day to be in charge of sharpening all the pencils at one time. Or, you may prefer to have the individual students sharpen their pencils themselves, but only at the beginning of the day. For the sake of those class members who break their points frequently, request that they have on hand several pencils at the beginning of the day, or you might have an extra set from which they may borrow and then replace.

Emergency Items

Since children sometimes forget clothing and other items during bad weather, make a collection of discarded things over the years. Label these with your name and room number, so that if and when overshoes, umbrellas, rainhats, and other items are borrowed from your supply, they are more likely to be returned to you intact. One way to display these borrowed items is to suspend them from clothespins on strings attached to an inverted frame of an umbrella suspended in the corner of your classroom. Or have a clothesline stretched across your classroom to serve the same purpose.

Emergency Kit

Salvage a child's lunch box and decorate it appropriately to serve as an emergency kit. Place inside it items that are often needed on short notice, such as safety pins, bandages, buttons, scissors, thread, needles, pins, an extra undergarment, a special compound for deodorizing sick rooms, a pair of shoestrings, etc. Another idea is to provide a tool box filled with the ordinary tools that are sometimes needed to make simple repairs in your classrooms: a hammer, several different kinds of screwdrivers and wrenches, and assorted nails and screws and bolts. In either container, provide a list of its contents.

Emergency Response

Since children tend to model their attitudes and behaviors after the significant adults in their lives, it is particularly important that your reaction to emergencies be appropriate for them to imitate. Students should be shown that emergencies are an inevitable part of life and that a person who has been trained to handle them is more likely to do a good job than someone who is not so prepared. For that purpose, post prominently in your classroom some of the basic first aid procedures, particularly if medical personnel are not readily available. Caution the children, however, not to act unless there is a clear and present danger, such as copious bleeding or cessation of breathing. Also display the emergency telephone numbers for a doctor, the local hospital, the fire and police departments, and ambulance service. Procedures for fire drills and other disaster drills should be placed on large brightly colored charts with animal figures or other attractive pictures to remind the students of procedures. Make a point to review emergency procedures with greater regularity than is ordinarily required by school administrators or school board policy.

End-of-Day Clean Up

Taking care of the cleaning up and putting away at the end of the day is not always pleasant or challenging to your children. So engage them in a variety of activities:

1. While tidying, let the children sing a song they all enjoy. A simple parody of a familiar tune, such as "This is the way we . . . (clean the room)" for younger boys and girls, will do nicely. Older students might prefer to make up their own parodies of familiar tunes. Or, play the children's favorite records to accompany these clean-up efforts.

2. Provide colorful containers for storage purposes. For example, bright plastic dishpans can be color-coded to match their contents. The children can then carry these from place to place as they pick up the items that belong inside them. Similarly, a coaster wagon or a caster cart can be moved from place to place to accommodate the larger pieces of equipment.

3. If time is short, set a kitchen timer for a specified number of minutes and challenge the youngsters to beat the clock. Or better yet, ask a class member to set the timer, sight unseen. A minor reward may be suggested in the event the students can complete their tasks before the timer rings.

4. Have well-labeled spots on shelves, in closets, and in drawers for each item. In some instances, have large, plain colorful labels and/or symbols for each spot. Also, outline with felt-tip markers the shapes of objects that are to be stored in each spot.

5. Assign each child or group of children just one activity to be responsible for. For instance, one group can be asked to take care of the condition of the floor, another to replace all the books on the shelves, and a third to put the chairs on the tables.

6. Decorate the sides of empty plastic jugs and cut out holes in the sides just under the handles, making them large enough for the students to insert their hands. One container might hold puzzle pieces or building blocks. Another container can contain detergent solution for washing off toys and hands.

7. Obtain from a toy store a child-size cleaning set, including a mop and a broom, and decorate these with red fabric tape to represent candy canes. They will then be more visible and more fun to use.

8. Set up a "bucket brigade" with plastic pails of the same size. The children can have fun by passing things along a line of classmates, until each bucket is filled. Or, distribute the pails randomly to the pupils to use in picking up items.

9. Convert the cleaning process into a game by giving clues such as "find a red item," "find something under any desk," and "find something large."

10. Divide your rows or clusters of desks into streets or neighborhoods, each with a label familiar to the children who live in your area. Challenge the students to see which sections of the territory can quickly and satisfactorily arrange things properly.

Fabric Noise Control

Where acoustics are not conducive to learning, attach carpet scraps that have been salvaged from local stores or donated by family members. These pieces may serve double duty by being used as seating on the floor during a portion of the day. You might provide a strip of wood on which hooks are attached to hold the carpeting. Or, provide panels made of salvaged draperies or curtains that have been washed and dyed or painted by the children themselves. Suspend these panels from the ceiling or drape them on the walls. A third suggestion is to obtain large sheets of fiberboard cut to size and ask the children to decorate these as an art project. Various colorful banners of educational as well as class interests, holidays, or seasons may also add interest to the children's activities and to the acoustical properties of the room.

Faces and Figures Helpers

Combine miniature photographs of the children or their miniature self-portraits by making an array in a circle like a clock and connecting hands to which you have attached labels of some of the main classroom jobs. These hands are moved about the face of the clock each day or week, pointing in turn to the pictures of the class members who are to undertake each matching task.

A second idea is to have an envelope for each child posted on the classroom display area. On each envelope have a face to represent the child in charge of the task, and write and illustrate the job at hand. Inside the envelope place a brief description of what to do, or insert a small finger puppet that each child can use during the performance of his or her duties.

A third suggestion is to attach miniature portraits to springtype clothespins. Attach these pins to a cardboard poster on which you have written the names of the tasks required in your classroom. Each morning these clips can be moved from place to place on the poster.

Give-a-Hand Helper

Let the children make helper charts by tracing their hands onto pieces of cardboard and making two copies, each one of a different color of paper. On one hand the children write their names and on the other hand the name of a classroom job. When it is time to assign tasks, these can be mixed up and placed face down. Each child in turn may draw one hand from the jobs pile and a second hand from the names pile. The match of name with job is then set for the day or the week. You might also use these hands as labels on the actual part of the room where the job originates. For example, the person in charge of the lights should put his or her name and the job hand near the light switch.

Help-Wanted Helpers

Emphasize the importance of routine jobs by handling these responsibilities as if they were regular paid-for jobs. For example, at the beginning of the year post on a display board a series of want ads in which you describe the nature of each task, and the qualifications you would like to have in the person who is interested in performing that job. Hold a series of interviews in which each applicant must explain why he or she is capable of handling that particular chore. Match pupils with tasks as best you can and, as each position is filled, have each person decorated appropriate to the task assumed. For example, let each person wear a badge or an armband during the school day which enables their classmates to view clearly the responsibility undertaken.

Jobs as Occupations

Ask young children to assume that your classroom is a rocket ship that will be traveling for the year through space. Each person will have a particular role on board: the medical officer, the logistics officer, the communications officer, the loyalty officer, the evaluation team, the chief botanist, the morale officer, etc. Provide each pupil a suitable headband, an apron, and tools of that trade. Ask the students to make cardboard signs to stand on their desks indicating their particular contributions to the welfare of the group embarked on the imaginary venture.

Messy Dressing

Many learning experiences, especially in art, involve the children getting dirty. There are several useful ways to protect clothing from the inevitable spills. Wearing plastic bags on the feet is one such possibility. Wearing large plastic garbage sacks pulled down over the head, each one with holes cut out for arms and head to poke through, is still another option. Oversize shirts and blouses salvaged from the children's families are also helpful. If complete protection is needed, however, get discarded coveralls that loosely fit the youngsters. These can be worn over school clothing and then hung up to dry at the end of the day.

Nature's Helpers

Adapt any element in nature to the classroom job chart. A tree with leaves attached to a branch or a beehive with labeled bees are two possibilities. An octopus with name-gloves on each hand, spots on the backs of ladybugs or giraffes or leopards, and sections on a turtle's shell are further examples. You could also make a bright and cheerful daisy on which the jobs on the inner portion match the names on the petals.

Noise Abatement Ideas

Reconsider some of the traditional materials and techniques you are using if the matter of noise is a problem in your room. Give some time to approaches such as these:

- Anything that is tossed in a game might be made of sponge rubber or plastic rather than wood, metal, or other hard material. Number cubes, letter cubes, and balls for games can then be silenced in this way.
- Soft plastic dishpans, instead of wooden boxes, can serve as storage units.
- Use plastic and cardboard blocks and other building materials in place of wooden ones.
- Minimize the scraping of desks, chairs, and tables on the floor by placing them on large squares of salvaged carpeting that can be slid around easily.
- Obtain pastel egg cartons of styrofoam, along with other styrofoam scraps, and hang these attractively around the classroom walls.
- As required, let the children wear old socks over their shoes or, in balmy weather, let them go only in socks.

- Cover work tables with pieces of pressed fiberboard salvaged from construction sites or lumber yards. Use carpet samples to muffle the sound of pounding.

Noise Control Signals

Several techniques can help your children remember not to make too much noise. One suggestion is to obtain from a hardware store a flashing red light. This can be turned on as a warning to quell disturbances. You might have a similar amber light to caution the boys and girls before the red light completely discontinues their activity. A second idea is to tape record the extreme noise and then play back this tape when you have regained their attention. It is also a good idea to ask a noisy class to close their eyes; experience proves that when children close their eyes their mouths usually close as well. If you have just one or two individuals who are forgetful, choose a "noisemaker" student to be the next "noise watcher" for the coming period. In this way the miscreant is given some small responsibility for order in the classroom and must therefore serve as a good example to the rest of the group.

Quiet Spots

Provide one or more "silent spots" where the children can retreat to be alone without distraction. In some instances, a large closet without a lock or latch can serve this purpose, especially if it is lighted and has enough room for at least one desk or a cushion for the floor. Otherwise, convert a large cardboard container into a special place as you pad it with carpet squares and line the inside of the box with pieces of acoustical tile. Make this booth sufficiently portable so it can be moved from place to place. Label this place with a clever name.

Random Helper Choice

Sometimes it is interesting to make the assignment of tasks unpredictable. For instance, the children might want to toss number cubes for the privilege, with the high score winning the job. Or, let the children fish for the jobs, using a magnet to catch slips of paper that have paper clips attached to them. Snapping a spinner is yet another way to decide. Make this spinner in the shape of a pointing hand and attach it to a cardboard circle, using a small brad to help the spinner move freely.

Safety Inspection

Examine your classroom regularly to make sure there are no safety hazards. Be careful with trunks, closets, drawers, and other containers large enough to hold a child. Replace all latches with magnetic catches. A more general suggestion is to introduce each child to the appropriate and safe way to use all the equipment associated with their learning experience. More than that, place beside each piece of equipment a permanent set of instructions that the children are to read and follow before using it.

ACCOUNTING FOR KIDS

Absentees

A child who is absent from school for a long period of time is often at a distinct disadvantage when he or she returns to the classroom. One way to help solve this problem is to assign each member of the class a buddy or a compatible peer group, whose responsibility is to keep track of daily assignments for the classmate. These companions can be asked to take one copy of each worksheet or other study item distributed during the day, write the name of the absent pupil on it, and place it in the absentee's desk or classroom mailbox. The partners may also be asked to help explain new concepts to the persons. You might try to assign such assistants on the basis of geographical proximity in the neighborhood or similar interests, activities, or abilities.

Attendance Clothespins

There are several ways to use common clothespins in the attendance procedures. One idea is to attach to them miniature portraits taken with an instant camera in order to give a visual accounting of those members present and those who are absent. Another idea is to ask the youngsters to make small puppet heads to attach to these pins, and use them as counting objects during the preliminary procedures as the day begins. These clothespins can also be clipped to the edges of other charts during the rest of the day to indicate which children are participating in certain groups or who are at specific learning centers or who are out of the room on special assignments.

Bookkeeping

When you have your own books in a classroom library collection, provide a set of colorful cardboard space holders for the pupils to use as they remove volumes from the shelves. This place holder has the title of the book at the top, so the child simply signs his or her name underneath. This bright piece of posterboard shows the student where each volume belongs in its appropriate place on each shelf. The sign-out cards may also be color-coded to represent certain subject areas, making the task of returning books even easier. You would also do well to cut these cards to an exact size to fit inside the pocket attached to every book. New cards may be made as the old ones are filled in with signatures. A published record can then be made of the number of times a given book is checked out, thereby recommending it to other readers in your class.

Calendar Compartments

Combine daily calendar activities with learning in several different ways. One suggestion is to staple together 31 small boxes in an array to resemble a three-dimensional calendar. The child whose turn it is each day must count out small objects in keeping with the date or must perform some other mathematical computation appropriate to the number of the date and the individual child's abilities. These same compartments may be used as storage boxes for small items brought by the children to share with their peers, particularly in the middle grades where such objects may be in keeping

with special dates of note in a given month. In addition, when
you have papers that must be distributed to the group on a
certain day, place them in the appropriate compartment so
that the children will remember them when they're needed.

Calendar Lift-Ups

Enhance your children's use of the calendar by incorporating original art. For example, collect from parents discarded seasonal greeting cards and trim these to one size. Set
up these cards in an array to form the days in the present
month. As each next day arrives, the children in turn may
open up the greeting card for that day and read the message,
from which you have marked out the personal name and any
other remarks. You might also ask the children to make their
own lift-up items—each day of the month a different child
might then bring an original drawing that can be attached to
the monthly array. Or, you might prefer to ask one child to
draw at the end of the day a picture that shows the best or
most interesting activity that was done during the session.
When the seasons change or in the midst of a month with holidays, children might also choose to make lift-ups consisting of
signs of the season or of the holiday at hand.

Choosing Sides

In activities involving two or more teams, too often the
most popular pupils are asked or allowed to choose sides.
Thus, the same boys and girls tend to end up on the same
teams and a small number of class members are chosen last.
Being either chosen first or last is not necessarily healthy for
children's self-concepts, particularly if it occurs repeatedly.
This problem can be prevented by having the sides chosen by
lot. Or, you might have the leaders selected randomly and
then ask them to select peers for their teams. Setting up
teams by rows in the classroom, by first letter of last name, by
months of birth, by color of clothing being worn that day, by
section of the neighborhood, or by tossing dice are all ways to
introduce an element of chance and surprise into the
proceedings.

Class Lists

When you are preparing a master list of your class at the beginning of the school year, remember to defer this task for at least several days to allow latecomers to be enrolled. Then make a list on which you have alphabetically written the last names of your children, allowing at least one blank space between each name. This provides a space for further additions to your group, comments, or descriptive information about each enrollee. Such a list might include columns for taking attendance, keeping track of grades, and making any other suitable bookkeeping data.

Dial-a-Day

A large poster-like device can be made to designate not only the day but the general seasonal conditions as well. For example, you might cut several slots into a large piece of cardboard and make circles from cardboard on which you have indicated several elements appropriate to such statements as: "The month is . . . , " "The weather is . . . ," "The name of the day is . . . ," "Today's date is . . . ," "The season is . . . ," "The temperature is . . . ," "The sun is . . . ." Designate a student each day to check the data to be displayed on this dialing device and then to set each circle appropriately. A second related idea is to make several concentric circles, one with the labels "Today, Tomorrow and Yesterday," and the others indicating the day, the week, and the calendar date.

Diary Calendar

Obtain large sheets of plain newsprint and have one for each month of the school year. Stack these sheets in one pile and measure off the weeks of a month on the top sheet, making the lines with a felt-tip marker. These markings will bleed through onto the sheet underneath, leaving faint lines for you to trace in making the subsequent ones. Then, as each month progresses, let the children at the end of each day write in the appropriate space on the sheet the most interesting, humorous, helpful or most important things that happened dur-

ing that session. This monthly summary may also be used as
the basis of a weekly or monthly newsletter that your students duplicate and send home to parents.

Food Count

Simplify the task of taking milk counts and lunch counts
by asking the children to cut out from the front sections of
clean empty milk cartons a set of tags into each of which a
hole is punched. As the children arrive at school every day,
they are to use one of these tags on their own name cards
which have been displayed prominently in the classroom.
Similarly, a different but comparable set of pictures of food-
filled plates can be cut from magazines and glued to sturdy
cardboard tags. A student can then be assigned the job of
counting the number of milk and/or lunch tags every day.

Head Count Hangers

Use ordinary wire coathangers to help with taking attendance each day and counting noses for other purposes as
well. Set up and label as many hangers as necessary and then
ask each child to sign his or her name on an ordinary spring-
type clothespin. These may be colored differently front and
back to signify "yes" and "no," for example, or "absent" and
"present." Instruct the children that they are to move their
pins from one spot to another to show the type of participation
in each activity every day. Assign one pupil the task of
counting or recording the number of participants, and then
moving all the pins back to their original positions at the end
of the school session.

House and School Counters

As an interesting device to record the daily presence of
your children, decorate two small boxes to resemble a simple
house and an old-fashioned school. Leave the tops open on
these two containers. Have spring-type clothespins with each
student's name written on it. As the boys and girls come into
your classroom each day, ask them to remove their pins from

the edge of the house and place them on the top edge of the school. Around the top of the house you will find the pins of those students who are absent.

Keeping Control

You can simultaneously maintain greater interest and keep better control as you incorporate several handy techniques. One of these is to fasten to your chalkboard pointer a miniature toy car, doll, insect, or any other eye-catcher. Or, have a child make a puppet head for the pointer. Add a touch of intrigue to your presentations by having a nonsensical incantation precede them. Or, designate one small section of a rug or the floor to be your "listening spot." Whenever you are standing on that spot, the children must give you their complete attention. Or, you may prefer to have any inattentive child stand on that "magic" spot.

Lost and Found

When your students forget to put their names on their papers, post the papers on the face of a large cardboard cutout of a labeled "Mr. No-Buddy." Clip the papers around the perimeter of this comic character until they are claimed by their owners. Another suggestion is to make from cardboard a large outline of a child to which you have attached at various points around the perimeter clothespins on strings. These pins can be used to hold the various items found in your classroom.

You might also want to add interest to the reclaiming of lost items by decorating a cardboard carton to resemble a treasure chest. Whenever a child needs to look into this box for some lost item, require him or her to provide a "password" in the form of an answer to a simple question or by performing an easy stunt. Such activities may stimulate your boys and girls not to forget their items again.

A third suggestion is to identify some central spot in your school that is heavily traveled during the day and set up a used volleyball net to which you have attached a colorful set of spring-type clothespins. Cut out an outline of a child and color it attractively to catch the attention of the passers-by. Attach to this net mittens, pencils, purses, scarves, hats, shoes, and other items that have been found. Stipulate that these items be dated when they are posted and then removed after a certain reasonable period, to be donated to persons in special need.

After the Christmas season, salvage a large sturdy tree and strip the needles from each branch. Spray paint this in an interesting color and collect a set of clothespins. Set up the tree in some central location in your school or your classroom, and place a box of colored pencils or crayons, along with some colorful scraps of paper, nearby. Instruct the students that they write and post on this tree appropriate notes whenever they either lose or find an item anywhere on the school property.

Personalized Attendance

Let the children keep track of their own attendance by setting up a chart for all the days of the marking period, and then marking in those squares that indicate presence or absence. You will be able to tell at a glance the patterns of attendance by certain days or by individual students.

Another suggestion is to have the boys and girls cut out felt shapes resembling dolls, labeling each one with the name of a student. These cutouts may be displayed appropriately on a flannelboard every day to indicate that the particular pupil is present.

A simple self-portrait drawn on the end of a tongue depressor is yet another idea. These objects may be kept in a piece of sturdy plastic or fabric that has been stitched together to create as many pockets as there are children in your class. Students who are absent on any given day will have their sticks still located in the "absent" pockets once all the present students have taken their sticks in the morning.

Random Grouping

There are many times during a week when you need to have your children in groups for certain learning activities.

Games in the gym or on the playground, study groups for researching topics, and clusters to work on major art projects are just three examples. While it is appropriate on some occasions to group your students either by ability, by interest, or by peer choice, it is also wise from time to time to randomly select group memberships. You will thus avoid the twin problems of having the same persons in the same groups, and will not have children last-chosen or late-chosen repeatedly when the students elect their own group leaders for the purpose of selecting members. Try to group by an arbitrary criterion, such as the letters of the children's names, their birthday months during the year, counting off by fours or fives, the color of clothing worn that day, the size of families, or unique neighborhoods in the community. As each group is formed, encourage the children to think up a name for themselves, such as an animal, a famous character, or a place mentioned in a familiar story. Let the students also make and wear original name tags to indicate the groups to which they belong that day.

Restroom Markers

When the students must take turns in using the restrooms in your school or your classroom, provide one or more pieces of cardboard that is cut to the shape of a stop sign. One side of each sign is painted red and the word "STOP" is added in white. The opposite side is painted green and "GO" is added in yellow. In instances where a bathroom down the hall is to be used, this sign may be posted inside the classroom door or on the doorknob, but be turned over by the user appropriate to his or her departure and return. Children can tell at a glance when the restroom is being used by someone else, so they will no longer have to ask.

Roll Call

Occasionally choose to have the children take the daily attendance by answering a roll call rather than marking names on a chart. Each child whose name is called in turn may respond with the name of a pet or a favorite animal, a special activity or hobby, a cherished food, or some other interest. Similarly, each child may also be asked to respond to a simple cognitive question within his or her ability. Another possibility is to assign each child a number that indicates his or her numerical order on the alphabetical class list. The roll is then simply taken by calling off these numbers in order. As the pupils develop skill in numbers, you might also pose questions in manipulating and computing these numbers, such as simple addition problems or other arithmetic operations.

Sign Out Symbols

If it is necessary for your students to have permission to be out of your classroom during the day, make a set of sturdy cardboard or wooden symbols that can represent the reason for the temporary absence and may be handily worn on a string around the neck, leaving the pupils' hands free for other purposes. A large key might suggest the use of the bathroom; a book, the library; a telephone, the office; a flask, the science room; a mathematics symbol, the math room. If you require a more specific naming of the places and times of departure for these persons, set up a miniature chalkboard or bulletin board at your classroom exit. Use the same symbols for headings for sign-outs, and let the children keep track of their own comings and goings.

Spinner Wheel Calendar

Cut from cardboard a large rectangle and then cut out three cardboard circles. On each circle write appropriate information to be used in keeping track of the day. One circle will have the five school days on it, the second will show the months in which school is in session, and the third one will display the days of the month. Each school day, the child who is in charge of the calendar will simply move each wheel forward one spot to show the appropriate day and date.

Sunshine Calendar

Make an unusual calendar by cutting from bright yellow posterboard two large circles. Write on one of these the months that school is in session, each month in the shape of a separate ray or sunbeam coming out of the sun. Attach these two circles together in the center with a brad so that one may be moved about after the display has been posted on the wall. As the months change, a child may come up and turn the device so the appropriately named sunbeam coincides with the label on the face. A second variation of this idea is to have each child make his or her own rectangular calendar of a given month. At the end of each school day, instruct each student to take from his or her desk a yellow crayon or felt-tip marker and mark on that day's space a face to show what kind of a day it was: a bright smiling face to indicate a happy day, a frown to suggest an unhappy or a frustrating one, and a straight-line mouth to represent an indifferent day.

6

Using Resources
Inside and Outside
the Classroom

The school building is no longer the exclusive preserve of learning. Today's teachers realize and appreciate the fact that children can learn anywhere. Professionals know that the community is one of the most important sources of instruction, for it provides children a diverse set of experiences that is quite different from the activities offered within the classroom. The community is a rich source of hands-on encounters vital to boys' and girls' understanding the world at large, promoting relevance between what is happening in schools and in neighborhoods.

In addition, the community is useful as a source of assistance from the persons who can introduce many appropriate discussion topics by appearing in the classrooms from time to time. Here again, the same story told by a different voice, a new interpretation or point of view, or some unique expertise which the teacher cannot in person provide all justify the involvement of parents and other citizens in face-to-face encounters with the students.

Where it is impossible either to interact with the community firsthand or to benefit from nearby representatives, teachers must rely on vicarious experiences presented through a variety of media. For one thing, media capitalize on the visual and auditory imagery to which youngsters by now have become accustomed and to which they are closely attuned in their activities. Furthermore, media, by presenting the same or similar information in a quite different manner, entice children into the topic at hand.

Most schools have several major types of media for regular instructional use. However, not all professionals are trained to operate this equipment effectively; and even those who have been schooled in the operation of the major machines could benefit from some of the shortcuts and alternative uses that experienced media persons recommend.

Basic to the use of any resources, of course, is parental support. While some schools develop major campaigns for enlisting parents in developing and assessing instructional programs, most educational establishments do not have such a structured approach. Whether or not parents and teachers work together on a formal basis, however, they can participate informally in many activities; this both involves parents in assisting and observing teachers at work, and also extends and deepens their understandings and appreciations of what a teacher accomplishes with children during the year. Equally important is the fact that teachers can enhance the importance of the parent's role. And as these parents come to school, their offspring will begin to see how the educational process is truly a cooperative venture involving many different people.

PLACES TO GO, PEOPLE TO SEE, THINGS TO USE

Alternatives Afield

There are many situations that arise during field excursions that call for sudden changes and ready adaptability on the part of children and teachers alike. Before the field trip begins, give the students some advance idea of what contingency plans you have in mind. In this way they will see the value of planning for all possibilities, and will not be disappointed if things do not go as they anticipate. You may have to contend, for example, with bad weather, vehicle failure, illness, or traffic delays. You can prepare for each contingency by having on hand alternative places to visit in the event of bad weather, interesting story papers or worksheets or puzzles to distribute if the children are forced to wait for service, and sources of aid in the event a child becomes ill. Have in mind or at hand a variety of simple games to play that do not require much equipment. Such activities can be used for rest time during an all-day outing, as well as for emergencies. Explore beforehand the site you are about to visit to see if it might provide other learning experiences and sites besides those originally intended.

Bag of Tricks

When substitute teachers come to your classroom, have available for them in a special spot in your site a collection of materials that are particularly interesting for your pupils, but which you reserve for only those times when a substitute is in charge. Typical items are games, poems, puzzles, books, and no-contest quizzes. Place these in an interesting container such as a suitcase, a picnic basket, or a toy chest, and rotate the items occasionally to keep them fresh and interesting. Have as well some small nutritious snack, such as dried fruit, peanuts in the shell or fruit rolls, that the children may have during the instructional day when you are gone.

Catalog Sources

When you are looking for free information and ideas, catalogs are important resources for two reasons. First, specialty catalogs can provide a lot of picture material to cut out, mount, and incorporate into your instructional program. Solicit from parents special-interest catalogs that have to do with their own occupations and special hobbies. Activities include building vocabularies by naming the items pictured in the catalogs, classifying items, describing their applications and uses, and including items in many different arts and crafts experiences.

Second, catalogs pertaining to educational material are also excellent sources for learning. The pieces of educational equipment discussed, the learning aids described, and the games depicted are good ways to expand your own instructional materials simply by adapting the ideas presented and making your own items. Let the students help as you collect discarded items to adapt.

Commercial Suppliers

Most of the major industries that produce goods and services on a nationwide basis have a variety of free things to offer for classroom instruction. Perhaps the single best source of such commercial supplies is the set of reference books published annually by Educators Progress Service in Randolph, Wisconsin. Each year this company produces more than a dozen books that tell teachers the current offerings of posters, charts, diagrams, coloring books, booklets, pamphlets, free rental films, etc. Each item mentioned is described in considerable detail, and note is made regarding the age of pupil for which it is most appropriate. While it would be impractical for a single school to purchase all the volumes in the series every year, there is compelling reason for a district of size to maintain a current set every year in a central office, since approximately 30 percent of the contents are new every year. If nothing better can be managed, a given school building ought to invest at least every second year in the volume that lists free curriculum materials, as well as the volume that lists free rental films. The cost of such an investment is well paid back over any school year in terms of the value the students and the teachers derive from these free items.

Construction Sites

If you require scrap materials for a variety of projects, it is often to your advantage to explore new building sites, or sites where a building is being razed in pursuit of things you can use in the classroom. In regard to old buildings being torn down, there is a number of applications of items to science classes, for example. Often it is possible for you to salvage panels to use in making partitions for your classroom. Think also in terms of scrap lumber from which you might construct major playground equipment or build a loft in your classroom where the students can study and read.

In regard to new building sites, investigate the possibility of rescuing scraps of lumber, siding, scrap metal, and wire. Occasional bricks or concrete blocks are usually not wanted and, with permission, may be removed. Pieces of interior siding and acoustical tile are thrown away, along with scraps of tile and ceramic and linoleum that might work well into a crafts program. Keep alert for scraps of rugs and carpeting for soundproofing your classroom and for giving your students comfortable seating on the floor. Be on the lookout for large cardboard cartons in which built-in appliances and cupboards are shipped. Ask for crates, bits of finish trim for the interior, and shingles that can be incorporated into a construction center in your classroom. If nothing else, ask the children what they could do with the scrap items you have salvaged from these sites.

Counting Noses

On any field excursion, your main responsibility is to keep track of the students at every point. One convenient way to accomplish this is to be sure that there are enough adults present to chaperone and count the group, appropriate to the age of students you are escorting. Have each adult helper identified by color and by symbol, and give him or her a list of children in that cluster who are similarly coded by color and by symbol. When the attendance must be taken at various checkpoints, the adult in charge of each section merely tallies his or her small group and reports to the person in charge of the trip.

A variation of this idea is to assign each child a partner. When taking roll, the partners must stand next to each other. Numbering off these pairs is yet another possibility. If you are responsible for young children moving through a large and confusing crowd of people, or where there is any danger of difficulty, provide a long rope into which you have tied either knots or loops. Call this rope your "magic rope," and ask the children to cling to the knots or loops as they move from place to place. If this rope is elasticized, it will provide some "give," thereby making the tugging and pulling less strenuous on small arms. Yet another idea is to assign several students to hold on to a plastic hula hoop at the outside, thereby giving them a point of reference as they move about a congested or dangerous area. Older boys and girls can be shown a distant landmark at which they are all to assemble, particularly if any member or any pair should happen to become separated from the total group. If you assign seating on a bus or other conveyance, your checking is also simplified as you only need to examine the seats for occupancy.

Emergency Trip Provisions

When on a field excursion, make sure you have supplies for emergency treatment. For one thing, have with you a foil-lined bag for motion sickness. Also include at least one light-weight plastic raincoat and/or a fold-away umbrella for the purpose of summoning assistance in inclement weather. Have a small kit on hand for simple clothing repairs: a set of safety pins, needle and thread, extra shoestrings, and disposable tissues. An extra pair of undergarments for young children would also be thoughtful. Simple supplies for sterile treatment of emergency cuts and bruises might also be included, depending on your school's policy in this regard. You might include mints for upset stomachs. Make a point beforehand to see if professional first aid is available at the site you are to visit. Be sure you have abundant coins for telephone calls, in the event a major crisis occurs.

Evaluating Excursions

As you participate in a field trip, have on hand a set of note cards or a notebook in which you can record the main elements of the trip, the questions raised by your students, and their reactions to the points of interest, as well as any problems you encounter. After the trip is over engage your students in an evaluative discussion regarding the most interesting or the most useful aspect of the trip. While younger children may choose to dictate experience stories or write their own, older boys and girls are not necessarily so eager either to write reports about the activity or engage in a prolonged discussion. You might suggest, therefore, that these students dramatize with hand puppets certain exciting, interesting or useful aspects of the venture. Or, they might produce paintings or drawings or other representations of the expedition. Some children might want to write thank-you letters. Tape recording impressions of the trip is yet another possibility.

Excursion Booklet

When your students genuinely want to write extended impressions of an excursion, suggest that they write original stories and then combine these into a booklet to share not only with their classmates, but also with the hosts at the site of the trip. Your own trip booklet might include quite different information, however, for as you have occasional opportunity to visit many sites, combine your own data in one place: the telephone number of the host, the visiting hours, the name of the person to contact, the street address, the best mode of travel and best route, facilities for eating, toileting, playing, and parking, free or fee-basis nature of the place, safety precautions, and special management problems. Include in your professional booklet questions about each site that might stimulate the visitors' curiosity and interest. Encourage your co-teachers to add their own impressions and information to this booklet and let it be readily available in some central location for all your colleagues to use.

Factories and Agencies

When exploring your community for free and inexpensive items to convert into learning materials, first contact your local chamber of commerce to see the names and the nature of the businesses and service agencies. Make a point to visit each likely source and ask about the availability of either commercial items prepared specifically for children to use, or discarded items that easily could be recycled into things for play and for learning. Many members of the community readily contribute such things to school personnel if they understand clearly that the appeal is made on behalf of children. This is particularly true when you also add that such donations of discards will be recycled, thereby benefiting the environment. Furthermore, you can point out that any materials given to your class members will save the taxpayers indirectly by providing ready materials for instruction instead of necessitating their purchase.

If, in your examination of local businesses and agencies, the managers are not sure if there is anything you could use, you might suggest that they give you a tour of the facility, thereby not only showing you what they do or what they produce, but also familiarizing you with their contributions to the area. If and when such items can be found useful for your classroom, send on school stationery a thank-you letter, with carbons to the local chamber of commerce, to the president of the company, and to anyone else who might appropriately be given a good word regarding the accommodation of your requests. Wherever possible during the school year, arrange either a field excursion to these local plants on behalf of your students, or ask the persons who work in these nearby establishments to come to the classroom to explain their work and their products.

Folders for Subs

In fairness to both your children and to the person who must replace you when you are absent, always have on hand a brightly colored folder prominently placed on your desk, in which you include and keep current the essential information needed by a substitute teacher. Include in this folder the plans for at least the next day. Indicate the location of your main teaching materials and manuals. Have available a master schedule of your instructional day. Add the emergency procedures, such as disaster drills and evacuation routes and fire drill instructions. Provide an up-to-date roster of your students' names, including phonetic markings for correct pronunciations of unusual names. Indicate on a seating chart where the children are customarily located during instruction. Have available the addresses and telephone numbers of the children. Indicate how and where the substitute can get in touch with persons in the event of emergencies. Make a special point to include in the folder the names of several students who can be relied on for accurate information and assistance during the day. Point out potential problem areas and those children who might need special support and attention.

Fun for Subs

Leave instructions with both the substitute teacher and with your students that a portion of the day toward the conclusion of the session can be set aside for freely chosen activities. Have on hand items of high interest, or simply allow the students to engage in activities they have selected themselves. Leave instructions that at the substitute's discretion, this period may be shortened if the class has not responded well at any time during the day.

General End-of-Day Critique

Whenever a substitute teacher is engaged for your classroom, ask that person to leave behind a general evaluation of how things went. Such a critique might be in the form of a series of anecdotal cards. Let the children know that the substitute will be asked to do this, and that he or she will be encouraged to solicit from the children themselves their own impressions of how the day went, while receiving, in turn, the impressions from the temporary teacher. Mention to the class that if the general report is satisfactory, upon your return they will be given special privileges as a thank-you for their cooperation. To add interest to such an assessment of the interaction between the substitute and your children, encourage the use of a tape recorder in which the teacher may actually register the events that happened during the day, and/or ask the pupils to voice their own impressions of how the day progressed.

Helpers at a Distance

It is not possible for every adult to come to school to help you in classroom activities. It is important, therefore, that as you sample the skills, the interests, and the time represented among your parents and your community, you identify those persons who would be willing to support your program without necessarily being present in the school building. For instance, there are many senior citizens in private residences or in nursing homes who would be more than willing to prepare simple materials for your instruction, assuming that you provided them appropriate and adequate instructions beforehand. Still other adults of any age would enjoy corresponding with some of your children. Perhaps some of the members of your community would be interested in being "adopted" by your class. Think, too, of the parents who can build pieces of equipment for your students to use, who can repair items that are not functioning well, and who otherwise are glad to give you a hand without necessarily coming to school.

Introducing Substitutes

To help your students respect and respond appropriately to the substitutes, ask these professionals to come to your classroom beforehand and get acquainted with the youngsters. Suggest, too, that the people who come to your classroom under any supportive arrangement be referred to by an appropriate term: "parent teacher," "paraprofessional teacher," "professional replacement," "peer teacher," and "pre-service teacher." These new terms will intrigue the children, will point out that there are many different kinds of teachers, and will suggest that each competency or set of competencies ought to be respected.

Introducing Trip Concepts

Before a field excursion occurs, prepare the students by tying in the site with the concepts you have already been studying. Encourage the children to formulate questions they would like to have answered. Make a list of these questions as a means of comparing their queries with the results of the trip once it is completed. Let the class members suggest what they think they may discover at the trip site, and then compare these guesses with what actually does happen. List on the chalkboard the new words they are likely to hear and discuss the meanings of unfamiliar concepts. Send to the host at the site a list of questions that might be anticipated. If the children are riding any great distance to the site, prepare for them a checklist of interesting things to look for along the way. Make this list into a sort of scavenger hunt, as you ask intriguing questions such as, "What is on the sign next to the clock tower we will pass?" or "How many times did we turn right before we arrived?"

Kids as Tutors

Explore the skills represented among both your own pupils and the children elsewhere in your school system. In the grades higher than your own, there are almost always students who have unique talents in many different areas that might be incorporated into your instructional day. Send around a questionnaire to sample these interests and skills, and obtain the permission of the other teachers to release such children occasionally to share their competencies with your own class members. This is especially important in situations where students could use some boosting of their self-confidence by practicing their skills with less demanding pupils. While some schools have long ago established training programs through which older pupils learn to interact with younger ones, all too often these arrangements involve secondary students in menial activities such as checking papers and listening to youngsters read. Thus, it becomes important that you select students who will have an opportunity to present their special skills and interests to your class.

Lost on Trips

Before any field excursion takes place, discuss with your children the procedures they should follow in the event they get separated from the group or otherwise disoriented. Remind the students of the adults to ask for assistance, whatever the need. Remind the class, too, of the information they have placed on their name tags. Recommend that each child bring along on any trip at least enough money to make one telephone call, if necessary. When you are at the site, point out landmarks for the students to remember visually. Identify one gate or entrance at which all persons are to gather in the event separation occurs. Recommend that all items of clothing, such as hats and coats, be labeled by name, address and telephone number. With older students in your group, distribute maps of the site and orient the students regarding where they will be moving within that facility.

Name Tags for Trips

Depending on the age of your children, have them or adult helpers make name tags with information such as name, address, the name of the school and the school address, the home and school telephone numbers, and the name of the place visited. A name tag can be cut from scraps of plastic jugs or bottles and worn with a safety pin. Or these can be fashioned to be worn in the pocket, around the wrist, or from the neck on a piece of yarn. Use fabric tape to color-code the name tags appropriate to each sub-group, and involve the children in thinking up an interesting name for each cluster. You might want to make a name tag appropriate to the place being visited: for example, a tag can be cut in the shape of a zoo animal or an Indian feather. Young children might enjoy wearing their name tags as hats cut into interesting shapes and tied securely under the chin.

Parents in Classrooms

While most schools have not established a tradition of having parents involved in classrooms as helpers, there is much to be said in favor of this practice. In the first place, teachers are more likely to take special care to implement the best methods if they know they are likely to be observed from time to time during the year. Second, as parents are involved informally in instructional programs, the children begin to grasp the importance of what occurs in their own classrooms. Third, teachers begin to view parents as co-teachers with the best interests of their offspring at heart. Finally, and most practically, since the demands on a teacher's time are increasing by the year, there is no good reason to turn down a willing pair of hands.

In the beginning, it is important to structure parent assistance. This might be done by circulating among your pupils' families or the neighborhood at large a questionnaire to discover what talents and time the parents and other community members might be willing to share. In order to get better acquainted with your parents, at the outset of this program schedule their appearances in your classroom to give you a chance to see which persons best fit in with your instructional necessities and the personalities of the children at hand. Later on, you may decide to liberalize the scheduling, encouraging certain parents and members of the public to come more often for a greater varietyof service opportunities.

It is also essential that you do not entrust parents with the pedagogical tasks for which training is required and which rightfully are your own responsibility. However, in suggesting routine types of help they might give, allow them to select some of the more interesting tasks to engage in. Do not simply expect them to do the unpleasant or boring tasks you have neither the time nor the interest to perform. Where possible, encourage parents to demonstrate specific skills associated with their own hobbies or livelihoods. There are many ways in which they can demonstrate what they ordinarily do as a part of an interesting instructional day and thereby enhance their children's sense of worth among their peers.

Permission from Parents

Whenever you are planning a field excursion, make a note to obtain from the children's parents a form granting you permission to take their offspring along. Provide the parents with an information sheet, giving full details of the nature and the purpose of the venture, and have a tear-off portion at the bottom that is to be returned to you. Allow ample time for this to be done to avoid anxiety among the pupils regarding whether or not they may attend. Most schools insist that written permission be obtained before any such trip is taken. Discuss the manner of transportation, and indicate that such carriers are insured against accidents. Indicate special fees, the food to be sent along, if any, and the appropriate clothing to be worn. Set a deadline for such a response, but make sure there is at least one day leeway for the forgetful parent or the careless pupil to make adjustments in getting the permission slip. When you go on a trip, take along with you these permission slips to protect you in the event an emergency arises. Have a photocopy of the slips left at your school for back-up proof of permission. In the rare situation a parent might prefer his or her child not participate in such a venture, provide appropriate alternative activities for that child with another teacher or at home, depending on the policy of your school administrator.

Rest and Refreshments Afield

Allow ample time for resting and change of pace, particularly if there is much physical energy required on the trip. You can help yourself in visiting a multi-story building by beginning your exploration at the very top and coming down during the session, rather than climbing stairs when the pupils are tired later on. Take along in a knapsack or other convenient container several simple items for play. For example, a long jump rope could be used for several jumpers at the same time, beanbags or an inflatable beach ball are other suggestions. Locate play areas near the site you are visiting. Locate the drinking fountains and restrooms. Include in your supplies quick-energy food items that quench thirst as they restore vitality. Take along picnic jugs with juice or water, and include a nested set of small paper cups for the children to use.

Rummages and Auctions

In looking for free items to use in your classroom, be aware of the tremendous possibilities represented by garage sales, rummage sales, auctions, and other such sales. You are likely to find there clothing that can be cleaned and adapted to dramatic endeavors, hardware appropriate for science experiments, books to stock your library shelves, play equipment and games, rugs and carpeting, pieces of furniture such as rockers, desks and tables, and other items to be adapted for your class. Tools, fabrics, and storage containers are other frequent possibilities, along with speciality magazines. Make a point to appear at the conclusion of some of these sales and offer to cart away free of charge any items the owner may care to donate to your children, assuming that such an item might be appropriate to your needs.

Seating for Subs

Whenever a replacement teacher is to be in charge of your classroom, prepare beforehand a personalized seating chart in addition to the one you regularly choose. Using large movable pieces of stiff cardboard, indicate on each one the age of the child, the general ability level, outstanding achievements, close friends, birthdates, special learning needs, particular interests, and any other personal data that might help the substitute to become quickly acquainted with that child and also to be able to help him or her learn. To accommodate these cards, prepare a chart in a folder form that enables you to place the cards in appropriate slots to represent the seating arrangement on any given day. These cards can be moved about as the children change their location in your classroom.

Secondary School Sources

If you maintain close contact with your colleagues in the local junior and senior high schools, you may be able to salvage many useful items to enhance your program. For example, the shop teachers may be able to provide scraps of metal, wire, wood, and electronics that are no longer useful. These items may be included in play or dramatic activities, or incorporated into interesting constructions in your classroom. The home economics teachers, in turn, may be able to provide remnants of fabric, ribbon, or yard goods. From time to time there may also be damaged cartons related to the kitchen experience. A print shop might be a good supply of print books for alphabet samples, discarded type, and paper printed on one side. The business education people might be able to furnish computer paper, computer cards, carbon paper, duplicating masters, envelopes, and folders.

Senior Citizen Aides

The elderly members of any community are a logical and rewarding source of much assistance. In the first place, senior citizens not only often have time that needs to be constructively occupied, they also need the social contacts that keep them in touch with what is happening in the neighborhood. Seniors also have many skills and much information to contribute to children still in school. Furthermore, it is to the children's advantage to be frequently exposed to the elderly, because with frequent contacts youngsters are more likely to accept them as fellow human beings with much to share, thereby avoiding the usual prejudices and stereotypes so often associated with the process of aging and the nature of the aged. In addition, seniors can provide a willing pair of hands to tend to many routine aspects of your instruction, particularly those that require much patience but no planning or pedagogical training. Here are just a few good examples of things seniors might help with.

- Demonstrate games they played as children.
- Teach popular songs of the "olden" days.
- Share some of the history of the community, complete with a photographic display.
- Relate how your school has developed and changed, comparing early enrollments, school textbooks, children's library books, report cards, and curricula.
- Bring to school some of their favorite storybooks and read these aloud to the children.
- Engage in a storytelling session, retelling some of their childhood narratives, or reminiscing about their past experiences of note.
- Demonstrate on a map where their ancestors came from and show how the migrations populated your own region.
- Bring to school examples of antique devices and explain how each one worked. Compare these with modern machines and inventions.

- Dramatize in costume the dress and mode of life of people who lived long ago, particularly the colonial era or the pioneer times.
- Demonstrate how foods used to be prepared and preserved. Show the children how to bake bread or how to churn butter. Compare their typical menu with what is customarily eaten today.
- Compare the kinds of stores available in your town years ago with those presently in use. Note the difference in merchandise available and the ways in which advertising and merchandising methods have changed.

State Department Sources

One place of information often overlooked in one's search for free and inexpensive data for instruction is the governmental body. For example, at the state level the departments of tourism and transportation are good places to request folders of the state's points of interest, along with maps and other travel information. The department of agriculture or forestry can share professional items in areas of soil conservation, ecological concern, and the like. Sometimes items of furniture and equipment are available at low prices from surplus stores maintained around the state. The state office of education occasionally has on hand publications in various areas of program development and curriculum, which give you good suggestions for enhancing your methods, activities, and materials. Museums often have exhibits that travel from school to school, and sometimes share through the mails items of interest in natural or historical areas of study. Films and filmstrips are often lent without rental by various state agencies. Make a point, too, to contact your city governments, council of the county, and other regional representatives. All sorts of personnel are working in extension to tell people about their services and their products. Thus, they can serve as resource persons in many areas, such as social studies. If nothing else, have some of these local municipal and agency people talk to your students about how the local government works.

Stores and Businesses

The local commercial enterprises are a veritable gold mine of supplies, simply because they represent such a wide variety of discarded and close-out items you can add to your collection with no trouble and at very little cost. The ever-present grocery store, for example, is a source of banners, streamers, posters, flats, stand-up figures, and cartons and containers of all sizes and descriptions. A department store or an appliance outlet can supply you any number of large cartons, fabric scraps, packing materials, etc. Office supply businesses can provide trade-in machines such as adding machines and old typewriters. Feed stores, mills, and grain elevators often throw out burlap bags and sometimes have seeds and seed catalogs. Any agency that uses business machines and computers has discarded paper, tapes, computer cards, and outdated forms. Where appropriate, leave your name and telephone number with these suppliers, promising that you will come to collect upon request or once a month, for instance, those items that you can use in your classroom. In this way, they will be helping you and the children learn, and at the same time be reducing the number of things they must discard or otherwise waste.

Textbooks to Salvage

While old textbooks are not always appropriate for routine instruction, good thinking and planning can convert much of their content into appropriate learning activities on an individual basis. For one thing, children might be permitted to work from outdated items on a strictly voluntary basis, since youngsters are often attracted to such "historical" items. You might also decide to cut out some of the practice exercises and attach them to cardboard panels for individualized instruction. If you laminate these pieces, the children can write directly on them and check their own accuracy before rubbing off their work for the next person in line. Check the textbooks for small maps, diagrams, illustrations, pictures, and similar representations that might be similarly removed, attached to a card for adding to a growing file of resource information. In addition to collecting discarded and worn textbooks, be aware that schools often accumulate sample copies of new textbooks that are sent for examination purposes when series are being reviewed. Use as many of these as possible for individual students who may be studying either at, above or below your present grade level of instruction. By diversifying the materials on hand, you will help prevent the comparisons of abilities that children otherwise make when they are all working in the same textbooks.

Timing Your Trips

Keep in mind that the timing of a field excursion is crucial to its success. For one thing, the trip ought to coincide with a legitimate and generally-held interest on the part of your students. Things that are seasonal prompt certain types of trips, as well as those that coincide with holiday celebrations. Wherever possible, avoid huge crowds by trying to schedule trips to places during their off-season. Resist the temptation of trying to see everything in one given spot; rather, concentrate on only those few activities and exhibits that best relate to your classroom studies. Visit those spots that are the most appropriate to the time and the attention of your students. Schedule the trip to reach the climactic moment when interest is still high, rather than having an anticlimax later in the event. Plan for the most demanding activities, whether intellectually or physically, to occur early in the day, with less taxing demands on your students later in the venture. Allow some extra time in your schedule to accommodate unexpected events. Plan for a return to school or to your neighborhood well before the point of exhaustion of either your children or the adult chaperones.

Trip Impressions

To aid your children in recalling the trip later on take along a camera and photograph the children participating in the various activities at the site. These pictures can be displayed later at a parent meeting. Take along a tape recorder, too, and use it to register the children's impressions, questions, and responses, as well as the explanations offered by the host at the site. In addition, tape record the background noises during the trip to and from the site and challenge the children to identify what made each sound. A tape recording of animal sounds or airport sounds or farm machinery could also be useful in providing a background for later dramatizations.

Walking Tours

There is no need to think that a field excursion must take place at some distance. On the contrary, there are many advantages of observing the local neighborhood you can reach on foot. The local schoolyard, nearby parks and backyards have tremendous possibilities for science exploration, and local cemeteries and points of historical interest can involve the children in thinking about social studies. You can examine firsthand how local people go about their work, asking them questions and seeing what they produce. Sidewalk science can involve something as simple as observing what happens to concrete when it's poured or what lives in the cracks in the sidewalk. Use the school building itself as a laboratory for

looking at heating and cooling systems, the diversity of occupations, and the examination of commonplace machines. In the event you take small children on such an excursion outside the school grounds, you might consider pulling along a small coaster wagon to carry supplies on the way out, and transporting tired children on the way back.

MAKING MEDIA MEANINGFUL

Chalkboard Lines

Provide lines for practicing handwriting on your chalkboard with the aid of a commercial music liner. But instead of using chalk to make erasable lines, use a felt-tip marker in each arm of the holder. Select a section of chalkboard that can be permanently marked, and then make lines that cannot be erased except with a thorough scrubbing of the chalkboard. Let the students use this same music liner loaded with chalk for marking areas of the chalkboard that are to be temporarily used for handwriting practice. Encourage the children to use such sections of chalkboard to write their original stories on during composition period, and also register their mathematics practice problems. A second suggestion is to place small screw eyes into the frame of the chalkboard at either end and tie stout twine to these. Using soft carpenters' chalk, snap a chalkline across the board for handwriting practice.

Chalkboard Questions

Several suggestions may help you use your chalkboard more efficiently. One trick is to write test questions on the chalkboard before class begins and then pull down a roller map to cover these questions until the children are ready to work on them. Aspects of regular routine classroom discussions may also be registered this way. As the class gets involved in the activity of the moment, raise the map roller slightly to expose the item next higher up in the listing. Add interest to this sequence by numbering these items in reverse order, aiming for a "Blast off" or "Lift off" legend at the top of the list. Or, you might ask the children in turn to walk up to the chalkboard and erase each item as it is completed or discussed.

Chalkboards in General

The chalkboard still has great appeal for students who rarely tire of writing or drawing on it. They particularly enjoy serving as the demonstrators of a procedure for the other members of the class. They like to use the chalkboard as welcome relief from paper and pencil exercises. It can serve as an effective art medium, too. Make a point when the children are working at the board to check the contrast of the chalk with the surface they are using. Some yellow chalks do not show up well on tan or green shaded surfaces. You might use good quality white chalk if this is a problem. Stand at the farthest limit of the classroom and examine what effect different chalks have on the board. Make a point not to use artist's chalks on your chalkboard until you have made sure these will erase completely.

Look around for discarded chalkboards that might be salvaged from schools being remodeled. Then cut these into small fragments resembling the old-fashioned slates, one for each child to use as an individual surface for practicing handwriting, spelling words, math combinations, and other kinds of personalized efforts. When groups of children work on the same kinds of questions, check their answers all at once by asking them to hold up their slates.

A further suggestion is to distribute to your students bits of sponge and let them use water to explore the large movements that are necessary to handwriting and art activities. Involve these sponges in other practice experiences, such as those requiring several persons at the chalkboard at the same time. As problems are given or tasks are assigned, the children can write their responses on the surface. The answers will evaporate by the time the next task is presented.

Chart Uses

The chart is a versatile item because it can be adapted to many purposes. Language experiences of many kinds can be recorded as part of a reading program. A chart can register the children's best handwriting efforts. Charts can also serve as pages of oversize books for the students to read themselves, share with classmates, and share with younger children.

If you choose to preserve charts for long-term use, laminate them with clear vinyl. Make a point, however, to do any lettering of captions with water-based felt markers before you laminate or otherwise cover the chart; if you do not use the water-based felt markers, the colors have a tendency to "bleed" underneath the covering. If you are not sure beforehand, experiment first and see which types best retain their colors.

If you have quantities of unlined newsprint, convert the paper into lined charts by inserting three or more felt-tip markers in a music liner. To make sure that your lines are straight, run the holder along a meter stick laid across the chart paper. In some instances, if you have the newsprint stacked neatly in a pile, the top lines will bleed through and will make a faint impression on the next sheet in the stack. This will eliminate the need of measuring each successive sheet of newsprint.

Charts from Shades

Salvage from your children's families or obtain at auctions or rummage sales discarded spring-type roller window shades that are of a single light color and relatively clean. Use felt markers to convert these into charts, posters, diagrams, and other kinds of permanent information of general interest to the members of your class. Facts about the solar system, phonetic generalizations, multiplication tables, and conversion tables for metrics are just a few examples that can be kept at the ready. Mount the charts on brackets at the top of the chalkboard. When these items are no longer needed during the school year, carefully store them away in the long corrugated boxes in which fluorescent light tubes are sometimes shipped. Label the end of each container appropriate to the chart inside.

Duplicator Masters

Any time you run off a complicated drawing or a diagram that might need to be traced again at a later date, save yourself much time by running off as many good copies as you can possibly manage from the very first impression, putting these aside in well-marked boxes or folders for subsequent use in later months or years. Whenever you make such a complex item, do it in dark carbon pen so there will be adequate contrast, in the event your school has a machine that can make duplicator masters from thermal copies.

Another way to save time is to run through a fresh duplicator master as one of the first copies. In this way the initial impression will be recorded on this second master. Later on you will only need to trace the details of this fresh master.

One way to diversify the children's art work and other efforts is to salvage from the school office and from your colleagues scraps of duplicator carbon in sizes of sufficient nature to give the students at least appropriate working space. The children can then be encouraged to make original drawings and other projects to be duplicated for distribution to their peers and their parents.

Films in Action

Motion pictures are more dramatic than most other media, although they are also more expensive to rent or to purchase. Some schools develop a film cooperative that buys movies, thereby minimizing costs. Another approach is to discover sources of free rental films produced by major commercial organizations. It is always wise to preview films for appropriateness of contents, and to formulate questions to ask the children before, during, or after the showing. From time to time, stop a film in mid-reel to discuss its contents. Sometimes show the movie first without the sound track or narration. Then let the children invent or predict their own story. Show the film a second time to confirm or compare their suggestions with that of the producer. A further idea is to stop a film before its end and ask the students to guess how it is likely to end.

Filmstrips

The filmstrip is virtually a universal medium. It is not too expensive to own, and can be used over and over. It does not necessarily have to tie in with a mandatory time frame, particularly if you have the narration in print as well as on tape. The mechanical aspect is even usually within the capabilities of even young children. In addition to the basic informational aspects of a filmstrip, use the medium in any or all of these ways:

- Show several frames of a strip and then ask the children to recapitulate the order and contents.
- Project one frame of a strip onto a kraft paper background and let the students outline main shapes and areas for a class mural, or simply as painting or coloring activities.
- Project an interesting image onto a white sheet or muslin. Explore ways in which this image can be used as the background for a dramatic production.
- Since children like to make shadow figures in the light of the projector lamp, immediately after a story filmstrip is concluded let them invent some of the characters of the story using their hands. Or, have them assume silhouette poses of the action in the scenes depicted.
- Explore the possibility of using blank filmstrips that are sold in long rolls and in complete kits. The children may use these blanks for drawing original miniatures. Then they may compose a caption or a story segment to accompany each frame. If you do not want to keep these segments year after year, let the students write on these with water-washable inks.

Flannelboards

The flannelboard is a convenient medium for both younger and older students. Many fabrics can be adapted to this purpose, and remnants or salvaged items reduce the cost considerably. Much of the materials for flannel presentations can be stored in flat boxes also recycled from clothing stores, department stores, or the children's families. One of the best fabrics for this purpose is Pelon, a commercial material obtained from a dress shop or a fabric store. This material is sufficiently translucent to permit you to trace large bold figures, such as those in coloring books. Pelon will absorb line drawings from felt-tip pens without running. You can easily cut the fabric with scissors, and if you choose to make large backgrounds, it can be rolled up and stored inside a tube or stored flat between two sheets of cardboard.

In regard to other elements of flannelboards, experiment with scraps until you find the ones that best suit your needs. Rough fabrics, styrofoam scraps, carpeting samples, and sandpaper can all be adapted to this medium. A sample carpet square serves nicely as a miniature flannelboard all by itself. You can use flannel to enclose a magnet board simply by sewing it into a pillowcase and inserting the magnet board. The magnetized letters and numerals and other items you have in your classroom will thus adhere to this fabric-covered surface.

A flannelboard box is made by obtaining a large sturdy shallow container, such as a shirt box or a hosiery box. Cover the inside of the lid with flannel, and store the cutout shapes of fabric inside the box. Prop up the lid whenever the flannelboard is to be used. Cover the box and put it away when it is not in use, making sure beforehand that the edge of the lid is labeled with the contents of the box.

Frieze

A frieze is easily made by having the children draw a series of pictures on the same or similar subjects and then gluing them to a cardboard backing. You can then tape these units together into one long continuous line of related pictures to be displayed above your chalkboard or bulletin board. If the children are interested in adding more dimensionality to the elements in this frieze, show them how to cut out and overlay additional pieces of cardboard to make the items project farther into the room.

If the cardboard used in the frieze is sufficiently stiff and if the tape is durable, a frieze can be displayed upright on a tabletop, accordion-folded in a way that each element can be

self-supporting. The entire unit can then be collapsed easily for quick storage when the particular unit of study is concluded.

Still another good suggestion for a frieze is to make standard printing blocks from large pieces of cardboard and yarn glued to the surfaces. These items can be covered with paint, using a brayer, and then pressed down in turn onto a large and long piece of plain paper. The children can then embellish these printings with additional paint.

General Handy Hints

You can do a lot to make the use of your equipment more effective, even if your budget does not permit many media in your school. One important consideration is to have all major items mounted on wheeled vehicles. This provides greater mobility and allows you to share with your colleagues the supplies and the machines that are so essential to an instructional program. If the matter of purchasing wheeled vehicles is out of the question, contact some of your parents who have already expressed an interest and a skill in such matters to construct from scrap materials a satisfactory cart or conveyance. Where such a device might have several or many smaller items contained on or in it, it is also wise for you to have a listing of everything that belongs with that particular wheeled vehicle. If more than one cart is used in your school, make a point to color-code them to indicate what things are customarily included on each one.

A common complaint is from people not experienced in the operation of mechanical devices. You can do a lot to help your students and your colleagues use the machines successfully. First, post on any machine the exact operating instructions, including appropriate diagrams. Write these simply and in large type, with numerals representing the various steps in things that must be done sequentially. In addition, make a point to post a troubleshooter's list of common complaints which even young children can read and respond to. Further color-code the knobs to show appropriate settings for volume, focus, and the like. Paint the "start" buttons green and the "stop" buttons red. Have with each machine a carton containing extra bulbs or replacement items, with simple directions for their installation.

Magazines

Periodicals are appropriate for a variety of reasons. For one thing, you can subscribe to children's magazines and then use the stories as a regular part of your reading instruction. You can cut out story material from many magazines and incorporate these into composition and spelling practice. Magazines are also appropriate as sources of pictures to stimulate vocabulary development. Many high-quality publications contain pictures that are ideal for posting in a miniature art gallery. Other illustrations can be converted into greeting cards. To obtain periodicals at no cost or at low cost, frequent rummage sales, garage sales, auctions, and second-hand stores. Or, simply appeal to your children's parents for back issues, making note of special interests they identify on questionnaires at the beginning of the school year—crafts, travel, hobbies, photography, and flying are just a few examples.

Maps

Maps of many kinds are readily available either free of charge or inexpensively from many commercial sources such as highway departments, travel agencies, gasoline stations, and chambers of commerce. Other good sources are the local junior high school, secondary school, or college where, on occasion, maps are upgraded and updated and the old ones thrown away. For greater durability, glue an entire map onto a large sheet of posterboard. Then cut out the various elements with a jigsaw and use the pieces as a puzzle to be reassembled on the floor or on a tabletop. A similar idea is to convert a large scrap of oilcloth or plastic into a map with the addition of scraps of colored fabric tape. This latter kind of a map can be rolled up and stored in a cardboard tube.

Murals

A mural involves children in informative and constructive activities at the same time. One approach to a mural is to assign each of several groups of students a different but related subtopic. Children can then work simultaneously on different portions of the project, and the entire work assembled for display at the conclusion of the group effort. Another approach is to divide the responsibilities for the mural in this way: one group might do the preliminary drawing, a second group might undertake the background painting or shading, and the third group could add the details or the attachments. To add variety, show the children how to cut flaps into the surface of the paper so that the flaps can be lifted up and opened out to reveal something hidden underneath. At the conclusion of the unit of study, the mural can be cut apart for distribution to the various students who were involved in its preparation. Or, you might choose to roll it up and store it for the coming year. Then it could be used to show the new class what the other children did along the same or similar lines of inquiry.

Overhead Projector Activities

An overhead projector is appropriate for many projects. One is to enlist the children in preparing a movie roll by cutting to size and length the heavy-duty strip of plastic obtained from a hardware store. Attach both ends of this to cardboard tubes salvaged from the children's families. Let the children make it either in one long continuous strip or mark off the strip of plastic like segments of a filmstrip to be shown one at a time and then moved ahead.

As a more direct instructional tool, the overhead is helpful in letting the students see the actual handwriting, spelling, composition, mathematics, and other skills demonstrated like a wall-size image. The children can be engaged in examining this work for possible improvements. To protect the sensitivities of your students, however, make a point to collect from year to year those examples of children's work that would be the best to the points at hand. Do not give the names of these children so that your present students will not have to worry about public embarrassment.

Overhead Projector Tips

Sometimes teachers are not aware of some of the ways they can enhance the use of this projector. One of the common mistakes with the overhead is that the person making the presentation sits or stands in the line of sight of the viewers, so be sure you are not in the way. A second suggestion is to cover with a piece of paper or cardboard the items being projected that you are not interested in discussing right away. If your transparency is revealed in its entirety the very first moment, the children will lose interest. Instead, it is better to reveal the items one by one.

If you are in need of inexpensive transparencies, cut to size and shape pieces of sturdy but flexible plastic purchased by the yard at hardware stores or lumber yards, or salvaged from your children's families. Add color to the overhead with scraps of cellophane that can be taped to a transparency. This same set of cellophane scraps can be used in examining color-mixing as a part of an art or science experience.

The overhead projector is also invaluable in its use as a source of enlarging for bulletin boards cartoons and other drawings you have collected from catalogs, comic books, and coloring books. By simply adjusting the distance of the projector from the wall, you can make an image virtually as large as you would like it to be. Such images would first need to be traced on something transparent so the projection against the wall is clearly seen. Sometimes you might want to project the image onto a large piece of kraft paper as a part of a bulletin board decoration. After you are done with that particular motif, you can then roll it up and store it in long cardboard tubes salvaged from gift wrapping. Make sure each tube is identified regarding the rolled-up picture inside.

Overhead Projectors and Science

The stage of a projector helps to examine many real objects in the world. For example, sprinkle iron filings onto the stage and demonstrate the magnetic field as you lay a fairly large bar magnet onto the stage and tap it until the filings arrange themselves accordingly. A clear glass fishbowl is also useful not only for the study of fish shapes and swimming, but also to introduce color mixing as you add food coloring to the bowl. Dissolving materials in this water is yet another activity. Or, you might choose to sprinkle sugar water on the stage and then study the insects that are attracted as the classroom windows are briefly left open. Mealworms and other slow-moving insects might also be the objects of examination.

Posters

A well-executed poster can add a dash of color to your classroom or convey a direct instructional message. Decorative and informational posters are often discarded by commercial groups, such as travel agencies and major organizations that make automobiles and foods. If you want your children to salvage and prepare their own, instruct them to contact a local supermarket or department store to request they donate to your classroom their weekly or seasonal posters which otherwise are destroyed. These large pieces of paper or cardboard can be cut apart for the colorful motifs, as well as oversize letters and numerals. Some of them, of course, can be used intact. If nothing else, use the plain back sides of each poster for the children to produce their own inventive creations on themes of current interest.

Programmed Materials

Work experiences that your students can check themselves are useful because they free you from the task of checking up. Second, the students do not have to wait to find out how well they are performing. Their mistakes are quickly found and corrected, rather than being perpetuated while they await your appraisal of their efforts. There are several useful ways to convert ordinary items into programmed materials. Write on the edge of every worksheet the answers to problems being worked on that page. The boys and girls can fold these underneath during the time they are working on that page. Or, the answers may be printed upside down at the bottom of the page, or printed on the reverse side of the worksheets you duplicate. In many instances, you could provide a tagboard overlay with rectangles cut into it that match the positions of the questions on a particular page. The children can thus place the overlay on top of their papers when their work is done, comparing the accuracy of their efforts with the answers inside each cutout section of the tagboard.

Proper Patterns

There are some occasions when you would like to have on the chalkboard the pattern of a picture or a design that is to be filled in later. If there is ever this need, first make on a large piece of posterboard the outline of the object to be made, and then with a compass point prick holes to outline the picture. Press the posterboard against the chalkboard and load an eraser with a lot of chalk dust. Tap this eraser against the posterboard. Remove the drawing to reveal a series of dots in place on the chalkboard. Dots will enable you to make a drawing to complete the image at the appropriate moment.

Realia

Give your pupils many opportunities to share the real objects they accumulate during the school year. One suggestion is to make a collection of gift boxes, each with a plastic lid, such as greeting card boxes. These can be used to display interesting shells, stones, or other souvenirs of travel. Another possibility is to assemble realia in one place by topic by salvaging from a retail store a carton that has inserts which form a matrix. A third suggestion is to assemble an assortment of colorful egg cartons, each one labeled in keeping with its contents. Collections contributed by the children can be incorporated into learning centers as well.

Sand Table

While sand tables have historically been associated only with young children, they are useful devices for older students as well. Realistic dioramas can illustrate many concepts of science and social studies. Place the sand in a large plastic swimming pool on the table or on the floor. Place a rug directly underneath the table to catch any sand that falls. When the sand becomes a problem in cleaning up the classroom, you might consider substituting materials such as a box of sawdust usually obtained free of charge from a lumberyard. If you live in a rural community explore the possibility of using soybeans, millet, wheat, oats, rice, or other small grains for this same purpose. Such loose materials are also appropriate for a variety of activities involving measuring.

Slides Suggestions

Colored photographic slides are easy to take and have many applications in the classroom. If you are an active summer traveler with a camera, examine your own collection of photos taken during recent years. Many slides fit well into studies of geography and history. In addition, some slides work well in art appreciation or may stimulate art production. Slides of your pupils' year-round activities are most appealing to parents and can serve as the basis of discussion in parent-teacher meetings conducted during the school year. There are also readily available sets of slides for purchase that can enhance the children's understandings of many of your typical subjects of study.

You can easily make your own slides for special purposes by projecting line drawings, diagrams, and constellations of stars prepared by scraping the emulsion from underexposed or blank slides that you salvage from the children's families. You might also consider salvaging discarded filmstrips, cutting these apart into separate frames, and letting the boys and girls embellish them, or scratch away parts of the emulsion, and then enclosing them in holders that are available from camera shops. Whenever you happen to use any slide, cut one corner off or make a notch in the appropriate corner to let the operator know in the darkness which is the proper display of each image.

Tape Recorder Activities

The tape recorder is a commonplace object that has many instructional possibilities. One of these is to tape record instructions for your children to use in accomplishing specific learning tasks. Tapes of assignments can be made routinely each day for those persons who are absent from the classroom. You can use the recorder as a listening aid or to register original stories, poems, and music performed by your students. Another idea is to tape informational programs broadcasted on radio or television. These might serve as the natural narration to the students' interpretations of stories or news events in a dramatic setting, or as a vocal background to original illustrations being made as an art experience. The tape recorder is also handy for dictation given by children too young to write their own stories, to dictate spelling lists to students who are working independently, for interviewing persons in and out of the school building, and for registering impressions on field trips.

Tape recorded materials can also be exchanged with teachers and students in other schools. They can be sent along to persons of varying ages who are confined to bed at home or in hospitals or nursing homes. The tape recorder can help children polish their speaking or conversational skills, as well as reveal to you your own instructional style during the day.

Textbooks

Because they seem to be present everywhere, textbooks sometimes fail to attract the attention they deserve as learning aids. Many teachers plow through them page after page, trying to cover all the material, whether or not the topics coincide with their students' interests, the season of the year, or other subjects of study. The textbook, therefore, is not best used when the number of pages is arbitrarily divided up by the number of days of school remaining. Furthermore, the textbook should usually serve as a reference rather than as a reader. Children should never be asked to read orally from a text unless they have become thoroughly familiar with it beforehand.

Since the children in any classroom read at different levels, you might inquire into diversifying the titles available to you on the same or similar topics, rather than purchasing the same book for every child enrolled in your class. In this way you are much more likely not only to have content presented within the reading capabilities of all the persons in the classroom, but you will also, without spending any more money, provide your group different editorial points of view and greater range of subject matter. The textbooks can be arranged on one shelf and then checked out to the students as they are needed.

Tracings

Children of many ages enjoy tracing, which can be used with many subjects. One simple approach is to set aside a portion of a window that admits direct sunlight. Have a pile of onionskin paper or other appropriate thin paper and provide tape for the students to use to adhere the paper to the window for their tracings. A stage of an overhead projector might also be used instead of a window. Another idea is to salvage scraps of carbon paper from the school office and let the pupils use these. A light bulb placed inside a glass terrarium is still another suggestion, if a clear piece of sturdy plastic is placed across the top of the container.

Another variation is to have the children make rubbings of different items, such as coins used in mathematics explorations. Use the side of a soft lead pencil for this purpose. Other rubbings can be made with the side of a dark crayon. A sun fade is yet another type of tracing. Make this by taping various posterboard shapes onto a larger piece of posterboard and placing this in the window facing direct sunlight. After a few days, remove the large posterboard from the window and remove the shapes. Shadows are left behind. Projected shadows made with an overhead or an opaque projector are also interesting elements in the learning environment: shapes of states in geography, shapes of geometric forms, and shapes of animals are just a few possibilities for shadow tracings.

Typewriter

Every classroom ought to have some kind of typewriter, even one that has been salvaged from home, purchased as a trade-in at an office supply store, or bought at an auction or a second-hand shop. The students generally enjoy learning how to spell their words by typing them out. You can also use the typewriter to record the items your children dictate to you. Older students can use it to prepare their own stories or make a class newspaper or booklet. Regardless of the quality of your machine, however, provide appropriate instructions for the children in its use and care, and encourage them to protect the life of the machine with consideration for it and for their classmates who also might want to use it.

When a typewriter is not readily available, inquire into the possibilities represented by purchasing or obtaining a toy printing set, complete with movable type that the students can manipulate themselves in making legends and captions, and in practicing the appropriate selection of letters for new spelling words.

TELLING PARENTS TALES OUT OF SCHOOL

Communication Competencies

Taking special pains to communicate with parents pays off in many different forms during the year. First, it anticipates and clarifies points of potential misunderstanding. Second, it provides information that lets the parents know what to expect during the year. Third, it presents you as a person rather than as a disembodied name at a distance, and shows your parents that you take the extra effort needed to maintain two-way communication.

Perhaps the most obvious and most effective means of producing this communication is to have a variety of interesting and well-prepared student projects going home day after day. The parents will see the variety of activities you introduce to their children and will be able to see the general level of competency their offspring attain. Frequent supportive notes are also essential here. Find many opportunities in your day to reward and reinforce and recognize your students by sending home congratulatory messages. Utilize a simple form that can easily be reproduced. Make a point to telephone the children's parents for many positive reasons during the year, too, since parents often think that any communication from a teacher is problem-related. Provide the parents your own telephone number at home and at school and encourage them to contact you when genuine concerns arise.

The production of a classroom newspaper not only gives the parents some notion of their children's activities and skills, but also allows the students to demonstrate special abilities as they prepare and distribute it. Such a publication is easily made if you allow the children to use their own duplicating masters as they do some of their better work from week to week. At the end of a given unit of instruction or simply at the conclusion of a given period of time, each child's efforts can be run off quickly and the students themselves can staple them together and take them home to share with their families.

One important application of good communication has to do with parent conferences. Whenever these occur, make a point to give the parents specific examples of certain achievements, behaviors, and needs. Jot these down on a daily basis in the margin of your plan book. These examples will stick in the mind long after the conference is over. Remember to avoid technical language and jargon that only teachers use. Speak plainly and to the point. Avoid terms that are inflammatory, such as lazy, liar, troublemaker, and cheat. These words are stereotypic and non-describing, and are likely to close the mind of parents to further discussion. Make a point to identify behaviors, but do not label them.

Conference Considerations

The parent-teacher conference represents an ideal setting to exchange information about your children. While such events are primarily matters of common sense, several items merit special attention:

1. Begin any conversation with an itemization of the pupil's strengths and continue to stress the need to maximize potential.

2. Avoid making this encounter a gripe session. If the parent tends to complain a lot, redirect the conversation by asking him or her to make specific suggestions about how the situation might be remedied.

3. Be accepting of any negative feelings and frustrations. Everyone is entitled to his or her emotions. Assure the parents you understand how they feel, especially if you are a parent yourself. In this context, liberally use the expressions "We teachers . . . " and "We parents . . . ," indicating the fact that parenting and teaching are very much alike.

4. Be prepared to offer several options or alternatives for the solution of any problem. Have at hand the names of professionals or agencies that might help resolve difficulties.

5. Ask the parents to suggest the kinds of things that seem to work well with their offspring at home. Make the point, however, that a child in a large group of peers in a highly structured setting is not necessarily the same person they may know in the privacy of their own homes.

6. Whenever you give suggestions of things the parents might help with at home, ask for a commitment to at least one measure of support, and be sure the parents understand what is expected of them and agree that it seems reasonable. Do not overwhelm them with things that ought to be corrected, but give the opportunity for success with one or two major and most pressing factors or methods. Mention that after an agreed-upon period you will once again contact them and find out how things are going.

Educational Experiences Inventory

In assessing your students' backgrounds early in the school year, make a survey to sample the things they have already done and learned. You can then suggest they share their expertise with their classmates from time to time. This will not only demonstrate to them that important learning occurs outside the school, it also reinforces the notions of confidence and competence that are so essential to making a reasonable effort in acquiring new learnings in schools. The simplest way to compile such a questionnaire is to ask all the students the very first day of school to write down a sampling of all the interesting things they have ever done or the most interesting or worthwhile things they have learned. Then combine all this information into one list, casting out the duplications. Once again ask the children to respond to this extended list prepared by the class as a whole. A few sample items might include:

- visited a museum
- talked long distance on the telephone
- went camping
- visited a national park
- took a bike hike
- paddled a canoe
- did a science experiment
- went up in a tall building
- flew in an airplane
- rode a train
- went to an ocean
- made a collection
- played on a team
- invented something
- cooked something to eat
- made something to wear
- appeared on television
- won a prize
- found something valuable
- met someone special

Enrollment Data

Whenever the students in your school enroll for the year, in addition to the usual information the institution might request, prepare your own parent survey to give yourself added insights into the nature and the needs of the children you will be teaching that year. Here are several sample questions:

- What is your child's attitude about coming to school this year?
- What are your main expectations of what your child might learn in school?
- How does your child generally behave in a group?
- Who are your child's best friends?
- Does your child have any problems I should know about?
- Is there anything your child fears?
- When does your child usually go to bed?
- Who usually lives in your household?
- What television programs does your child generally watch?
- What languages are spoken fluently in your home?
- What pets, if any, are in your home?
- What community activities does your child participate in?
- What major travel experiences has your child had?
- What regular household responsibilities does your child have?
- What special interests or hobbies does your child engage in?
- How does your child get to and from school?
- What is the most effective method of discipline to be used with your child?
- What previous group experiences has your child had?
- What did your child best like about last year's school experience?
- Can you write down several words that best describe your child?

Facilitating Conference Attendance

Whenever you need to confer with parents, make it as convenient as possible. Suggest that you would be glad to meet in their own home, in your home, or at a neutral site, such as a local coffee shop. Offer to provide transportation if it is needed. Schedule conference sessions as flexibly as possible to suit the hours of the parents. Late afternoons or evenings ought to be considered. Open the school building and the gymnasium equipment for all school-age children properly supervised to use, in the event two or more teachers are involved or two or more families must come. Engage qualified older students to serve as supervisors of younger children.

As the parents arrive for their conferences, make the school building and the classroom as agreeable as possible. Many parents have had unfortunate or unhappy experiences in schools, and some of them are fearful of teachers as a group. Ameliorate these negative sensations by serving light refreshments in a central place, such as a lobby or a lounge. Have comfortable furniture, such as easy chairs and rockers, at the conference site. Remove the teacher's desk or table as a barrier between the participants. Have on display the projects the children have done, and provide scrapbooks of typical products of their efforts. Decorate the conference site cheerfully with potted plants or fresh-cut flowers or children's art work.

Handbook Hints

Whenever you or the school administrator prepares booklets containing enrollment information, involve a group of children in preparing the covers before they are sent home to parents in the summer or the fall. Challenge the older students to think of drawings and suitable captions: "Getting A-Head," "Back to School," "Facing the Year," "What Everyone Nose," "Eye Can Do It," and "What We Kneed" might appeal to the older students in your classroom. If the number of covers is not great, you might also have the students prepare colorful paper by using any number of interesting effects: printing objects, fingerpainting, stencils, marbelizing, or simply making interesting drawings of things related either to home or to school.

Handbooks for Parents

Whether or not the school itself issues a handbook, you might help your parents know what to expect by distributing the first day an informal handbook to include items that might otherwise be overlooked. Include topics of interest such as:

- when and how to let off and pick up children at school
- when report cards are issued and what they include
- when parent conferences and parent-teacher meetings are scheduled
- symptoms of the most common childhood illnesses
- the general school calendar
- what to do and whom to contact when the school is closed due to emergencies
- how to mark clothing and other materials for ownership
- the main fees that are required and how and when they are to be paid
- the principal expectations in terms of conduct
- the main learning goals, units of study, and subjects
- how to send money and important messages to school
- how children are to dress appropriate to the weather or to school activities
- specific ways to help the children learn
- times and conditions under which parents are encouraged to visit the classroom
- policies on birthday celebrations, holidays, and other special events
- the nature, officers, and function of the local parent-teacher organization
- the policy on reporting absences
- the purposes of homework and how best it may be completed
- special requirements associated with certain subjects, such as physical education
- statutory requirements regarding physical examinations, vaccinations, medical records, emergency numbers, etc.
- ways in which parent volunteers can help at school

Parent Assessment

Just prior to a parent conference or as an end-of-year evaluation, engage your children's parents in a simple survey that asks questions about the child, the classroom, and the school. Where you request confidentiality, prepare a form to be sent back anonymously. Questions might explore such areas as:

- What does your child discuss most often that relates to school?
- What does your child enjoy most about this year in school?
- What does your child enjoy least about this year in school?
- In what does your child think he or she is most capable in school?
- What does your child generally do when school is not in session?
- How successful have I been in helping your child learn this year?
- How successful have I been in communicating with you this year?
- What might you like to have me change in my procedures next year?

Parent-Teacher Organizations

The groups of adults who support the school programs can only be as strong as the individual members. While teachers tend to complain a lot about the lack of interest on the part of parents, the teachers themselves sometimes fail to fulfill all their obligations to such an organization. For one thing, at any meeting in which both professionals and members of the public are present, make a point to intermingle and not sit only and always with other teachers. Similarly, when you are engaged in informal conversations with parents, forgo shop talk for the sake of finding out what the parents are interested in discussing.

Engage your children in modest contests to see how many parents attend week after week, preparing a simple graph to record the results. Have in your classroom a child serving as host or hostess. Let the adults sign in on a guest register. Have many interesting things made by the children for the parents to explore. Encourage the students to write messages for their parents to read and respond to as they visit the classroom.

Enlist the children in preparing appropriate art projects that further interest their parents in coming to school for parent-teacher meetings. One obvious suggestion is to have the children outline each other as they lie down on large sheets of kraft paper. Let the students paint in their clothing in keeping with the garments worn on the day of the parent-teacher session. Then see if the parents can identify the figure of their own offspring simply by examining the clothing. If the children are more ambitious and if you have enough time, let the students cut out two identical outlines, and after decorating them front and back appropriate to their clothing, staple these together and stuff with wads of newspapers.

Another idea is to prepare large cardboard cutouts suitable to a nursery theme, such as The Old Woman Who Lived in a Shoe. Let the children take instant photographs of each other (or draw freehand) and then post the self-portraits in small windows cut into the cardboard replicas.

Banners in the windows or on the doors welcoming parents are always well received by adults. Tape recorded messages are also appreciated.

Pupil-Parent Conferences

Some children become fearful of what goes on in parent-teacher conferences, especially where student progress reports are used as threatening devices or as disciplinary measures. In such instances, it might be better to confer with the child first, explaining what you plan to tell the parent at some other time. Another suggestion is to tape record the conference, with the permission of the parents beforehand. As you gain the confidence of both the parents and the children, schedule occasional three-way conferences with yourself, the parents, and the students. In this way, all members can hear what everyone else has to say without the need of interpretation.

Scheduling Conferences

While some schools set aside after-school hours for days of early dismissal, or else close school completely for a day or two annually, scheduling a conference is sometimes better done if there is a particular need at any time. In fact, parents are sometimes more receptive to a conference when there is no need for them to worry about the next person waiting in line. This special effort is almost bound to pay off in terms of greater respect for you and for your concern for their offspring.

Welcome Visitors

To encourage your children's parents and other adults to visit your classroom during the year, make a replica of a welcome mat that you hang on the door or place near it. You might also make a hardboard or plastic replica of a large key which you offer to any visitor who comes to your room. Also ask a child to serve as a host or hostess in finding seating and materials for the guests, to introduce them to the other members of your class, to share major items the students have made for just such a purpose, and to make the guest feel at ease.

7

Assessing
Students' Progress

The assessment of students' progress has always been one of the main tasks of classroom instruction. The information generated by the various instruments and techniques has for years constituted the backbone of this evaluation. However often and in-depth professionals have assembled data about their pupils, though, the key to successful measurement is how well and how extensively these findings are incorporated into subsequent instruction.

With that goal in mind, teachers do well to examine how many child study techniques can be utilized in examining the backgrounds of their students and the qualities that these pupils bring with them to the school. In addition, wise teachers become well acquainted with all the standard measures that are customarily used to determine yet other capabilities and learning needs.

An element of interest may be added to assessment as the students themselves are included in self-checking activities. In this way, the youngsters quickly ascertain their progress in the various subjects of study. In addition, students are able to detect their errors of fact and judgment as they occur; such a detection of error not only minimizes the anxiety that some children experience in assessment, but also reduces their time spent waiting while the teacher tends to his or her red pencil. Besides, as the teacher adds elements of fun and humor to the process of self-evaluation, the students are motivated to both take charge of their own learning and to engage in it with greater enthusiasm.

Qualities of high interest can also be used in stimulating the regular review experiences that are so necessary to acquiring the main skills at every grade level. Whenever a teacher can turn a chore into a challenge simply by introducing a game or by converting some drudgery into a high-interest activity, he or she is much more likely to foster longlasting learning. What is more, students who cope with concepts in a happy climate are much more enthusiastic and persevering about continuing their practice activities whether or not the teacher requires them.

The matter of rewards can also do much to spur students' best efforts. While many teachers choose to recognize and reward only those few pupils who achieve at the highest levels in each class, more insightful and compassionate professionals realize that many students have skills that are only rarely accommodated on the traditional honor rolls. Then, too, the matter of greater effort and appreciable gain are qualities that deserve all the public attention they can get. Since there is theoretically no limit on how much any one person can learn, the matter of rewarding as many students as possible is consistent with the goal of helping all students achieve as much as they are capable of, interested in, and need. By adding different techniques and various dimensions to the pedagogical repertoire, teachers can accomplish these instructional objectives.

THE CHALLENGE OF CHILD STUDY

"All About Me" Booklet

Periodically during the school year, ask your children to write on personal themes that explore their feelings regarding various aspects of their relationships with family members, friends, and peers. These can be free-form stories done on topics such as "Brothers are ...," "Sisters can be ...," "Sometimes parents ...," etc. Other elements from time to time might include their feelings and insights about pets, home responsibilities, television viewing, athletics, reading, hobbies, and similar subjects. Ask the students to combine some of these compositions into booklets titled "All About Me." Because some of this information may be quite personal in nature, it is wise for you to indicate before each assignment in this series that the stories will be read only by you and will not be shared with the other members of the class or their parents. To encourage the students to be even less inhibited about their personal expressions, assure them as well that you will neither grade these items nor correct them.

Autobiography

Early in the year each child ought to write a summary of his or her life thus far, with the understanding that such a report might deal with personal feelings, life ambitions, learning goals, and other information that will give you insights into how to plan a learning program for each student. If there is general agreement that such personal writings might be produced for general consumption, encourage the students to rewrite their compositions and bind and decorate them attractively to be added to the materials in the classroom reading center.

Fantasy Stories

Encourage the children to freely exercise their imaginations as they write original stories. Such compositions may not only provide insight into their creative instincts, but may also suggest their values and their self-perceptions. Topics might include some of these at the beginning:

- "If I Had a Million Dollars"
- "If I Were King (Queen)"
- "If I Had Three Wishes"
- "A Magic Carpet Ride"

- "The Rainbow's End"
- "When I Grow Up"
- "A Trip Through Space"

Free Play

Play activities have long been used as a way to find out about children's feelings and relationships and to help the students cope with life's problems. Young children often respond well to either doll play or puppet play, expressions that allow students to speak through the make-believe characters they manipulate without fear of criticism for their opinions. This security of the impersonation shelters them from blame, conflict, or argument. Older children may choose to use role play as their medium. Sometimes this involves donning a costume and/or a mask to represent someone or to act out an incident. Role play also occurs naturally in the housekeeping center in the preschool and primary classrooms. This medium can also be applied in the unstructured play on the playground at recess or before or after school. Even as children interact on the swings and the games, the observer can gain valuable insights into their interests and their ability to relate to peers in social settings.

Inventories

In order to plan an appropriate instructional program for your students, you need to collect much information from them early in the year. One useful device to use is an interest inventory. You can either ask the children to list the various things they are interested in under various categories of activities, or you can provide your own checklist and have them mark off the appropriate interests. A second related idea is to have the students complete an educational experiences inventory. This instrument simply asks the children to list or mark a list of learning experiences they have already had. They can thus briefly indicate what they have already accomplished in athletics, reading, science, travel, and many other areas that are allied with their in-school tasks. If you need more specific information, you can develop a checklist of concepts and/or skills to sample learnings already acquired.

Listing Rules and Rights

Your children can share with you the various school-related behaviors they think are important in one of several ways. One idea is to have them share the rule-making process that must regulate the general order and the discipline in any classroom. Do this the first few days of the school year by engaging students in extended discussions concerning what elements of self-governance might be included in an original list of regulations compiled by the students themselves. Or, ask the youngsters to write an original list of "Ten Commandments" that might condition their conduct in the classroom. Also engage them in identifying a "Bill of Rights" for children that would guarantee them the respect and consideration they are entitled to during the year.

Parent Checklists

At the beginning of the school year, send home a checklist of attributes for the parents to fill out, providing you impressions in advance of their offsprings' capabilities, interests, and needs. This will help you to compare the outlook of the parents with the actual attitudes and achievement of the children. Include a wide variety of elements on the checklist, or prepare more than one checklist to sample attitudes, values, habits, playmates, discipline, home responsibilities, fears, relationships with siblings, preferences of subjects to study, and personal problems. Make a point to assure the parents that all such information will remain confidential with you.

Picture Clues

Sometimes it is possible to gather data about your students simply by having them create pictures. One possibility is to provide photographs or other pictorial materials where the meanings are ambiguous. Tape record, if appropriate, the children's free discussions of their pictures, or record the highlights anecdotally. A similar idea is to have the children draw their own self-portraits, past, present or future, and then talk about them. Have the students draw pictures of their own families and discuss their relative position in the cluster. Or, make captions for cartoons, or complete unfinished sketches.

Self-Reports

During the year ask the children to share with you some of their occupational aspirations and interests. This information can help you plan reading and social studies projects. It also might lead you to let each child think of him- or herself as preparing for a particular adult role, to the extent that they might dress appropriately and accumulate pictures of tools and equipment that are used by that particular occupation. A second type of self-report is an "I Think I Am" checklist consisting of many different personal characteristics. These might call for a "Yes-No" forced choice, or require an "Always-Sometimes-Never" ranking.

Sociograms

A good way to study the social relationships among the students in your class is to give them an opportunity to provide data on a sociogram. For example, the children are asked to list three people they would like to work with on a given classroom project. Represent boys with triangles and girls with circles, and use arrows to show attractions, mutual and otherwise, as you plot the relationships indicated on the queries. You will find that some pupils are highly regarded and others are virtually isolated. Since your aim is not to devastate any person's self-concept, make a point to assure that everyone has a chance to have at least one choice in the persons who work together. Also, set up each situation as a legitimate opportunity for persons to work together, so the students will not focus on which class members chose each other. Another good suggestion when using sociograms is to allow several different opportunities during the year, because friendships do change from time to time. Also, there is the consideration that a person might choose another to be on an athletic team, but would choose someone else quite different to make a mural.

Story Situations

Children often provide you with information about feelings, aspirations and values through creative writing activities. Provide the group an unfinished story, particularly one including a problem situation. Then ask the students to resolve the issue either individually or as a group. A similar suggestion is to ask the students to interpret a fable or a parable that is presented to them. Acting out in dramatic form some familiar tale from a reading class also gives special insights into children's creativity.

Unfinished Sentences

This projective technique taps the children's first or most thoughtful answer to an open-ended stimulus. You can get special insights into self-perceptions and peer and family relationships as the students respond to such situations as:

- I feel worried when . . .
- My parents think I am . . .
- I believe my brother (sister) is . . .
- The nicest time was . . .
- I get mad when . . .
- At school I like . . .
- I would change . . .
- When I'm sad, I . . .
- The trouble with teachers is . . .
- My favorite teachers all . . .

Values Scales

There are several good ways to find out what your students believe about various events and relationships as the year progresses. One possibility is to give students a list of statements, attitudes, or beliefs and have them rank these elements, listing the most important item first, the next most important item second, and so on through the list. Another possibility is to give the children cards, with a different statement written on each one. The students then sort these cards into two piles: agree or disagree. Several piles may be used if you need several degrees of agreement or disagreement. Or, you may use a checklist that registers these same statements. The students then mark their papers to show the extent of their agreement with these remarks.

ACTIVITIES TO ENLIVEN REVIEWS

Color-Coding

When children are permitted to correct their own papers, suggest that they use crayons, colored pencils, or felt-tip markers of a hue that contrasts clearly with the pen or pencil used for the actual exercises themselves. This procedure allows both the students and you to see at a glance those elements that require further practice. Similarly, when the children are performing routine practice such as tracing a letter form or a numeral, have the students select different colors of crayons or pencils for each successive tracing for ease of evaluation, or just to add variety to the experience.

Computer Carton

Let the children make a computer from a large cardboard carton salvaged from a department store, a furniture store, or an appliance store. Cut a variety of slots in this carton and

label each one appropriate to a different subject area. Decorate the entire carton so it resembles a gigantic computer. Inside the carton attach boxes or other containers underneath each slot. Let the children take turns sitting inside the computer, either answering the questions orally or returning answer cards through these same slots. The interchange of review cards ought to enhance the children's acquisition of the desired information.

Deliberate Mistake

From time to time play a game with your students in which you make some deliberate errors in your verbal exchanges or as you write items on the chalkboard. Offer a small token or a treat for that child who first detects your error. This will sharpen your students' enthusiasm for catching your intentional mistakes of format or fact, and also keep the learning environment light and upbeat. Invert this activity by having the students keep track of their correct answers, along with your own, in a low-key competition to see whether the class as a whole or the instructor will get the higher score in simple review activities. The students will be delighted with the possibility of surpassing the teacher at some activity.

Diary Details

Ask the children during a given grading period to make a journal entry every day that indicates their general impressions of their progress, with specific details as to what they mastered during that session. At the end of the time, such journals may be shared with each other and with their parents as well. Let the students make interesting covers for each document. When the school year is done, these journals may then be taken home to serve as mementoes of the time they spent together.

End-of-Day Review

At the end of each day, make a point to identify the main learnings that occurred. This will help fix in your children's minds their individual accomplishments and will assist them in reporting these learnings to their family members once they get home. Have a large calendar posted near the doorway of the classroom and select one person each day to note on this poster the most interesting or more useful thing that happened that session.

Expert Panel

As an end-of-week or end-of-unit review, one Friday afternoon let the children submit to a panel of classmates slips of papers with questions covering any of the material that was studied during the period stipulated. Choose the members of the panel on a rotating basis so all class members have a chance to practice their skills. Stipulate that for each question submitted, that person must also provide the correct answer to it. Another idea is to set up a question box into which the children during the week drop cards with questions on them. At the Friday review session these cards are withdrawn and randomly assigned to the panel members for response.

Fact Mats

When the children are in need of special reinforcement of facts, make a laminated set of place mats for them to use at their work places. Each mat then serves as a source of information for review, and can be carried to the lunchroom for study while waiting to be served or while having the meal. Add to each mat some interesting cartoon characters, symbols and/or colors before the lamination is done. Sets of mats may be exchanged among your students or may serve as the basis of games. Those persons who master each set of facts might autograph the mat.

Fix-It Shop

To help the children develop a sense of accountability for accuracy in arithmetic, spelling, and other written work, let them take turns manning a table labeled "Fix-It Shop." Set up in one corner of the classroom a set of cardboard panels to represent a workshop, with original drawings of tools and equipment, particularly those devices that are used in the learning process. Let the students take turns as the fixer-in-residence. Their task is to examine their peers' daily papers for correctness by proofreading them and checking computations and other elements.

Game Formats

Any childhood game can be adapted to review purposes. Identify a game that all the children know and ask them to help you convert it into an appropriate review. Or, simply play a game according to the usual rules, but before any given player in the activity may take his or her turn, that class member must respond accurately or appropriately to whatever questions are posed. A mistaken response to the query means that that particular student must forfeit his or her chance to take a turn until the other students have all had their turns.

Good Guesses

Before you begin a new unit of study, write down in detail what you think your students already know about the topics to be undertaken, in effect making a pretest of their knowledge. Then administer this pretest and compare your guesses with what the students actually do know. Or, make a prediction of how well your students will perform over the unit of instruction. Seal this prediction in an envelope and post the envelope conspicuously in the classroom. At the end of the unit of instruction, compare your guesses with the students' actual performance. Your students will be challenged to outdo your preliminary assessment and try to prove your underestimates wrong.

Peer Helpers

Whenever you have students who are in special need of assimilating information or acquiring skills, let them share whatever competencies they do have with younger children who are enrolled elsewhere in the school. Contact other teachers who will allow your students to come to their rooms and share their reading or mathematics skills or any other competencies with the younger persons. Your students who work at slower speeds and lower levels of expertise will be delighted to share their knowledge with other persons, and will develop a heightened sense of worth.

On the other hand, if you have capable students in your class, let them work as buddies or partners with classmates who are in need of tutoring. However, arrange this situation so the capable students are not always at the command of their peers, for they should not be penalized by virtue of their talents and abilities. Nevertheless, many able students are delighted to share their time and their talents with classmates and often understand how to explain concepts to their peers better than teachers do.

Puppet Tutors

Use a puppet to demonstrate to slower or younger pupils how to perform certain skills. Youngsters naturally relate to such characters. As the students themselves use these puppet figures to explain the same processes to someone else, the puppet is entitled to make unintentional mistakes and the child is not put down. As classmates correct the puppet, there is no threat to the self-worth of anyone.

Puzzle Papers

Combine puzzles with any routine paper-and-pencil exercise the students are assigned to complete. After you have produced a set of worksheets for the children, for example, simply cut these into several large irregular shapes. The students using the sheets will first have to recombine the pieces before they can proceed with the work called for on the worksheet itself. Or, you may want to reverse the procedure by allowing any person who completes a worksheet satisfactorily to cut the paper apart into a puzzle and exchange that puzzle with a classmate who has similarly completed the cognitive exercise. Store each set of pieces in a salvaged envelope.

Quiz Slips

At the end of a unit of study, write on slips of paper the main facts that the children should have mastered. Pin these slips at random to your clothing and then walk around the classroom. Let individual students either answer a slip they have plucked off, pose that question to the class as a whole, or call on one student for the correct response. In any case, print the correct answer on the reverse side of each slip so the students can check the accuracy themselves. Later on, place these slips in a file box for review in other game formats.

Shingles to Show

Focus the students' attention on their individual and cumulative expertise by asking each child to make a "shingle" to stand up or hang down from his or her desk or table space. On this sign, which is made from light wood or sturdy cardboard, each child can identify one area of the curriculum that is his or her forte in which he or she can serve as an expert. Such resource persons can then take turns helping classmates during the day, particularly when reviewing familiar material.

"Show Me" Cards

There are many times during the year when your students may be expected to respond to simple single-concept questions posed to the entire class. You can readily check the accuracy of every member of any group simply by having them write down every conceivable correct answer to a set of queries, especially in the area of mathematics, where students might make themselves arrays of numeral cards. Use a different color of paper for each different answer, however. As the leader of the review activity poses a question, the students are given a few seconds to examine, but not touch, all the cards laid out before them on their desks. When this several-second interval is over, the leader says, "Show Me!" Immediately, all the children select and raise above their heads the card or cards that indicate the correct answer. The leader of the activity can quickly check the accuracy of all participants just by examining to see if the colors on the cards are all uniform. Repeated errors may then be identified and remedied.

Signal Systems

When you are checking the responses of a large group of children for mastery of simple factual information, invent a signal system to show you quickly how many students know the correct answers to the questions you pose. One suggestion is to have each child cut from sturdy paper or thin cardboard a circle that has a face drawn on each side, one with a hearty smile and the other with a frown. Whenever you ask a "yes-no" or a "right-wrong" question, the children can hold up the appropriate face so you can see how many correct answers are presented. Similarly, you can ask the children to use their own faces for a ready response: a happy grin for affirmative, a scowl for negative. Or, use the old Roman custom of "thumbs up" for agreement with a statement and "thumbs down" for disagreement. Here, again, a quick check of the students' hands will tell you how many pupils know the answers.

Teacher for a Day

Let the students occasionally take turns acting as the teacher of the class. You, in turn, pretend to be a pupil, sitting in the desk just vacated by that student and responding to any questions asked of you by the "teacher." Provide a special garment, a headband, an armband, or a badge to signify which student has the honor for that hour.

Trouble Spots

Children sometimes have difficulties with certain elements of learning. When that happens, label each major trouble spot with the name of one person who is having the difficulty. For example, the inability to handle multiplication of fractions might be referred to as "Mary's multiplication monster." A humorous cartoon picture might be placed on that person's desk. In this way the class members are made more aware that everyone has trouble from time to time, and that they should work together to assist their peers in overcoming them.

Wizard Cap

Adopt the old-fashioned dunce cap to bring recognition and satisfaction to your students. Fold a large piece of stiff paper into a conical shape, and decorate it with stars and crescents. Label it "The Wizard." Any child who wants to serve as an expert in a given subject area may, in turn, wear the hat for a portion of the day. Set up a stool or a special cubicle where the resident expert may answer questions.

Wrong Answers

For an interesting turnabout in review activities, suggest that on a given exercise only *wrong* answers will be accepted for an oral drill or an informal quiz. The children will then have to think doubly hard not to give the correct responses! Similarly, at examination time, instead of having the students think up questions to ask, suggest that each child bring a cluster of answers to the review session and challenge their classmates to provide any appropriate question to match these answers. Several responses may conceivably be appropriate in each case.

MEASURING THE RESULTS

Anecdotal Records

Maintaining a narrative record of what your students are doing during the year provides you with much information and gives the parents more information than a report card could ever convey. In addition, anecdotal records properly maintained are free of comparative judgments because the point of writing down the narrative is to chronicle the pupils' progress in relation to their own growth, regardless of what the other members of the class are doing. In addition, by keeping a written summary of achievement and behavior during the weeks you will not need to rely on your memory for data that is important in evaluating your students' development.

While some teachers find it difficult to establish a routine use of anecdotal recording, others have discovered that by committing just a few minutes at the end of each day to this task, their impressions are fresh in mind and there is an incentive to report before leaving at the end of the day. One approach is to report on only a few children each day. For example, if you have 25 pupils enrolled, write complete reports on five children every Monday, another five on Tuesday, and so on. Choose a standard size of index card, such as 3″ × 5″, that will control the amount you write each day. File these cards in a convenient file box, with each child having his or her own tabbed divider.

Another suggestion is to have anecdotal index cards in your pocket as you walk around the classroom or playground at recess during the day. You can write on these cards brief impressions as incidents occur. Or, you might have the cards, each with a hole punched in one corner, attached to a ring that opens and closes conveniently. Another variation is to obtain a set of different colored cards and color-code them so that one set will identify a certain project, a group, or a subject area. Such cards might be similarly associated with given learning centers in your classroom, each spot with a name incorporating that particular color label.

Averages

While grades as such convey very little information about either special skills or how a child compares with peers, many parents still insist on some statement of normative behavior. The comparisons ordinarily associated with issuing grades can be minimized, however, by making a list of expectations or learning objectives during a certain grading period. As each child accomplishes one of these tasks, keep a running tally of the total number of children in your class who have also achieved that particular goal. At the conclusion of the grading period, you will be able to show on a checklist that a given student has either attained competency at the task or not attained it; and you will also be able to show parents the number of students who have mastered that same skill or concept. The parents will then have some better knowledge of where their offspring stand in relation to their peers.

Bowling Scores

Whenever the children keep track of their own progress in spelling, arithmetic, or any other area that is relatively easy to score and record, reproduce replicas of score sheets for bowling, complete with the little boxes in the corner. Then as each student proceeds through a set of lessons, you can stipulate that for a perfect effort (or for one you mutually agree is worth special mention), the student can mark in the crossed lines indicating a "strike." A "spare," on the other hand, may be assigned a stipulated percentage or a number right. At the end of the ten "frames," ask the children to total up how many strikes, spares, and misses have been accumulated. Also suggest that inside each box the students write the name of each activity that is being evaluated. If you would like to get even more involved with this method of scoring, find a way to convert it into an actual bowling score and challenge the children each succeeding unit of instruction to improve their scores.

Can-Do Can

A good method of stimulating self-checking is the "Can-Do Can." Indicate the specific skill, along with a picture, on individually duplicated slips of paper. Have each child bring from home a medium-sized can and decorate it appropriate to a different skill. As either a concept or a skill is completed, a child may write his or her name on the matching slip of paper and drop it into the appropriately labeled can. When all the children's names are correctly represented in one can, a new can may be decorated and substituted in its place. Or, you may prefer to have just one large communal can and stipulate that the students write on the slips the particular skill they are trying to master. At the end of an assessment period, dump these slips out of the cans and have the children sort them out, then combine them into personal booklets with brass fasteners. These items may be sent home to parents as a multi-page report card.

Card Log

Where there is not enough interest or time for pupils to report weekly or daily achievements in a personal journal, give them index cards. Let the students write down the main things they accomplish daily, and also the special new skills learned any given day. Have them date each item and file it chronologically in a master file that is alphabetized by last name. As their parents come to school for conferences, the children's own written records can give some hints of the major activities and achievements they experienced. Suggest, too, that the students use these cards to give their opinions regarding what they liked or disliked about the day's studies, how well you as the teacher fulfilled your own responsibilities, and other feedback that will furnish you more complete data concerning how well the time was spent in school.

Checklist

Using a checklist either in place of the usual report card or as a supplement to it has several advantages. For one thing, the checklist provides parents with specific information regarding the skills you expect of the children. Second, it shows plainly which items have been mastered during the year and when they were accomplished. Another positive aspect is that the checklist records only successes, not making a point of enumerating failures. A checklist can also give the parents a general notion of the sequence of learnings as the child continues to add check marks during the course of the year. The children themselves can help check off these items as they are achieved, giving the youngsters immediate reinforcement and personal satisfaction.

Cumulative Folders

During the course of the year, have available in your desk or cabinet a set of folders, one for each child. Into these folders place representative work that the students produce during the course of each grading period. As you schedule conferences with parents during the year, the contents of these folders can be shared with them. You might also include the checklists of the major skills expected in the various subject areas you teach. Transfer to more permanent folders the more valuable or representative items.

Cumulative Grading

Lessen your students' anxiety over the course of the grading period by setting up a point system under which each performance earns a given number of points rather than a grade. At the end of each term, total the points and assign the grades to cumulative efforts. This technique can help in areas where it might be difficult to assign letter or numeral grades to minor exercises. A second idea is to provide a contracted approach, where you indicate the minimum number of points required for an "A," a lesser number for a "B," and so on down the scale. Under this arrangement, the children may select a level of accomplishment they can work toward during the grading period in a given subject area. You might also allow them to improve their grade by submitting more projects than the minimum number called for. Control the quality of the work submitted by stipulating that all work for credit must be acceptable, or must otherwise be corrected and resubmitted.

Diagnostics

The first few days of any school year ought to be spent largely in diagnostic procedures. In this way, you are less likely to expect children to learn things for which they are not ready, and not bore other students by having them repeat activities they have already mastered. One way to conduct diagnostics is to use the usual end-of-year or end-of-unit tests early in the year or ahead of the actual instruction of a unit. Instead of consuming actual test booklets, let the students use sheets of plastic or acetate to mark on. They can have the added satisfaction of knowing that the tests will not count toward their grades, and will have the personal satisfaction of knowing what they do know and don't know without having to make public the results of these self-checked tests. Use the information you collect to plan your instructional year.

HappyGrams

In most schools children are accustomed to having a progress report only at the end of a certain grading period; and even then they too often expect a summary to be expressed in mostly negative terms. Change this routine by duplicating at the beginning of the school year a ream of yellow paper, each page divided into sections, and each section with a symbol on it. Leave space for your personal messages, and then cut the paper into the designated pieces. A ream of paper will provide you with as many as 2,000 personal message blanks to use during the year! From time to time, surprise a child by noting something unexpected to comment on favorably. Or, suggest to your class that they look out for special commendations to be passed along to the parents. You will find most children are more highly motivated both to come to school regularly and to perform well and behave appropriately if they are regularly recognized and rewarded.

Marking Papers

When there are many papers for you to check, save your-self time with several different techniques. One of these is to have on a worksheet a pattern planned, into which the an-swers will fall if they are named or written correctly, such as, two on the right, three on the left, etc. Then, as you check the answers, you will only have to follow the pattern instead of looking at each response on the page. Similarly, if you assign a worksheet with a lot of answers on it, such as a mathematics page, cut out from light cardboard a template for each page. On the template write in the correct answers where they would appear appropriate to the questions that are on the pupils' worksheets. As the students answer each query, they are to write in their responses in the appropriate boxes on their papers. When the template is laid over each worksheet in turn, you will be able to quickly compare your answers with those of the students. You might also permit your pupils to check their own answers on routine assignments, thereby saving you considerable time.

Measurement Message

At the conclusion of the school year, it's a nice touch to send to the parents personal comments in a letter, either indi-vidually handwritten or duplicated. When the students are measured for height and weight in the spring, obtain an inex-pensive plastic or fabric measuring tape and cut it into snip-pets, each piece equaling the exact gain in height and weight attained by each child in the class. Tape this small item of tape to the top of your letter as an eye-catching introduction to your discussion of growth of other types registered by that particular child. The parents will be reminded of the physical development of their offspring, and will also be encouraged to notice other ways in which the children grow during the school year.

Measuring Line

Somewhere on the classroom wall, alongside a tape you have attached, keep track of the boys' and girls' physical development during the year. This will give them a good indication of the relative physical growth of their peers over the months, and will show the great diversity of measurements represented even in the same-age grouping of boys and girls. Expand this concept by also posting a tape on which you have written the major skills and concepts expected of your stu-

dents. Each member of your class can maintain as well a shorter version of this master list. As the students accomplish the learnings expected of them, let them fill in with a colored pencil or crayon the spaces on their own tapes. At the end of a reporting period, these tapes may be folded up and inserted into a small envelope to be sent home to parents.

Open Report Cards

When traditional report cards are used, children usually glance only at their grades without thinking about their needs or prospects for improvement. Change this attitude by presenting the students a blank report card and letting them estimate in pencil their own achievement, assigning themselves tentative grades in each subject area. Then compare these approximations with your own estimates and help them understand any reasons for serious disparities. Another approach is to send home blank report cards and ask the parents to bring these items back to school for parent conferences. This will give them a chance to review the criteria you should have listed on the reporting device. Then, when they come to the conference you can fill in the grades and comments on the actual report forms.

Original Report Cards

In situations where the official report cards are not adequate for your own purposes, make up a reporting device to supplement those supplied by the school. Make sure that the parents understand that these efforts represent a personal interest on your part, that they do not represent any other person's approach. With such a device you can provide anecdotal information about your pupils, credit personal qualities, reward effort, show growth in comparison with the individual's capabilities, solicit parents' comments in reply, and differentiate between objective facts and professional judgments of behaviors. Make duplicate copies of these more elaborate forms by inserting carbon paper between the sheets, and filing duplicates in the children's cumulative folders.

Parent Report Cards

In connection with your sending home the children's report cards, suggest to the parents that they send one back to you. Such a device might take one of several forms: you could prepare an informal form on which you inquire regarding pupils' applications of subject matter to their home situations, their cooperation with parental requests, and the like. It might also ask the parents to list in some detail the kinds of pupil expectations they think are reasonable for you to work on during the year. Or, have the parents evaluate your own pedagogical performance as understood and appreciated by them. Include on such a form the elements of teaching you think are important and/or ask them to suggest some.

Parent Visits

Encourage your children's parents to freely visit the classroom, especially when there is a need for them to examine the progress of their offspring in relation to the growth of the other class members. To facilitate these observations, provide parents with a checklist of skills and expectations of behavior that they might want to look for. A few examples might include:

- How does the child relate to the other boys and girls in the group?
- Is your child's language development and use about the same as that of the other pupils?
- Can your child work independently without difficulty?
- Does your child demand a reasonable amount of attention?
- Does your child show evidence of special abilities?
- Is your child confident and consistent in work habits?
- Does your child seem interested in what is going on?

Passports

Add interest to older children's efforts by having each person make a small booklet resembling in size and shape a passport. This might include personal information, interests, and learning goals. Then have the students record on each page the outcomes from a particular unit of instruction. Ask the students to salvage from their daily mail at home cancelled postage stamps. Whenever a given child completes a certain set of learnings satisfactorily, let him or her stamp with a library stamper the date of the achievement and then glue a stamp to that particular page or portion of a page in the passport. You might also suggest that each page be labeled with the name of a country so that the children can "travel" through a continent as they progress through their various projects.

Peer Assessment

Vary your evaluation procedures by asking the students to help evaluate each other's performance in school. This can be successful only where there are no high levels of competition for a limited number of rewards, and where the members of the class are reasonably mature and responsible. Peer evaluation gives a different perspective, for the students are made aware of their responsibility to promote the overall progress of the group and to act in ways that will permit everyone to succeed. The peer groups can meet in small face-to-face encounters, making comments on each member's strengths and suggesting ways to improve. Or, you might prefer to ask the students to respond anonymously to a questionnaire on which they name members of your class (including themselves, if appropriate) who have made significant contributions in specific areas identified on a form made up for this purpose.

Physical Measurement

Children are usually interested in being weighed and measured because these statistics serve as visible proof of growth. Add even greater enthusiasm to these events by having a measuring tape incorporated into a wall display of a rocket ship, a tree, a giraffe, or something comparable. Encourage the children to find and bring to school their measurements from earlier years. Or, as the students are measured in your school, prepare beforehand miniature "fortune" cards, such as were associated with weighing machines years ago. As each child is weighed, for example, he or she is randomly handed a card on which some amusing prediction is made.

Pupil-Made Tests

Once in a while ask the children to help you invent a test. Ask each class member to contribute questions and answers, and then explain why those particular items should be included on the test. Or, you might ask several of the students to go through an entire instructional unit or textbook or notes and select the most important items to include. This kind of review can be even more useful than making the children guess what you think important enough to put on a test. You might also vary this procedure by distributing well before a test a list of everything that will be on it, and challenge the children to see if everyone in the class can get 100% on the examination.

Pupil Products

Make a collection of student projects gathered during the year and lay these out for casual inspection whenever parent conferences are scheduled or during American Education Week in November. The parents will develop an appreciation of the varieties of activities you plan for their children, and will begin to understand the diversity of pupil performances on them. In addition to accumulating written work and art products, make arrangements beforehand to tape record examples of children's oral reading, musical performances, or class discussions. Or, ask each child to dictate a brief report into the microphone, telling the main things he or she has learned during the recent grading period. In turn, let the parents tape record a message in response to their children's efforts on display in the classroom.

Questionnaires on Growth

Collect evidence of growth from your pupils' parents by submitting to parents a questionnaire at the conclusion of every major reporting period. Such a device will prompt the families to be more alert to their children's development, and will also inform them of some of your more urgent interests and objectives. You might pose such questions as:

- Does your child voluntarily read at home? If so, how many hours each week, and with what materials?
- Is your child curious and interested in the natural world? Can he or she apply learnings to actual problem-solving situations?
- Does your child seem to like school? Is he or she glad to get up every day and come to school?
- What is your child's favorite subject or subjects? What does he or she say about it or otherwise show this interest?
- Does your child willingly do whatever homework is assigned? Does he or she have a place and a time set aside for this purpose?
- Does your child have friends at school? With whom does he or she usually play when school is not in session?

Reinforcement Techniques

As your children increasingly assume personal responsibility for checking their own learning, foster this initiative by using positive reinforcements rather than negative ones, encouraging rather than criticizing their efforts. Treat pupil mistakes as examples of forgetting rather than as cardinal sins. Evaluate papers in terms of numbers of answers right, rather than the number wrong. Provide an ample display space on your bulletin board and request each child to identify his or her best work for public notice. Ask the pupils how they would go about improving the quality of their efforts. Give smiles and partial credit for good effort and for nearly-correct answers. You can point out that a certain paper has one mistake on a given line of a composition, for example, but the student must find his or her own mistake. Or, convert the search for errors in usage or other fact into a treasure hunt or a scavenger hunt: "Find the one mistake on problems in row four within the next five minutes."

Self-Checking

By charging your students with the task of checking the accuracy of most of their routine work, you will save yourself and them much time and will offer them immediate feedback on their correctness, thereby minimizing subsequent errors. To help keep accountable those students who are too immature to handle this task or who rush through their assignments or who cheat to get a higher grade, build into the self-checking a safeguard: stipulate to the students that after a unit of study is completed, you will administer and check yourself a mastery test. If they can pass this test with a satisfactory grade, you will permit them to continue checking and studying on a new unit of instruction. But if they do not do well on the test, they will have to go back and review and rework some of their earlier exercises that they themselves checked. This should provide ample warning to the members of your class to proceed with care and conscientious effort, and to check their own work accurately and thoroughly.

Summer Carryover

At the conclusion of the school year, instead of just providing the report card for your pupils, prepare a set of anecdotal records that can be passed along to the teacher who will be receiving these students in the next term. Include comments on traits of character and work habits, along with specific accomplishments and levels of proficiency in the various subjects of study. If you have children who need special help during the summer, sign out some of the textbooks and other materials and exercises they did not complete during the regular school year. In addition, provide them practice papers that will help to maintain their skills during the vacation period. Where it is feasible, let them also have early access to the books for the coming school year so they may get a head start on the next set of instructional activities.

Tape Recordings

As a part of a home visit or a parent conference, you might prepare tape recordings of children's work. This technique is also important for you in keeping in touch with class members who are confined at home with illnesses or disabilities, who are in the hospital, or who are absent from school on extended trips. Such tape recordings can convey to the absentee what you are working on in class. In turn, the student may use the tape recording as a way of sharing his or her understandings of activities that are conducted away from the classroom; this will help you to assess how well he or she is maintaining pace with the other class members.

REWARDS FOR WINNERS

Achievement Tree

When the students are all working on the same skill, give each child a ball of plastic clay and a twig salvaged from a tree branch. Whenever any child has accomplished the mastery of the task at hand, let him or her stand the twig upright on his or her desk to show completion of the assignment. On each subdivision of the twig, pupils may attach a different leaf cut out from tape or paper, each leaf representing an additional learning objective achieved.

Animal Piecework

An interesting visual stimulation of achievement is a wall treatment of a dinosaur, an elephant, a giraffe, or any other creature of large dimensions. As each child completes a task, he or she may attach to it a small bit of colored paper or tape, or color in a part of the paper on which the huge picture is outlined. Or, the pupils may individually fill in the feathers on a peacock or the stripes on a zebra. The more familiar bookworm also has many possibilities.

Badges of Honor

From time to time during the year make badges from cardboard and cover them with foil of silver or gold wrapped tightly around each shape. Use stars, shields, or any other "official" shape. Add to the badges legends such as "Perfect Pa-

Room 34 - Proud as a . . .

per" or "Most Improved." Or, write in the special skill mastered. Make up your own captions, such as "C.I.A." which might stand for "Carefully Improving Arithmetic," or "F.B.I." for "Far Better Information." Let the pupils who earn these symbols serve as the classroom "marshals" during certain class sessions, such as spelling and mathematics.

Bank Deposits

Let the children "deposit" and "withdraw" privileges from a special "bank" you have set up. Whenever a child has accomplished a stipulated goal, he or she puts "money" in the form of coupons of various denominations into the bank, which is credited to his or her "account." Selected members of the group may serve as tellers, taking turns during the day. In return, the "interest" accumulated in the bank is withdrawn in the form of privileges that are issued only as a certain number of credits have been accrued. Some of these privileges may be represented in the form of coins and currencies, each one telling what the bearer is entitled to.

Certificates of Honor

Coinciding with the usual honors assemblies or other recognition of only a few children in the school, schedule your own recognition day when you make an attempt to reward with a homemade certificate any child in the class who has made significant progress in any kind of endeavor. Get a ream of good quality bond paper and obtain wax seals and pieces of ribbon that are affixed to the certificates which you duplicate in the school office. You might include categories such as "Growth in . . . ," "Improvement in . . . ," and "Outstanding Effort for . . . ."

Chest Decorations

A unique way to recognize special achievement is to make cross-chest sashes, similar to those worn by Scouts, on which the children may display homemade attachments that tell in symbol form their main achievements. Athletic-type letters for special accomplishments might also be fashioned from fabric scraps, with each letter representing one subject area in your curriculum. Cut these from fabric to represent the school colors. Or, you might make these letters from colored paper and write on each letter the specific achievement being honored.

Currency

Invent your own currency to circulate in the classroom, including both coin replicas and bills. Ask the children to help design these items, including a motto for the bills. Include several different denominations of coins and bills. Make these items from colored paper and designate the children in turn as the persons in charge of "paying" those persons who complete their tasks satisfactorily every day. Make a point to recognize as many pupils as possible. Let the students swap coins for privileges and services they render to each other as well.

Eatable Items

Once in a while as the children are playing educational games in your classroom, have on hand small cereal, nuts, marshmallows, or raisins to use as their markers on the game board. As each class member completes the game, he or she may eat the marker. Use this same general approach in basic mathematics activities where items must be manipulated to develop an understanding of the concepts involved. As the children answer these problems correctly, they may eat their counters.

Fancy Phrases

Add interest to your verbal reinforcers by learning a few compliments in a foreign language and then responding to your children's achievements by using the appropriate expressions. Contact a teacher of a foreign language for suggestions. Or, make and use a list of the many ways you can compliment a child in English, instead of using the usual trite expressions. On the other hand, discover alternatives to the negative reinforcers that are so commonly heard in classrooms as well; there are many different ways to tell a child an answer is incorrect besides saying "you're wrong." Another suggestion is to find large words in the dictionary and use these expressions liberally as you compliment your students. The boys and girls will learn new vocabulary items as they develop a sense of worth.

Group Goals

Devise a display that will engage all the children in a communal effort toward a major goal, such as a party in the classroom. One example of a group goal might be to spell correctly a large cumulative total of spelling words. To record the progress in spelling and to show the move toward a class party as the reward, fashion the display like a rocket ship on its way through the solar system, for example. Or, make a representation of a person climbing a mountain. Each set of achievements from the class as a whole will thus advance an appropriate marker along the display. Of course, the faster learners will move the marker along faster than will their peers. But the goal will be attained only as all the pupils cooperate on the project at hand.

Hall of Fame

Set up in the classroom a "Hall of Fame" in which different children each week are honored for their contributions to the progress of the class. In addition to their individual accomplishments, include in the display some of the favorite items belonging to the students being honored in the Hall of Fame. Take photographs of these students and have an album in which each person, along with his or her major contribution, is listed. As this Hall of Fame is maintained over the years, the younger siblings of these persons will be pleased and encouraged to view the information about their predecessors and will be encouraged to make comparable efforts.

Hats and Headbands

To give students special recognition, prepare sets of hats for them to wear. One suggestion is a "halo" hat, made by cutting from a portion of a plastic jug a section that fits the head like a headband. The other matching shape stands up on a stem from the headband to serve as an elevated halo above the head. The headband portion can be tied to the head in the rear with string. Let the child being honored wear the halo hat home, bringing it back to school the next day. A second variation of this is to use a band cut from a plastic jug to make a headband with feathers. Each feather may be labeled with the particular task accomplished. As the boys and girls progress through the year they may staple new feathers to their headbands.

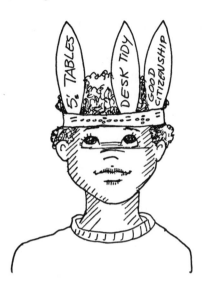

Military Markings

Instead of distributing to the children gummed stars affixed to a chart of achievements, make sturdy cardboard
strips just large enough to accommodate five colored stars.
Point out that military generals may wear from one to five
stars indicating five different levels of rank. Issue these cards
or tabs to the children in keeping with their efforts from week
to week. Use paper clips to attach these tabs to the lapels or
collars or shirt pockets of the students. Oak leaves, bars, and
chevrons may also be used for the same purpose. Investigate
some of the insignia of the other military services and challenge the children to adapt some of these symbols for this use.

Quick Games

There are several easy ways to engage the children in
game activities. One idea is to let a child place several questions on the chalkboard. That person may then call on classmates to answer the questions or problems. Anyone who can
respond accurately may then come up to the board and erase
the question. A second suggestion is to provide a stuffed toy or

mascot and let any child who answers correctly hold this object for a while. A playground ball or a beanbag may be tossed around the group under similar circumstances. Introduce the element of time into these informal activities by asking one child to count to ten while a classmate tries to answer a question posed.

Real Objects Motivators

In the early grades, offer an incentive that is directly related to the skill being learned. For example, obtain a set of special pencils or pens and offer one to each child who attains a particular level of competency in handwriting or composition. A pair of shoestrings might be the premium for the kindergartener who has learned to tie his or her shoes. Small notebooks might help to stimulate those children who have mastered certain reading activities. The children will cherish these mementoes and will use them to further their skills.

Secret Messages

Surprise rewards foster learning and build enthusiasm for the daily learning tasks. From time to time, hide inside some of your library books, textbooks, desks, or drawers secret messages that are to be found accidentally by the users of these items. One idea is to plant a slip that says, "If you have read to this page, we will stop our class and let you share this story with all of us." Or, "If you can tell me the names of the main kinds of clouds, you may go outside and look at the sky for ten minutes." Or, "If your desk is neat right now, you may go to the library and get a new book and read it for ten minutes."

Stamper Use

Young children like to use the special stampers that are available from commercial school supply houses. Get a set of those having positive comments, happy smiles, or other reinforcers on them. Let the students use these stampers to evaluate and mark their own work. They should be more aware of the quality of their products if they have the responsibility of assessing how well they have done. Another possibility is to obtain from a toy store a play set of letter stamps that can be made up into original slogans by moving the print. Then you can custom-make your own messages of approval and encouragement. You might also contact a business agency for discarded stampers that might be adapted to this purpose: "Approved," "Certified," and "Received" are just a few examples. One last suggestion is to have a stamper pad inked and ready at the conclusion of each worksheet experience. When students certify that they have done their best work, let them affix a thumb print to the paper.

Stickers and Seals

In addition to using the gummed seals that are commercially available, ask the children to salvage comic greeting cards and seasonal cards from their families. Let them cut out the small figures from these cards and place them in a communal box. Then whenever a child merits special recognition on a paper submitted, attach one of these figures with a spot of glue. At other times, let the boys and girls select their own motifs and combine these into a mini-montage certificate, using one item for each major accomplishment during a grading period.

A further suggestion is to ask the pupils to bring to school trading stamps, stickers, seals, and other items salvaged from third-class and fourth-class mail, as well as from premiums given away in groceries and other stores. Collect, too, booklets to fill with these items. As any given task is accomplished, let that child attach one sticker to a page. When a page is filled, have on hand some special treat or privilege appropriate to the effort expended. Or, use individual stickers to attach to the top of the papers and other papers. If you would like to turn this into a group activity, ask each child to take a page in one of the stamp books. When all the pages are filled, the children can help decide what they would like to "spend" a book of stamps on, including merchandise that might be redeemed with the stamps.

Treasure Box

Obtain a sturdy carton and convert it into a treasure box that you fill with vermiculite, styrofoam granules, cornmeal, pea gravel, or any other sand substitute. In this box hide small items from a department store, gadgets from coin-operated dispensing machines, wrapped candies, or items donated by the children themselves. Wrap pennies in gold holiday foil to simulate fancy coins. Occasionally use these tiny objects as reinforcers for especially difficult tasks accomplished successfully.

A second version of the treasure box is to make a large rainbow crossing your classroom, constructed of crepe paper or other paper strips. At one end of this rainbow place a pot containing the main instructional tasks for your students. At the opposite end of the rainbow place a treasure pot filled with coin replicas. Give each child a cardboard replica of a coin, on each of which the child writes a task and his or her own name. Divide the rainbow into segments to represent progress through a unit of instruction. As the students complete their learnings appropriately, they may move their markers across the rainbow. When the unit is completed, they may withdraw other coin replicas from the treasure pot, each of which entitles them to a reward of their choosing.

INDEX

Art:
Assessing, 100
Brushes in use, 101
Chalk hints, 101
Clay helps, 102
Clay substitutes, 102
Clean-up time, 102
Crayon melts, 103
Display variations, 103
Fairs and festivals, 104
Fingerpainting surfaces, 105
Giving assistance, 105
Handling clay, 105
Mess made less, 106
Mini-gallery, 107
Mixing made easier, 107
Paint additives, 108
Paint alternatives, 108
Paint instruments, 109
Paint palettes, 109
Paint principles, 110
Paint storage, 110
Paper cutting, 111
Paper storage, 111
Paper uses, 112
Paste mess, 112
Paste pointers, 112
Patterns and models, 113
Personal participation, 113
Plaster possibilities, 114
Project keepers, 114
Protecting clothing, 114
Random reminders, 115
Recycled art, 116
Respect for the artist, 117
Scheduling, 117
Sculpture armatures, 118
Smocks, 118
Time and space considerations, 119
Water source, 119
Ways with paints, 120

Assessing Pupils:
Anecdotal records, 247
Averages, 248
Bowling scores, 248
Can-do can, 249
Card log, 249
Checklist, 249

Assessing Pupils: (cont'd)
Cumulative folders, 250
Cumulative grading, 250
Diagnostics, 251
HappyGrams, 251
Marking papers, 252
Measurement message, 252
Measuring line, 252
Open report cards, 253
Original report cards, 253
Parent report cards, 255
Parent visits, 255
Passports, 255
Peer assessment, 256
Physical measurement, 256
Pupil-made tests, 257
Pupil products, 257
Questionnaires on growth, 257
Reinforcement techniques, 258
Self-checking, 259
Summer carryover, 259
Tape recordings, 259

Attendance:
Absentees, 176
Attendance clothespins, 176
Bookkeeping, 177
Calendar compartments, 177
Calendar lift-ups, 178
Choosing sides, 178
Class lists, 179
Dial-a-day, 179
Diary calendar, 179
Food count, 180
Head count hangers, 180
House and school counters, 180
Keeping control, 181
Lost and found, 181
Personalized, 182
Random grouping, 182
Restroom markers, 183
Roll call, 183
Sign out symbols, 184
Spinner wheel calendar, 184
Sunshine calendar, 184

Child Study:
"All About Me" booklet, 233
Autobiography, 234

Child Study: (*cont'd*)
Fantasy stories, 234
Free play, 235
Inventories, 235
Listing rules and rights, 236
Parent checklists, 236
Picture clues, 236
Self-reports, 237
Sociograms, 237
Story situations, 237
Unfinished sentences, 238
Values scales, 238

Discipline:
Aggression and acting-out
 alternatives, 57
Anger alternatives, 58
Appropriate punishments, 58
Attention span, 59
Being fair, 60
Changing positions, 60
Confidential criticism, 61
Consistent treatment, 62
Contracted changes, 62
Cooperative involvements, 63
Corporal punishment, 63
Correcting mistakes, 64
Expressing feelings, 65
Furniture arrangements, 65
Giving compliments, 66
Giving help, 66
Handling aggression, 67
Helpful humor, 68
Making allowances, 68
Making comparisons, 69
Managing monitors, 70
Managing upsets, 70
Note-writing alternatives, 71
Sincere apologies, 71
Withholding blame, 72

Fitness:
Accounting for equipment, 74
Calisthenics to a beat, 75
Choosing partners, 76
Coping with competition, 77
Cue cards, 77
Instructional helps, 77
Motivating, 79
No-fault, 80

Fitness: (*cont'd*)
Signal systems, 81
Playground guidance, 80
Safety sense, 81
Skill centers, 82
Skills charts, 82
Squad setups, 84
Taking turns, 84
Team selection, 84

Icebreakers:
Adapted games, 27
Booklets, 27
Circle games, 28
Circle pass, 28
Guess Who?, 29
Letter and word games, 29
Mail call, 30
Mixed-up names, 30
Pair presentations, 31
Personalized tags, 31
Photo tags, 32
Pictures and portraits, 32
Plastic tags, 33
Puzzle names, 33
Puzzle pictures, 34
Reversed names, 35
Shape tags, 35
Song responses, 36
Special sharing, 36
Tag lines, 36

Learning Centers:
Adjustability, 146
Book bus, 146
Bulk orders, 147
Checking out items, 147
Color-coding, 147
Distributing systems, 148
Duplicating economies, 149
Free-fashioned furnishings, 150
Oilcloth covering, 151
Panels and partitions, 151
Paper for backgrounds, 151
Sending notes home, 152
Stepped effects, 153
Stuff and junk, 153
Substitute materials, 153
Tabletop treatments, 154
Worksheet ways, 155

Learning Climate:
Absentees, 39
Assignment excitement, 40
Bad weather, 40
Blah month, 41
Breaks in the action, 41
Calendar fun, 42
Ceiling suspensions, 42
Clock treatment, 43
Favorite things, 44
Garments glorified, 44
Gracious grading, 44
Graffiti spot, 45
Grand entrance, 45
Humor in action, 46
Inspiration at work, 46
Interest clubs, 47
Keeping in touch, 47
Loyalty, 47
Mascot, 48
Music and moods, 49
Names are neat, 49
Old hats, 50
Outside the room, 50
Personal touch, 51
Popular choice, 52
Questions, questions, 52
Ratings race, 53
Scrapbook, 53
Sharing, 54
Spontaneous events, 54
Spots of color, 54
Teacher challenge, 55
Wall treatments, 55
Windows well, 56

Media:
Chalkboard lines, 205
Chalkboard questions, 206
Chalkboards in general, 207
Chart uses, 207
Charts from shades, 208
Duplicator masters, 209
Films in action, 209
Filmstrips, 210
Flannelboards, 210
Frieze, 211
General handy hints, 212
Magazines, 213
Murals, 214

Media: (cont'd)
Overhead projector activities, 215
Overhead projector tips, 215
Overhead projectors and science, 216
Posters, 216
Programmed materials, 217
Proper patterns, 217
Realia, 218
Sand table, 218
Slides suggestions, 218
Tape recorder activities, 219
Textbooks, 220
Tracings, 220
Typewriter, 221

Parent Communications:
Communication competencies, 222
Conference considerations, 223
Educational experience inventory, 224
Enrollment data, 225
Facilitating conference attendance, 226
Handbook hints, 227
Handbooks for parents, 227
Parent assessment, 228
Parent-teacher organizations, 229
Pupil-parent conferences, 230
Scheduling conferences, 230
Welcome visitors, 231

Planning:
Bus procedures, 2
Color-coding, 3
Communications, 3
Community data, 4
Exchange teaching, 4
Idea file, 5
Library books, 5
Planning cards, 6
Planning notebook, 6
Plus planning, 7
Professional materials, 7
Room arrangement, 8
School helpers, 8
Summer planning, 9
Syllabus system, 10
Teacher orientation, 10
Teaching pictures, 11

Pupil Orientation:
  Alternate sessions, 11
  Bibliotherapy, 12
  Bus procedures, 12
  Circus theme, 12
  Coloring books, 14
  Convincers, 14
  Early open house, 15
  First learnings, 15
  Helpers, 16
  Home helps, 16
  Map study, 17
  Mascot, 17
  Moral support, 17
  Name recognition, 18
  Name tag spoons, 18
  Participatory planning, 19
  Parties, 19
  Promotions, 21
  Round-up, 21
  Routines, 22
  School helpers, 22
  School tour, 22
  Security items, 23
  Self-portrait, 23
  Special attractions, 23
  Summer letter, 24
  Summer preparations, 24
  Surprises, 25
  Transfers, 25
  Tree treats, 26

Reading:
  All-purpose advice, 85
  Book clubs, 86
  Book festival, 87
  Book report alternatives, 88
  Books in comfort, 89
  Clever containers, 91
  Compatible pairs, 91
  Diversified basals, 91
  Kits and kids, 92
  Libraries and librarians, 92
  Reading group alternatives, 93
  Reading materials, 94
  Reducing the race, 94
  Reluctant readers, 95
  Sign-out sensations, 96
  Story hour, 97
  Taping the action, 98

Reading: (*cont'd*)
  Title ticklers, 99
  Workbook woes, 99

Resources:
  Alternatives afield, 187
  Bag of tricks, 188
  Catalog sources, 188
  Commercial suppliers, 189
  Construction sites, 189
  Counting noses, 190
  Emergency trip provisions, 191
  Evaluating excursions, 191
  Excursion booklet, 192
  Factories and agencies, 192
  Folders for subs, 193
  Fun for subs, 194
  General end-of-day critique, 194
  Helpers at a distance, 195
  Introducing substitutes, 195
  Introducing trip concepts, 195
  Kids as tutors, 196
  Lost on trips, 196
  Name tags for trips, 197
  Parents in classrooms, 197
  Permission from parents, 198
  Rest and refreshments afield, 199
  Rummages and auctions, 199
  Seating for subs, 200
  Secondary school sources, 200
  Senior citizen aides, 201
  State department sources, 202
  Stores and businesses, 203
  Textbooks to salvage, 203
  Timing your trips, 204
  Trip impressions, 204
  Walking tours, 205

Review:
  Color-coding, 239
  Computer carton, 239
  Deliberate mistake, 239
  Diary details, 240
  End-of-day review, 240
  Expert panel, 241
  Fact mats, 241
  Fix-it shop, 241
  Game formats, 242
  Good guesses, 242
  Peer helpers, 242

Review: (*cont'd*)
Puppet tutors, 243
Puzzle papers, 243
Quiz slips, 244
Shingles to show, 244
"Show Me" cards, 244
Signal systems, 245
Teacher for a day, 246
Trouble spots, 246
Wizard cap, 246
Wrong answers, 246

Rewards and Reinforcements:
Achievement tree, 260
Animal piecework, 260
Badges of honor, 260
Bank deposits, 261
Certificates of honor, 262
Currency, 262
Eatable items, 263
Fancy phrases, 263
Group goals, 263
Hall of fame, 264
Hats and headbands, 264
Military markings, 265
Quick games, 265
Real objects motivators, 266
Secret messages, 266
Stamper use, 266
Stickers and seals, 267
Treasure box, 268

Routine Management:
Art clean up, 165
Assigning jobs, 166
Bad weather tips, 166
Clean up campaign, 166
Clean up concepts, 168
Clean up roles, 168
Distraction reduction, 168
Emergency items, 169
Emergency kit, 169
Emergency response, 169
End-of-day clean up, 170
Fabric noise control, 171
Faces and figures helpers, 172
Give-a-hand helper, 172
Help-wanted helpers, 173
Jobs as occupations, 173
Messy dressing, 173

Routine Management: (*cont'd*)
Nature's helpers, 174
Noise abatement ideas, 174
Noise control signals, 175
Quiet spots, 175
Random helper choice, 175
Safety inspection, 176

Spaces and Places:
Ceiling brighteners, 122
Desk arrangements, 124
Display surfaces, 124
Doing doors, 125
Dual-purpose items, 125
Easel ways, 126
Foldaways, 126
Glare to spare, 126
Lightening and brightening, 127
Mobility management, 128
Poles and posts, 128
Privacy carrels, 130
Room dividers, 130
Space conservation, 132
Special spots, 133
Table flexibility, 134
Table ways, 134
Work space markings, 135

Storage:
Aprons, 135
Bags and baggies, 135
Boxes and cartons, 136
Cans for keeping, 136
Cardboard carriers, 137
Clotheshanger reels, 137
Cubbies, 137
Gym shoes, 138
Handy hints, 138
Homework holders, 139
Interesting containers, 140
Irregular materials, 140
Labeling containers, 140
Large flat items, 141
Paper at the ready, 141
Paper in boxes, 141
Pegboard possibilities, 142
Phonograph records, 142
Plastic drawers, 142
Plastic jugs, 142
Puzzles places, 143

Storage: (*cont'd*)
Safe and handy scissors, 143
Shelving to shift, 144
Small hooks, 144
String, 144
Study papers, 145
Tubes, 145
Worksheet extender, 145

Time Management:
Activity signals, 157
Appointments, 157
Before-school privileges, 158
Dismissal, 158

Time Management: (*cont'd*)
Movement, 159
Quiet signals, 159
Scheduling cycles, 160
Share and tell, 160
Signal system, 161
Start/stop symbols, 161
Taking turns, 161
Time cards, 162
Timely reminders, 162
Timing turns, 163
Traffic lines, 163
Transitions, 164
Waiting for response, 164
Waiting in lines, 165